For Jane,

Thank you for supporting
ELCA World Hunger.

Kathy Hoffman

Christmas at Two Ponds
The Backstory

Christmas
at Two Ponds
The Backstory

Volume Two of the Two Ponds Trilogy

Kathy Hoffman

Proceeds benefit ELCA World hunger

XULON PRESS

Xulon Press
2301 Lucien Way #415
Maitland, FL 32751
407.339.4217
www.xulonpress.com

Paperback ISBN-13: 978-1-66286-941-9
Ebook ISBN-13: 978-1-66286-942-6

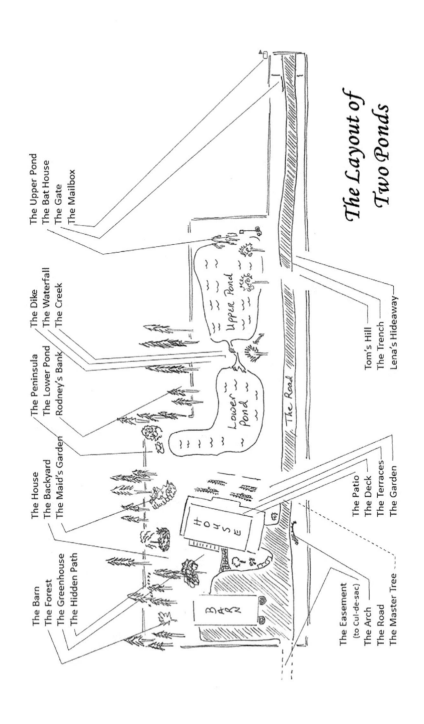

The Layout of *Two Ponds*

The Upper Pond
The Bat House
The Gate
The Mailbox

The Dike
The Waterfall
The Creek

The Peninsula
The Lower Pond
Rodney's Bank

The House
The Backyard
The Maid's Garden

The Barn
The Forest
The Greenhouse
The Hidden Path

Tom's Hill
The Trench
Lena's Hideaway

The Patio
The Deck
The Terraces
The Garden

The Easement
(to cul-de-sac)
The Arch
The Road
The Master Tree

Other Books by the Author

The Joyful Faces of Messiah

Brooklyn Art Library, The Sketchbook Project, Volume 18
An illustrated collection of close-ups (eyes, nose, and mouth)
of some of the 2021 members of Messiah Lutheran Church and
Preschool in Vancouver, Washington.

Life at Two Ponds

Volume One of the Two Ponds Trilogy

Autobiographical humor: Hoffman is very competitive. She finds
challenges in almost every situation. She finds ways to compete
with her puppies, her husband, Mother Nature, and even a little
mouse! Go for a walk with her through her married life as she over-
plans every event only to find that so many things can go awry.
Laugh with her as she carefully manipulates every situation until
it explodes in her face!

Main Cast of Characters

My husband of 40 years … **Harry** – a Man-of-Few-Words

Neighbors – **Morrie & Dorothy, Rodney & Dana,**
          Tom & Teryl, Brad & Gwen, Gary & Meg

Our Dogs:

- Westies – **Tori, Dietrich, Hector, Freddie Lu, Priscilla, Molly, Sara, Chatterbox, Toby**
- Corgis – **Angie, Lucy**
- **Jude** – Airedale
- **Bizi Bodi** (pronounced "busybody") – Boxer
- **Bo** – German Shepherd
- **Solo** – Bouvier des Flandres
- **Mickey** – Rat Terrier
- **Holly Bear** – Schipperke
- **Jud** – Lab/Doberman mix
- **Jack** – Border Collie
- **Cocoa Bean** – Chihuahua/Rat Terrier mix

Cat – **Jessica**

Parrots – **Ajax** (Orange-Winged Amazon), **Boris** (African Grey)

Turtle – **Tripod** (a three-legged turtle)

Duck – **Donald**

Christmas at Two Ponds

The Backstory

Volume Two of the Two Ponds Trilogy

They say you're supposed to have a bucket list. I've tried, but I've never been successful at making one, although I suppose a wish list is probably a close second. I've only had one thing on my wish list, but I have absolutely no control over it: When I die, I want people to tell the funny stories of all the stupid things I've done throughout my life. But I haven't died yet. My friends are getting older and more forgetful. Some of them are dying off. For the last several years, I've lived with the fear my wish would not come true and the stupid things I've done wouldn't see the light of day. Enter Covid: There I sat, isolated, mulling over my own thoughts. What was I to do? I'll tell you what I was to do: Write a book so those stupid things would actually see the light of day. I had a problem: There were too many stories. I asked Harry what I should do. "Write a trilogy," he said. And so I did.

Dedication

This book is dedicated to Dorothy Stamp. She's a good friend and neighbor. After her husband Morrie died in 2016, I made sure to look in on her from time to time. We'd have a cuppa and some long visits. She was inspirational … determined to make it on her own, and more than capable of doing so. Two years later, after I retired, I started visiting her more often … usually about six mornings each week. Neighbors have seen me drive up, rain or shine, wearing my bathrobe and slippers … mug in hand.

When Dorothy and I get together, we tell each other our life stories, laugh and reminisce, and laugh some more. Telling my stories to Dorothy has helped me polish them. I'm thankful for all the time we've had to share our meals, our lives, and our homes. At 88, Dorothy is still living on her large one-acre property and caring for her one house, one garage, three carports … and two ponds.

Mornings with Dorothy

Acknowledgments

I am grateful for my husband who seems to take it all in stride when I disappear to work on book stuff. One day, before I went to visit my friend Kay and her daughter Kathy, I walked into the TV room. There was a lot of machine-gun action on the screen. "I'm off for a little bit … (as I kissed him goodbye, he strained his neck to make sure he didn't miss any action on the screen) … Will you miss me?" The reply was unexpected: "Yes." "Why?" I asked. "Because I'm supposed to." All in stride!

I am grateful for those who have supported my efforts to raise money for ELCA Disaster Relief and World Hunger: my anonymous benefactor who provided matching funds during my first book project, my home church Messiah Lutheran in Vancouver through an Endowment Grant, others whose names were not available at the time of publication … and you, Dear Reader … your purchase implemented the matching of funds!

I'm grateful for Helene Johnsen, my muse. I've known her since grade school. We have a lot of shared experiences. In fact, she and I ended up at the same place for dinner after the Prom in our senior year.

My thanks to Sue Miholer. Everyone needs an editor. I found a gem! And here's what she did for you: (a) She struck out a ton of capitals, but sometimes I couldn't help myself … if you wonder why something is capitalized, just know that it is slightly special to me; (b) She saved you from wondering why I included so many hyphens; and (c) She pointed out places where you were likely to stumble over awkward phrasing. I happily made the changes … except for one story. I told her "hands off!" You'll know it when you come to it!

Many thanks to Paul Krueger who told me he'd like to see pictures with the stories. If you like the tiny pictures in this book, thank Paul.

I am grateful for the people at Xulon Publishing who make it easy for me to concentrate on writing and illustrating while they take care of everything else.

I give a nod to all the English teachers who will read this and roll their eyes because I have overused ellipses. Ellipses are most often used to signify omitted text in quotations. However, one can also use an ellipsis to indicate a pause ... or in my case, an afterthought ... or an aside. I grew into that style over the years. I hope you will enjoy the pace of this book a little more by pausing slightly ... and often rolling your eyes with me ... when you see an ellipsis.

And for these same English teachers, I know I should put a comma after the words *so* and *finally* ... but sometimes I don't. If you don't see a comma, just read through the text fast, because that's the way it will sound if I put the book on tape.

Give thanks for your blessings and be assured the royalties and more from your purchase will benefit the Evangelical Lutheran Church in America (ELCA) World Hunger. ELCA Disaster Relief and World Hunger are often among the first to show up and help when people are experiencing the worst days of their lives. To make additional donations, visit "www.elca.org." Poke the "Give" button at the upper-right portion of the webpage.

And finally, I acknowledge you, Dear Reader. In *Life at Two Ponds,* I promised to share my Prom story with you. It didn't fit within the parameters of this book, so I stuffed it into the Prologue ... just for you. I hope you cringe along with me each step of the way. But most of all, I hope reading my story gives you the courage to share yours with someone ... maybe with me!

Introduction

This book is a chronological account of Harry's and my married life as cataloged in our Christmas cards. As my Christmas card format developed, I decided three paragraphs would be sufficient to tell the tale of the year. But wait, there's more: Now you will be privy to some never-before-told stories behind the cryptic verbiage in the Christmas letters.

LET'S CATCH UP

Way back when, I lived in a three-bedroom ranch-style home. There was a grease-pit built into the garage floor. I learned how to change the oil in my car. I was an independent woman. In July of 1982, Harry and I had an unlikely meeting at his State Farm Insurance office. A month later, after shooting pheromones at me every time we talked, he was well on his way to landing me. I, however, had just barely realized I was in love. Another month later, sandwiched between my best friend Marg and Harry's brother Jon ... a few friends and family around ... we married and never looked back. Pastor Duane Sich officiated ... it stuck.

We lived in our little ranch-style home for four years. Being an insurance agent, Harry had lots of opportunities to see homes and properties for sale. He found one and invited me to take a ride to see it. I fell in love with it. We did the paperwork and moved to our little house on a hill with a view of our new two-acre property ... and two ponds. We named it "Two Ponds" ... we're so imaginative!

In Volume One, *Life at Two Ponds*, I made a promise to share the story of my Prom date. It occurred a dozen years before I met Harry, and so it is relegated to the Prologue. But first a note about ...

Boxes

We all build boxes around ourselves ... parameters within which we interact with the world. We have expectations ... of ourselves ... of others. No matter how much we believe we are free, we have these boundaries. On occasion, they remind us how confined we are. I had a lot of boxes, but I didn't realize how it was about to impact me. Here are a few that ended up biting me in the backside.

1. When someone performs a service for you, you tip them.

Restaurants, bars, hair salons ... think about tipping.

2. When relatives come to visit, they get a kiss.

Our family did a lot of kissing growing up. When younger siblings got ready for bed, they'd come for a kiss. A kiss was not slobbery, especially with relatives ... all you had to do was lean in, purse your lips, and make contact. A kiss was usually accompanied by a single-syllable sound ... similar to the double-syllable sound you make when you're calling a puppy to come to you. And so it was, when relatives came to visit, there was a little peck here and a little peck there. All was well in my little box.

3. Dinner is eaten at 6 p.m.

Mom and Dad had seven children. After Grandpa had a stroke in 1962, they arranged for him to buy the house next door. Dad worked in the treasurer's office at the University of Portland a few miles away ... no late nights. Mom was very efficient. We had a sit-down dinner every night at 6 p.m. With few exceptions, there were at least ten people around the table every night.

4. Listen to your teachers.

When I was a sophomore in gym class, Miss Lynch talked with us about a lot of personal things, including puberty. Among other things, she told us we would be afraid of boys. I heard what she said, but I thought it couldn't be true for me because I had six brothers. I figured I'd never have trouble talking with boys. Nevertheless, I tucked her comments away in a corner of my mind and tried to wait out this puberty thing ... while everyone else plunged right in. A couple of years later, we all went to the coast for a football game: the team was on one bus, the pep squad on another. Jay, a very handsome student in my grade, and a couple of his friends drove separately in Jay's Corvair. Somehow, I had heard there was a recall on Corvairs ... I assumed it was a serious one. When Jay and the other boys got to the restaurant, I went up to him and asked him if he was okay. It was the first time I had ever spoken with him. Just then, Miss Lynch flashed through my head and all my denial came crashing down around me. I knew I was going to have a big problem talking with boys.

Prologue

THE PROM: A COMING-OF-AGE STORY

One's first date can be a traumatic experience, especially for a late bloomer. It should have been something exciting to look forward to, but I was scared to death.

A ROCKY START

It would have been nice to have experienced a first date way, way, way before the senior Prom, but it didn't happen. In fact, while other girls were getting asked to the Prom right and left, I never expected an invitation. I was 5' 9" tall in my senior year ... taller than most of the boys in my class, although, mercifully, they were starting to gain on me. And who knows if I had a personality ... certainly I didn't know! When a tall boy in my class, Ray, invited me to the Prom, it was totally unexpected. I'm afraid I was taken off guard. I didn't know what to do or say.

Stepping back for context: When I was 17 years old, the summer before my senior year, I drove Grandpa to Southern California for an insurance convention. After his stroke three years earlier, he had recovered enough to continue selling life insurance, but not enough to drive. Now, I don't know where I met him, but there we were in Los Angeles and, out of the blue, a young man my age, Darryl, asked me to go to the movies. I didn't know him from Adam, so I thought it prudent to ask Grandpa if I could go. Well, Grandpa was always a pushover. Mom had him wrapped around her little finger all her life and I was a close second. Even though he didn't think it was a very good idea, all I had to do was ask him a couple of times.

I was pretty sure he'd eventually cave ... which he did. So there I was in 1965 ... totally inexperienced ... going out to a drive-in (I forgot to mention that detail to Grandpa) with a young man nobody knew. I was wearing an orange and white-checked summer frock I had sewn ... with the neckline way up to here. (If you're having trouble picturing what "way up to here" means ... picture higher.) It had a matching triangular mini-scarf, which was all the rage. Well, I don't know if it was all the rage, but it was easy to make, and I had made a couple. Pretty soon, Darryl leaned over and started making the moves on me. Well, I mean he kissed me ... at least he tried to. He leaned over and I saw him coming. I did what came naturally, minus the single-syllable sound. I didn't do a very good job of it: I pecked him. We had a moment! He critiqued our moment. He told me I wasn't supposed to kiss like I was kissing my brother. Who knew there would be a test on kissing! And so, after telling me I was doing it wrong, he explained how to do it right ... to open my mouth a little bit and lick my lips. We tried it again. Darryl seemed pleased at how well I learned. I figured since Darryl and I had kissed, we were likely to spend the rest of our lives together, so I invited him to the Prom ten months hence. He didn't say yes ... but he didn't say no. In fact, he didn't actually say much of anything. I think he wanted to practice kissing some more. I was a good Catholic girl, raised like matryoshkas ... Russian nesting dolls ... within eight boxes. Eventually, Darryl decided breaking through one box was sufficient for the evening and he took me back to my hotel. The next day, I wrote a postcard to a girlfriend back home. All it said was "Mission Accomplished!" I had no mission, but Linda knew exactly what I meant. Years later, someone asked me about my first date, and I told them about the Prom. Oddly enough, I had forgotten about going to the movies with Darryl.

And so, when Ray asked me to the Prom, I had a dilemma, because in my mind my "boyfriend" from California was going to fly up for the Prom. Never mind that we hadn't talked in nine months, never mind that I didn't have his phone number, never mind that he didn't have my phone number, and never mind that neither one of us had written because we didn't have each other's last names or addresses. And so, in the heat of the moment, I didn't have the courage to say Yes. I told Ray I couldn't go with him because I'd already asked someone to go with me. If I had had a job application in front of me and had to rate myself as to how fast I could think on my feet, it would have been a sorry rating, indeed!

It took me a few days to think it through. Mom helped me at one point, by noting Darryl and I had no way of contacting each other. I asked her what I should do. She suggested I call Ray and have a little talk with him. (Then and there, I realized a second time, how right Miss Lynch had been.)

I called. Ray's mother, a woman of strength and character, answered the phone. I blurted out my whole predicament in one long sentence, as if somehow, she would forgive me for the misunderstanding and make everything right. It never dawned on me to save a few words for talking with Ray. All I remember about her was she was very gracious and very tall, though I had never seen her ... (or maybe I was feeling very small). She calmly invited me to hold and she would get Ray so we could talk. That did wonders for my built-up anxiety. When he got to the phone, I told Ray I did not have a date for the Prom. I bit my lip hoping he hadn't asked anyone else, and hoping he still wanted to go with me. Mercifully, Ray didn't hold it against me. After my lengthy soliloquy, he was as gracious as his mother. And just like that, after a rocky start, Ray and I were going to the Prom!

*Y*ES

My life changed completely. I was now playing catch-up with all the flurry of activities that happen when you're going to the

Prom. All the girls were talking about getting their hair done for the Prom. They were booking hair appointments, and it seemed like the appointments were going fast. I had never had a hair appointment before, but all the girls were asking each other, "Have you made your hair appointment?"

"Yes!"

"I did!"

"Me, too!"

Everybody had. So I did, too. Perfect Look Beauty Salon was down on Lombard Street close to my grade school. I used to walk by it every day on the way home from school. It was the closest (and only) salon I could think of, and after all, I figured, all salons are the same. I went in and made an appointment. In retrospect, I should have wondered why I could still get an appointment at that hair salon. I was clueless.

DRESS

I never gave a dress or shoes or a wrap a second thought. The Prom was weeks away. I was oblivious, but Mom wasn't. One day she said, "Try this on." She handed me a beautiful vibrant coral satin dress: bodice and skirt. Unbeknownst to me, she had made me a Prom dress! (Much like the design of my little orange checked summer frock, the neckline came clear up to here!) Then Mom went about fitting a floral chiffon overlay to the skirt. The chiffon overlay had a multitude of large six-inch colorful pastel flowers and leaves. The effect was rather stunning.

Mom had taught me to sew. I knew what was right and what was not. As I looked down at the overlay, I saw a seam in the chiffon right down the middle. It was a nice seam, but even a nice seam is totally visible with chiffon. Mom was a perfectionist ... I was surprised she had put a seam down the front. Nevertheless, I didn't say a word. She had been kind enough to surprise me with a dress. What was I going to do? ... throw a fit? ... I don't think so. That wasn't my style, anyway. Mom had obviously put some thought into it and had done a lot of work. There was no way I was going to say anything negative. She continued pinning material until we were eventually through with the fitting session. As it turned out, the seam bothered her more than it bothered me, so she went right out, bought some more chiffon, and remade the front ... seam-free. I had no input at all. I don't know what I was thinking ... these things don't just magically appear. I've got six brothers ... it's not like she didn't have anything else to do. On the other hand, I was her only daughter ... she had only one chance at a Prom. I guess she wanted it to be perfect. Bless her heart ... it did just magically appear. It was very sweet.

Soon, I had a dress and white shoes ... flats because I didn't want to have even more height to deal with. I had little long white gloves to go with everything. My hands were built for the piano, perhaps the gloves weren't so little after all! As I look back, Mom seemed very much in touch with her children. She liked being a mom.

HAIR

Eventually, the big day came. It was time to go for my early-afternoon hair appointment.

Here's a question for the reader: Do you remember what hairstyles were like in the 60s? Bouffant on the top and a shoulder length flip ... That's exactly the way I wore my hair. I spent quite a bit of time every morning perfecting my hairdo. No hairs were out of place by the time it was plastered with hair spray. We had no tornadoes in Portland in those days, but if we had had one, it still wouldn't have messed up my hair. But I digress ...

I arrived on time for my hair appointment. In my purse I had money for the "do" and money for a tip. The first thing the lady said to me, even before I sat down in the chair, was, "I don't tease hair." Well, that comment was out of left field. Had she not been following the styles for the last twenty years? I tried not to appear crestfallen. There were absolutely no appointments left in the Portland area.

"Okay," I said. I had no choice but to tough it out. I sat down in the chair. One other thing I remember vividly was she was not very chatty ... not at all. And so I sat in silence, the joy slowly ebbing from my being as she worked whatever magic she had left.

The next question for the reader is: Do you remember what a girl's hair looked like when she was getting a perm and the curlers came out? Tikki-Tikki-Tikki ... wet, miniature S-curves rippling all the way down the back of the head. When my stylist finished her work, she asked if I wanted to take a look at it. I said, "Sure." My heart sank as I looked at the back of my head. My hair was plastered flat to my head, greased down with product ... shiny ... going Tikki-Tikki-Tikki all down the back. If I had had a flapper dress and a little round hat, I would have been right in fashion ... for The Roaring Twenties! Evidently, not all beauty salons are the same.

Still not a seasoned consumer, I was not able to think very fast on my feet. Oddly enough, not wanting to disappoint the stylist, I said it looked very nice and thanked her. Since I had a $5 tip in my purse, I paid her and gave her the tip ... because that's what you do. When I came home, Mom took one look at me, waited for a few seconds, and said in an encouraging pleasant-sounding voice, "Well, you've got a lot of product in your hair and your hair looks nice the way you fix it, so why don't you just go up and fix it the way you normally do." I never would have thought of changing it because I had paid good money for it, but Mom's idea sounded reasonable, and I couldn't make it worse! I got right to work and put it up in my big rollers. Within minutes, I was under a nylon hair dryer bonnet. When my hair was dry, I teased it like crazy, exactly like I normally did. Before long, I was my happy normal self with my bouffant flip shimmering in the bright lights of the kitchen.

RESEARCH

I was about to go on my first date. A few days earlier, while we were preparing dinner, I asked Mom about her first date with Dad. He had taken her to the soda shop in the afternoon and she ordered a chocolate sundae. I didn't think to ask her what I should do on my date. (Spoiler alert: There's something coming and it's going to be bad!)

GETTING DRESSED

Grandpa had gotten me a pretty little fur jacket to go with the Prom dress. Grandpa didn't shop. I knew Mom was behind it all. She had gotten the prettiest, whitest, softest little long-sleeved rabbit-fur jacket. This was a few years before fur was taboo. I wore it over the top of the coral dress ... it looked exquisite!

ARRIVAL

Ray arrived at our house, looking very handsome all dressed up in his suit, to take me to the Prom. And Ray was bearing gifts: a box of chocolates, an orchid corsage, and a dainty little purple and green floral handkerchief. In thinking back about the whole night, I wonder if he didn't ask that gracious mother of his what he should do on his first date. She probably thought back and told him what happened on her first date. Some traditions are worth keeping. That lovely handkerchief graced my special drawer for fifty years. I would open the drawer, look at it and smile at the thought ... and grimace at what happened later in the evening.

Of course, Dad took pictures. Dad always took pictures. He would make sure everyone posed perfectly before he snapped the shutter. My tolerance for Dad's picture-taking was about three seconds shorter than Dad's picture-taking. Consequently, when I look back at our family Easter pictures, I'm the one in tears. But now, for the first time I was all dressed up in my "Easter finest" and I wasn't in tears.

CONVENT

Everybody went to the convent before the Prom, to show the Sisters our finery and our good manners. It was a thing. The nuns must have looked forward to Prom night as much as we did. And so Ray and I went to the convent. Of course, I was self-conscious because I was all dressed up and fancy and whatnot. So I said, "Look at the beautiful flower he gave me." (I didn't know anything about orchids, except they are spendy and fragile. I had certainly never smelled one.) Sister Mary Virginette … a tiny little nun in a black floor-length habit and a large, black, starched, squared-off wimple … looked. Then I said, "Smell it." It was pinned to my dress, a little higher than the level of her smeller. I leaned over slightly. She said, "It's very nice." Well, of course, it had no scent, but neither of us knew that … at least if she did know, she graciously kept it to herself.

Prom Date

DANCE

We proceeded to the Prom. I'll tell you what, I don't remember anything about the Prom except Ray was very nice, very kind, and if I ever needed anything, it was right there, right now. I know there was dancing … it was the Prom … but I don't remember the theme. I don't remember much of anything, except thinking dancing is exercise, and after exercise, you're supposed to be out of breath. Consequently, after every dance, I returned to the table much like Blanche DuBois in *A Streetcar Named Desire*, fanning myself and letting out a little "Whew!"

Dancing was a risk. In those days, you didn't dress up without nylons, and going out on the dance floor without shoes would ruin the nylons. Snags, holes, runners … very unsightly. I couldn't wear shoes because I'd be too tall, so I crocheted a little pair of slippers with white yarn wrapped with silver filament. Given the reason for the slippers, they were quite elegant. My choice was shoes or slippers … I was taking a chance on crushed toes, but we had all taken ballroom dancing lessons at the Arthur Murray Dance Studio down the street from the church. Crushed toes were a minimal risk.

Dinner

Finally, it was time to go out afterwards. Several of us went to Palaske's Hillvilla, earlier named Simmons's Hillvilla … known for its "View of a Million Lights." It was a very nice restaurant high above the Willamette River … part of Portland's history There were twelve of us. The couples sitting across the table from us had the view.

Soon the server came around to take our orders. We really didn't have servers in those days … she was a waitress. I heard someone say, "I'll have the pork chops."

"And do you want soup or salad with that?"

"Salad, please."

Everyone was ordering big meals. The waitress was getting closer. "And for you, Sir?"

"I'll have the salmon, please … with a salad."

I was frantically trying to decide what to do: I already ate three meals … one of which was dinner … dinner is served at 6 p.m. …

don't eat onions ... or garlic ... it's not good to eat too late ... broccoli will get stuck in my teeth ... it's really late.

"And for you, Miss?"

Paulette was sitting next to me. She announced confidently, "Steak, medium rare, please ... with a salad."

I have never been adept with words when put on the spot. I was up next. "I'll have a Chocolate Sundae!" I said, a little too loudly.

"Are you sure?" asked the waitress.

"Are you sure?" asked Paulette next to me.

"Are you sure you don't want to have some dinner?" asked my date, Kindness-Personified.

"Oh, no," I said. I was even more embarrassed than before. I started to dig my heels in. "A Chocolate Sundae will be just fine." After all, how many dinners can you have in one night ... only one of course. Everyone was questioning my decision. I was dying a slow death. Perplexed, the waitress went on. Ray was next. He ordered a nice big dinner. After everyone had ordered, we all had a nice visit: eleven people who had finished passing through puberty ... and me.

I remember nothing, absolutely nothing, about the conversation except everyone seemed quite at ease laughing and talking while I sat there stewing about what might come next. While we were waiting for our meals, we must have had refreshments of some sort. I don't remember anything about them ... I must have had what everybody else was having. Soon the salads appeared. I was horrified when the waitress came directly to me and asked if I wanted to have my Chocolate Sundae while the others were having their salads or would I like to wait until everybody else had dessert. Well, if I knew anything, I certainly knew you don't eat dessert while someone else is eating dinner. She had given me an out. With as much of a worldly air as I could muster, I squeaked out, "I'll have it when everyone else has their dessert." Thank goodness she didn't belabor the point. And so everyone shook out their napkins, covered their laps, picked up their utensils, and tucked in.

I remember Paulette sitting gracefully to my left and Ray to my right. I'm a little long in the leg, which means I sit a little lower than expected. I think Ray must have been a little long in the torso, or maybe I was a little self-conscious, because … much like the fish that got away, my memory of Ray sitting there keeps changing … he grows taller and taller in the torso. To this day, I don't remember who was sitting at the right end of the table … after fifty years, he has totally blocked out the view!

Before Paulette started eating, she leaned over to me and asked, "Would you like some of my salad?"

"Oh, no thank you. I'm waiting for my Chocolate Sundae."

"Okay," she said, and without batting an eyelash, she took her fork and moved part of her salad to my bread plate. She pushed it over to me and I accepted it. I am eternally grateful for Paulette. I shook out my napkin, covered my lap, picked up my utensils and tucked into my half-salad … just like everyone else. Actually, I pitied the two or three people who hadn't ordered soup or salad. They had to sit there while everyone else was eating. What were they thinking?

I can't remember everyone who was there, but I remember James (very handsome in a James Brolin sort of way), Helene (always quick to smile and laugh with people), Bunny (a happy energetic organizer), Paulette (a lean-in type of low-speaker with a left eyebrow to die for), and of course, Ray (Kindness-Personified, sitting next to me all self-assured).

Paulette

The dinners came. I was looking around at the plates. With the salad having already primed my appetite, I realized for the first time I was really kind of hungry and, oh my goodness, the food smelled fantastic! Well, there was absolutely nothing I could do about it but wait until everyone ordered dessert. So I waited. Fortunately, with long-torsoed Ray sitting next to me, I could sit up straight without feeling out of place.

And there we sat ... twelve friends enjoying each other's company at Palaske's Hillvilla ... with view of the city ... and my back to the view.

After everyone finished, the waitress came along to take the orders for dessert. She started on the other side of the table. Like dominoes falling in slow motion, my fate played out slowly before me.

"Oh, no thank you," said the first person.

"I've had enough, thank you."

"Nope, no thank you."

"I don't want any."

"I couldn't eat another bite."

"I'm fine ... I'm fine."

It appeared no one ... absolutely no one in our party ... was going to have dessert ... except me. What was I going to do? I couldn't say I'd changed my mind and wasn't hungry. So the waitress brought out the Chocolate Sundae. It was glorious! Everybody "oohed and ah-ed" over it. I tried to stir up a little interest in having someone share it with me, but even Paulette said she couldn't eat another bite. I was eating alone! I was so embarrassed! I ate that Chocolate Sundae as fast as I could! I had to suffer through a little bit of brain-freeze, but I was eating like a woman on the clock!

HOME

When Ray brought me home, I was all concerned if there was supposed to be a kiss. I was thanking my lucky stars I knew how to kiss, even if I hadn't had any practice in ten months. But as it turned out, I didn't get a chance to use the skills I practiced down in

Los Angeles. I think the Prom was his first date, too. The optimum moment came and went. There we were, the two of us, standing on my parents' huge front porch ... Ray was one of the smartest boys in the school, I was one of the smartest girls. Boy, were we dumb!

The next thing I knew, I was in the house. I went over to Mom and Dad's bedroom, just off the dining room, to check in: They always waited up for their children. From the darkened room I heard Mother's voice, "Did you have a good time?"

"Yes."

"Go to bed, Dear. We'll talk tomorrow."

I had never thought of myself as a shy person, but after the Prom, I had to rethink everything.

THE REST OF THE STORY

Fast forward fifty years. I went to our high school's 50-year reunion. I went alone since reunions are not Harry's cup of tea. Ray was there. I got to talking about the Prom and apologizing. Because the dinner had been such a painful experience for me, I assumed it was for him as well, but he wasn't having any of that. Finally, I asked, "What did you think, when we went out?" He looked at me with a little pause and said, reminiscently, "I thought you looked pretty."

Five little words ... twenty-three little letters. In one millisecond, fifty years of anxiety dissipated into thin air.

Handkerchief

The Prom ... (sigh)!

Christmas at Two Ponds

The Backstory

Volume Two of the Two Ponds Trilogy

PART ONE

JOURNEY TO TWO PONDS

1982–1986

1982

The first year of our marriage was spent getting to know each other. I thought we might be a social couple. I invited another couple over for dinner. Harry was still building his State Farm Insurance agency and called to tell me he had an unexpected meeting. That killed our dinner party and our mid-week socializing. We found ways to adjust to this new married life.

FANNING THE FLAMES OF LOVE

We had been married a little more than a month when I got a telephone call as I was leaving work. Harry asked me to bring home some gloves. It was such an unusual request that I asked what he needed them for. It turned out he burned his hand. Things would have gone so much better for me if I had just said okay and let it go at that. But no, I just couldn't leave it alone.

Harry had been examining the house, specifically the third bedroom. He discovered boxes ... a whole room full of boxes! He opened the closet door and found even more boxes. I had saved several boxes to fit any size present possible. He opened some of them and found smaller boxes within boxes, sometimes four deep. Harry knew there were too many boxes and proceeded to take them out to the burn pile in the backyard. He lit them on fire but it was slow going. He added a little accelerant which did wonders to speed things along, but when he turned to go back into the house, he saw his reflection in the patio door and realized he was on fire! Being a man of few words, he only told me the reflection part. AACK! I'd waited until I was 34 to get married and my husband was going up in flames! There was no calming me down. I ran out to the car thinking as fast as I could about where to get a pair of little white gloves. I needed to get home to my new husband quickly. In retrospect, I should have concentrated more on "little white" than "quickly." Since I'd never seen white gloves at Fred

Meyer, I stopped at the only other store I could think of ... Army surplus. I darted in, got the only pair of gloves they had ... green wool ... and raced home. I got home quickly, but the gloves were a total disaster. Wool gloves on a fresh burn ... it does not compute! Thankfully, it wasn't as bad as I had imagined and he was fully recovered by Christmas.

A DIFFERENT PERSPECTIVE

When we had been married two months, the University of Portland, my Catholic alma mater, invited us to a seminar on comparative religions. I thought it would be interesting to go and listen. They had representatives from five different religions: Presbyterian, Methodist, Jewish, Buddhist, and of course, Catholic. All the presenters were interesting. I had never studied other religions, but I certainly had no interest in being anything other than Catholic.

On the drive home, for the sake of getting to know my new husband better, I asked him which of the five religions appealed to him ...

... and he said, "Buddhist!"

Holy Cow! I didn't see that coming. How was this going to work? Could I have a Buddhist husband and still be a Catholic? All sorts of things were popping in and out of my head. I couldn't keep anything straight, so I said, "Why is that?"

Without skipping a beat, my handsome Business-Major Insurance-Agent said, "Because they only tithe three percent."

I began to realize what it would be like to look at the world through someone else's eyes.

Forty years later, we had been watching some TV shows and bigamy came up twice as a common theme. Innocently, I asked, "Can you imagine having two different families?"

Harry was quiet for a few seconds ... imagining having two different families. Finally, he responded, "How would you do the taxes?"

HA-HA-HA, APRIL FOOLS!

When I was growing up, April Fool's Day was always a big thing at our house. Our father was a practical joker, a lot of it rubbed off on his seven children. We were a family of teasers ... I thought everyone was.

Harry and I had been married a little more than six months. I really didn't know him very well. And I certainly didn't know he wasn't a practical joker. I didn't fully appreciate Harry's need to wake up to a calm household. Nor did I realize a man raised in a small family might have a different slant on life than a girl raised with six brothers who enjoyed teasing and pranking.

So at the end of March, I had my antennae up and heard about several types of practical jokes. I selected three. On April 1, I was up before Harry and made orange Jell-O. I had no idea how long it would take for the Jell-O to set, but I held my breath and put it in a red Tupperware juice container. When Harry got up, I went about making special waffles. I layered a five-inch square of cheesecloth in the middle of Harry's waffle.

He stumbled out of the bedroom, scratching his head, still waking up. The table was nicely set with napkins, silverware, and juice glasses. I asked Harry to pour the juice. He let out a big yawn and reached for the container. "Shake it first," I said. Immediately, I turned toward the kitchen sink, bracing myself so he wouldn't see me shaking to stifle a huge laugh. He started to pour the "juice." The orange Jell-O looked like a fat worm in an apple poking its head out about two inches ... "Glug, glug, ... glug" ... hanging in the air ... defying gravity. He straightened the container, frowning and muttering "What the heck?" as the Jell-O returned to the safety of its red confines. I was beside myself. Unable to hold it any longer, I laughed like crazy. Failing to notice I was the only one who was thrilled with the prank, I went over to him and said, "Ha-ha-ha, April Fools!" Then I poured some real orange juice and told him, "Have a seat, our waffles are just about ready."

He sat down as I served the waffles. The butter and syrup were already in place. I sat down and, with the speed of a gazelle, I slathered some butter on my waffle and poured the syrup with a splash. He was barely starting to put on his syrup when I took my first bite. "Umm ... these are really good," I said. Out of the corner of my eye, I watched as he tried to cut his waffle with the fork ... and tried ... and tried! A few fumbles later, steam started rising from his reddening head.

I laughed out loud and said, "Ha-ha-ha, April Fools! ... I've got a good waffle for you over here!" I jumped up and hastily brought a real waffle, steamy and cuttable, promising him there were no more pranks for the breakfast fare. I was having the time of my life! Harry ... not so much.

I had one more thing planned. When he was nowhere to be found, I squirted a little bit of toothpaste out of the tube: Crest toothpaste on one finger and peanut butter on another. Deftly, I repacked the tube with peanut butter ... Sloop ... hiding it with a bit of Crest ... Sloop. It looked like it had never been touched. I had to wait all day for the prank. I'm not good at waiting. Early in the evening, I couldn't stand it anymore. I faked a yawn ... yaaawn ... nothing. About a minute later, I faked another ... yaaawn ... it worked: Harry yawned. With that, I said, "I think I'll get ready for bed." Well, he thought it sounded like a good idea and we each went to separate bathrooms to brush our teeth. As soon as I heard him go in, I tiptoed like something out of a Road Runner cartoon and stood quietly outside the door of the tiny bath. The door was open about one inch ... just enough for me to hear what was going on inside. It was a repeat of the JellO incident. "What the heck ...?" came the comment from the other side of the door. I laughed out loud and started to open the door. Instantly, the door was slammed ... right in my face! All I said was "Happy April Fool's Day!" All he said was, "God help you next year!" It was a very satisfying day for me. How did I know Harry wasn't a practical joker.

The following year, I knew my husband ever-so-much better, and though I was pretty sure April Fool's Day would be uneventful, I did hold out hope he would follow through with his threat. I was disappointed ... but not too much. By that time, I had learned that Harry was not a practical joker. Moreover, I realized we were two very different people, and I was going to need to be on top of our differences for the rest of my life!

Forty years later, I realized the continual process of getting to know the person you've fallen in love with is the best part of being married.

1983

FAMILY OUTINGS

We took Jude our Airedale with us wherever we went. In the late spring we took a trip to Victoria, British Columbia, and visited the Butchart Gardens. They were lovely … all the flowers had just been planted. Everything was orderly … nothing out of place. The gardens are quite large, having been built on the site of a retired limestone quarry. It takes about four hours to see the gardens. When we got about as far away from the car as was physically possible, Harry realized that Jude was under stress and needed to find a spot to take care of business. He reached into his pocket for a baggie and came up empty. Without so much as a boys-howdy, Harry took off as quickly as he could without calling too much attention to himself … and Jude. I wasn't used to taking dogs to that type of public arena and was left in the dust scratching my head.

I wondered if my new husband was pulling a runner! But no, they returned after a short while. Everything was well in their worlds, and mine too. I have a vivid vision of Harry and Jude on the move. My memory of them speeding through the grounds increases by a half a mile per hour each year. In another couple of years, I'll have to contact the *Guinness Book of World Records*!

Jude

WHAT SHALL WE DO WITH OUR LIVES?

We lived in our little ranch-style house with a grease pit and a large fenced backyard. That's where we discovered we liked raising dogs and gardening.

At the end of our first year, with our anniversary approaching, raising puppies came to the top of our list. We had been attending dog shows to find the perfect dog. We each had a pick. Mine was a six-week-old West Highland White Terrier (Westie). Westies are little white frou-frou dogs who look like puppies their entire lives. We spent quite a while looking for a female of good stock because we planned to breed them. At the end of August, we found an excellent litter in the Seattle area. Picking a puppy out of five identical puppies is a real challenge. I carefully learned about each one and twice made my decision … only to find out both times I had selected a male. Eventually, I got frustrated and realized they were all excellent choices. The breeder took charge and guided me to a darling little female, giving me the opportunity to declare for the third time, "This is the one." Because it was our anniversary, we named her Hoffman's Anni Victoria and never once called her anything but Tori. Six weeks later, Harry picked a pretty little twelve-week-old Boxer puppy already named Bizi Bodi (pronounced "busybody"). The name suited her well.

In addition to playing with puppies, we installed two large backyard decks. When we were engaged a year earlier, we installed cruise control on Harry's Scirocco. It was so fun to work together on a project. After we were married, we installed cruise control on our Suburban … it was not quite as much fun. But when we installed the backyard decks, we were pleased to discover we really could work well together, after all. As we began our gardening ventures, Harry said he wanted a big tiller. We decided it would be prudent to wait until we bought some acreage before getting one. It became part of our five-year plan.

1984

After two years of marriage, I decided to make our own Christmas cards ... the tradition was born.

The message included in the Christmas card:

Our 1984 started with a freeze that kept us indoors playing with our new puppies. They're great little lap warmers. We've been to four dog shows this year and are looking forward to some First-Place ribbons in 1985.

After we thawed out, we divided our backyard into six sections: two decks, one section of lawn and three sections of garden. We even converted some of the front yard to corn, squash, and marigolds. That kept us busy through June. We weeded during July. I don't remember having an August or September this year, but we did end up with a lot of canned food on the shelves by October.

We planted fifteen to twenty varieties of hot and sweet peppers, but as the seeds sprouted in the seed tray, Bizi (our little boxer) began to take an interest in gardening. She rearranged all the sweet pepper starts one morning!

Although we had a long, hot summer, I was cool the whole time. By Memorial Day Weekend, I had worked up enough courage to have Harry shave my head. Except for being cold all the time, having to shave every day, and having a five-o'clock shadow that wouldn't quit ... we both liked the result (and my ear healed pretty fast). The whole month I  *was bald was relatively uneventful except for one night during Rose Festival Week: We were driving through the heart of downtown Portland when Harry reached over while and WHIPPED OFF MY WIG!*

Make 1985 a Good Year!

GARDENING

When the third year rolled around, we went at gardening like there was no tomorrow: removing sod, stacking it upside down to make a planter at the high end of the yard, and tilling almost all the rest of the yard for a new garden.

Harry couldn't wait for the five-year plan to materialize. A big red Troy-Bilt tiller showed up at our place at the beginning of the year. He was like a little kid with a new toy. After tilling most of the backyard, he started looking at the front yard. I was scared! We had put an automatic watering system in the front yard ... I figured it was safe enough. (Two years later, I was excited about planting a new bunch of flowers. I jumped down on the shovel exuberantly, accidentally slicing right through the watering system. That was the last straw ... we moved.)

Harry showed what he was made of by amending the soil for the new garden. The next week, we made a run down to Nichol's Garden Nursery in Albany, Oregon, where we got fitted out with seeds ... and gardening paraphernalia to ensure the seeds would grow and produce all kinds of wonders. Produce, they did. Our first year of gardening was amazing. Snakes amidst the bush peas; cherry tomatoes hanging all around the back door jamb; multiple varieties of hot and sweet peppers surrounding the deck; Jerusalem artichokes rising to twelve feet seemingly overnight; flowers in pots on the deck and much, much more. The strangest crop was a special variety of squash called Guatemalan Blue. The squash grew three feet long! The package suggested they be put in women's nylons while they were growing. I had pantyhose ... they worked! The most precious crop we planted was the celery. Like he had with the corn, Harry started the celery in a trench. It was very sweet to see Harry squatting and fussing over his celery each week, packing soil around the growing plants to ensure they would be properly blanched. And he would coo to them! The celery plants had no idea they were so well-loved!

Tori was enamored with the Alderman peas growing up like pole beans on the back fence. They loved the constant shade and produced well. I never had to bend over to pick peas because Tori kept the lower two feet harvested while I took care of the top four feet. What a team!

Tori

SPEAKING OF HAIR

A Bald Woman: One day, I saw a striking woman on Star Trek. She had shaved off all her hair and was absolutely beautiful. I wondered what I might look like with no hair. I thought I might have a pretty good-looking head.

Fleshy Jowls: Another day, after a nice visit with my mother, I wanted to give her a kiss goodbye. I put my hands out to both of her cheeks and gently pulled her toward me. I was horrified to see her face come toward me while she remained stationary. She had the infamous fleshy Beaucage jowls. She usually kept them disguised by smiling. I suppose if we live long enough, we'll all look like Shar-Peis, but I wasn't expecting it from my mother. Worse yet, knowing I look like Mom, I knew this was in my future. I wondered what I might look like with no hair and fleshy jowls. I shuddered. Not a pretty thought!

Another Pesky Box: When you get something new, you treated it with reverence. My brothers may have had a different experience, but this has always been one of my boxes. In fact, I'd look at my "new thing" for a while … it would be days before I'd start using it. I'm still like that. (Harry doesn't understand.) For example: If you buy new shoes, you use them for good, and you use your old worn-out shoes for gardening. It's the hand-me-down principle. Everybody knows about the hand-me-down principle! Just to reiterate … When you buy shoes, you don't just go out and wear them in the mud!

Feelings: We had been married a year when Harry brought home a new pair of good-looking brown shoes. He took them out of the box, slathered leather conditioner on them, put them on, and proceeded to wear his beautiful new shoes out in the muddy garden! We weren't rolling in dough; in fact, we were a tad bit over-extended. I was just sick. Never having been one to confront my feelings, I coped in the only way I knew how … I burst into tears

"What's the matter?" he asked compassionately.

"I'm feeling left out." I bawled as I tried to zero in on the real reason I was blubbering. That wasn't it.

So he said, "Well … what do you want to do?"

And there I was. I had the whole universe in front of me ... I could choose anything. But what did I want to do? I made something up as quickly as I could without giving a whit as to the sensibility of the notion. I fired off, "I ... I want to shave my head!" For heaven's sake! Shave my head? Where in the world did that come from, I wondered. It just came out. When I get upset, or when I get nervous, stuff just comes out. Nobody, least of all me, knows what's going to come out! But it was out there, and I wasn't going to take it back.

And Harry, as cool as a cucumber, said, "Okay, when do you want to do it?" If he had thrown his head back and given me a belly laugh, we would have been finished with it. But he didn't. He was actually very sweet and supportive. And so we began to flesh out my pop decision into a goal with a deadline and a bunch of tasks.

It was not a well-thought-out plan! It just kept getting more and more real. I reverted to logic, saying, "I don't want to do it until the weather gets warm ..." (since we were starting into the winter months it gave me an opportunity to get prepared) "... Memorial Day." I suppose I could have changed my mind, but it would have cast doubt on the entire conversation. What kind of message would I have sent to my new husband? Harry said he would help me.

In my defense, it wasn't a purely off-the-cuff idea. I had seen the Star Trek episode with Uhura and her shaved head. And the visit with my mother was still pretty fresh in my mind. I soon realized if I wanted to know whether or not I had a good-looking head, I had better do it soon. Armed with these thoughts, we had the new-shoe incident and before I knew it, I had declared I wanted to shave my head.

If I was going to go through with this ... and I was ... I needed to have something for an everyday look. I wasn't planning to do this to shock my coworkers. I had a good job in a conservative engineering organization in the Northwest ... a federal agency ... Bonneville Power Administration (BPA). I bought a wig. It wasn't too bad. It looked a lot better on page six of the catalog than it did on my head, but this wasn't going to be a lifetime look. I wore the wig to work once a week during the late fall, but it got boring. I got a couple more wigs, tapping into the offerings from pages eight and nine.

The people at the office knew what I was up to, but they didn't know when. Mom knew, too … she wailed, "But Kath-leeeen, your hair is your crowning glory!" (Hers maybe … not mine.)

Wigs: By winter, I had gotten a lot of catalogs from *Wigs by Paula*. I decided to branch out and buy a Dolly Parton wig with brown curls.

When the Christmas party came along, I was part of a skit. I wore a long black midi-skirt and a button-down blouse with a blazer to the party. At the appointed time, I ran into the changing room, unbuttoned a couple of buttons, rolled my skirt at the waistband, ditched the blazer, slathered red on my cheeks and lips, rubbed purple on my eyelids, and topped off the look with the Dolly Parton wig. Within minutes, I sashayed out onto the stage. I noticed Dan and one of the guys from the billing section had started drooling. It was funny to see them almost choke on their drinks when they realized who was behind all the costuming and makeup. After that episode, I saved the Dolly Parton wig for date night with my hubby.

I had about four wigs and used them twice a week during the spring. People were getting used to seeing me in wigs. They'd ask about the wigs from time to time, not really wanting to know if I truly was going to shave my head.

One Friday night, I was wearing a mediocre wig when I stopped by Papa Murphy's for a take-and-bake pizza. I raced home and put it in the oven. I went through the mail and returned phone calls. In almost no time, the timer went off. I reached into the oven to pull out the pizza and heard "dzzzt." I couldn't figure out where the irritating sound was coming from until I took off my wig and examined the bangs … singed! Totally unacceptable. The hair was plastic … I had shortened several of the strands in the bangs. They each looked like a butterfly antenna with a little round blob on the end. Thank goodness they didn't melt together! But, not being one to throw something away simply because it's ruined, I made an appointment at the beauty college downtown. The poor little girl who had to cut my wig did her best, but it still looked pretty wretched. Sadly, I wore it to work the following week, and for the first time in all those months, I was complimented on how nice the wig looked ... by more than one person. I was disgusted, but I tried not to let it show.

The Deed: Memorial Day was getting closer and closer. Shaving my head was all I could think about. When the big evening came, neither of us said anything. It was just like a regular evening, except I sat at the counter and played solitaire ... non-stop ... for more than two hours! Earlier in the day, I had totally cleaned the house. It was like I was nesting: I was doing everything in the world, except getting ready to shave my head.

As the evening wore on, Harry said, "Well ... are we going to do this?" So I said yes. He filled a large bowl with warm water and got a razor and shaving cream. He laid out everything he needed on a little table including a couple of nice towels and the electric clippers we had purchased (and used!) for dog grooming. The whole process had me befuddled. I thought all he had to do was run a razor over my scalp and it would be a done deal. Not Harry. This was a serious production. He pulled out a chair for me and signaled me to sit. I sat.

"WAIT!" I yelled as I jumped up and raced for the camera. We took a breather while I posed in front of a large conversation bubble on an otherwise-blank wall. On the bubble was written "Hi Lar" (pronounced "lair") short for Larry, one of my bosses. He had a flattop all the years I worked with him. This seemed like a fitting way for me to mark this momentous event. Harry snapped a picture.

Before

There was to be no more stalling or I would lose my cohort. He plugged in the electric clippers and flipped the switch. The familiar groan of the blades filled my ears. Standing behind me, he ran the dog clippers over the center of my head leaving a swath about two inches wide and only an eighth of an inch long. Too late now, I thought, as he continued his mission. Next, he lathered my head with shaving cream and picked up a brand-new razor from the table. Finally, with great care and concentration, he shaved the last eighth inch of my hair clean off my head, using a dozen practiced swipes. I sat there looking in the mirror and thought, I'm going to need a lot more makeup!

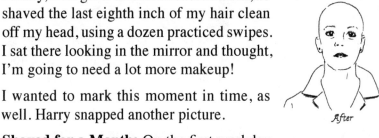

After

I wanted to mark this moment in time, as well. Harry snapped another picture.

Shaved for a Month: On the first workday after Memorial Day, I wore a wig to work as usual, but nobody said a word. They just knew ... and they sure didn't want me to take the wig off!

I wore different wigs each day. It was a hot summer ... we were setting records ... but I was so cold! Hair really keeps in the heat!

One day, about two weeks after the deed, I sat down with Dan. It was his turn to be the duty scheduler working through lunch. I asked, "Shall I take it off?"

He looked at the wig and said, "No, no, no."

We repeated the query-response pattern about five times, until finally, I reached up and whipped off the wig. Dan gasped! In retrospect, it wasn't a very smart thing to do. Dan had a weak heart, but thankfully, he lived through it. He was the only one at the office who saw me with no hair.

Waking up to no hair and no makeup every morning was startling. It made me think a lot about Auschwitz ... I had a reverence for the people in the concentration camps. But I didn't want to grow my hair back too soon. This was a one-time deal. I made a decision to continue shaving for a month.

Returning to Normal: After 28 days, I started to let my hair grow. The wigs became intolerable ... hot and itchy. I wore homemade turbans. BPA people would come for meetings and there I'd be, wearing a little cotton turban. One day, I noticed some of my quarter-inch hairs were poking through the material. Nobody had said a word. A year later, some of those people worked up the courage to ask me quietly if I was all right, now. I felt bad ... they had assumed I'd had major health concerns.

In September, I decided I'd keep my head covered until Christmas as I let my hair grow out to a decent length. Then I thought, "Shoot ... why wait?" I had gone to a hair salon down the street (will I never learn?) and they gave me a buzzcut. It didn't look too bad, so I slathered on the makeup and went to work. Larry, the big boss, was sitting at one of the consoles. I marched right up to him. I don't know what I said, but I was very assertive. I figured if I could get through a conversation with Larry, I could get through anything. Also, if everyone knew Larry knew, they'd have to fall in line. Taken slightly off guard, he took a close look at me and that was that. We ended up talking about work stuff, and I went on with the rest of my day.

A Real Card: But that wasn't exactly the end of it. Armed with Larry's acceptance, I was oblivious to what was to come. Roger, a real card, was on the rung of the corporate ladder below Larry. Well, nothing gets by Roger. He was walking by, took one look at me under all my makeup, and doubled over laughing. When he finally caught his breath, he choked out, "You look like a ... (mild expletive deleted) ... whore!"

Roger & Freddie

Soon afterwards, Roger married my best friend, Marg. Ten years later, Roger died ... bless his heart. At his memorial service we were invited to speak ... from our pews. I stood up and started telling the story about Roger laughing at me. I had it all written out so I wouldn't fall to pieces. Since it was a memorial service, I was sniffling like crazy. And because I had to look down at the paper to read, I knew I couldn't make it all the way through without a good blow. So right in the middle of the story, I sat down in the pew, pulled out a hand-kerchief, and did what needed to be done. Pastor Duane Sich was baffled. He waited a few seconds and finally said, "Well ... I guess Kathy's finished." I raised my hand and said "No, I'm not!" I put away my hankie and told the rest of the story. But, since the church was full of people, I took some editorial license with the punchline saying, "You look like a gosh-darn whore!" Everyone laughed ... everyone knew Roger ... they knew exactly what he had said!

1985

The message included in the Christmas card:

We had some odd gardening experiences this year. The broccoli that was supposed to flower last December finally came through in March. We didn't realize it until it was too late. We had already tilled most of it in. Later in the year, Harry wanted a greenhouse, and I wanted a solarium. We compromised and put a clear plastic tunnel over sixteen tomato plants to extend the harvest ... in the center of the garden. It worked pretty well, too ... except on the really hot days when we actually harvested stewed tomatoes!

MERRY CHRISTMAS
from
KATHY & HARRY

Since the harvest season, we've done nothing but play with the five Westie puppies. They're happy, healthy, and loud. They sound like a gaggle of geese when they get banished to their individual crates each night.

I'm pleased with my new pumpkin bread recipe. It's moist and full-bodied. I like to make it with home-grown sweet pumpkins for the naturally sweet flavor. One medium pumpkin makes about four batches. Enjoy!

```
            SWEET  PUMPKIN  BREAD


COMBINE IN MIXER               2 CUPS SUGAR
                               ½ CUP MOLASSES
                               ⅔ CUP SHORTENING

BLEND... THEN ADD              4 EGGS
     TO MIXTURE                2 CUPS PUMPKIN
                               ⅜ CUP MILK

SIFT... THEN ADD               4 CUPS FLOUR
     TO MIXTURE                2 tsp BAKING POWDER
                               1 tsp SALT
                               1 tsp GINGER
                               ¾ tsp BAKING SODA
                               ½ tsp GROUND CLOVES

ADD TO MIXTURE                 1 CUP RAISINS
                               1 CUP WALNUTS

GREASE & FLOUR TWO 9×5" LOAF PANS ... OR THREE 10×3" PANS.
BAKE AT 350° FOR 1-1½ HOURS (TEST WITH TOOTHPICK).
COOL ... WRAP AND STORE OVERNIGHT BEFORE SLICING

        ADAPTED FROM A "BETTER HOMES AND GARDENS" RECIPE
                        KATHY HOFFMAN  1985
```

WESTIES – TORI'S FIRST LITTER

In our fourth year, I was ready to scale back a little. I took some photinia cuttings and stuck them in the ground about two feet from the fence at two-foot intervals. They were lost amid the jungle of vegetables.

Meanwhile, Harry and I were hard at it, breeding our little Westie. I had read *The Comprehensive West Highland White Terrier* from cover to cover. But as the big day came, I read the chapter on birthing almost daily. The only thing it told me to watch for was whether or not her milk came in. If that was the only thing the book was concerned about, I wanted to be prepared for it.

When the big day came in September 1985, we were ready … sort of. All three of us were novices. The first time Tori screamed Harry took charge. I stood by with a can opener in one hand and a can of baby formula in another as Harry tried to determine if the scream was from normal contractions or something else. Finally, he realized it was something else. The puppy was breech. Aack! The book didn't say anything about that. I was useless, standing about two feet away, my elbows out to each side, the can opener poised, ready to pierce the tin lid in case Tori's milk didn't come in right away. I instinctively knew if the puppy didn't get milk within the first two minutes of life, it would die. I had no reason to question my instincts. Harry, on the other hand, instinctively knew if the first puppy didn't come out, the rest couldn't and we'd really have a problem. He reached up in there and did what had to be done. Thirty-seven years later, the memory has morphed into something akin to birthing a calf, but in 1985 we were only dealing with a twenty-five-pound dog … there wasn't a lot of "reaching up in there" that could be done. Once he got the puppy turned lengthwise, Tori let out a couple more normal screams and out popped a fat little fist-sized puppy in a sac. Harry broke the sac and did the routine cleaning with a soft washcloth. I was still standing there … frozen … with elbows still raised (to get good leverage in case I needed to open the formula tin quickly) taking it all in. When he finished, he placed the little one next to her mama's teat and miraculously, she started to suckle. Tori's milk had come in! I started to relax. It seemed I was not going to have to open the 49-cent can of formula after all. Tori didn't care about a thing, she just started licking her little one. Instincts. We all have them. Some are more finely-honed than others.

The first two puppies were born on Friday the 13th. I helped Tori with the second one. Harry retired at midnight. The remaining three came every couple of hours after midnight. Having been overly involved with the first four, I failed to realize Tori knew what her role was. It was almost 5 a.m. when the last one came. After helping her with her contractions (putting pressure on her sides to help her push), I relaxed and watched her do everything ... just like *The Comprehensive West Highland White Terrier* book said she would. She was a good mom.

The book advised it was a good idea to keep the first litter and raise the puppies for six months. We heeded the advice. Three months later, I realized the book was wrong! So were we. We had three large four-by-eight-foot chain-link dog pens in the garage: one for Tori, one for Bizi Bodi, and one for Jude. When the puppies ... Agatha, Woodrow, Rutledge, Dietrich, and Hector ... were big enough to climb out of their whelping box but too big to escape under the chain-link fencing, it was time for a change. Tori moved in with Bizi Bodi giving the puppies their own pen. For three months, those five puppies piled on top of each other on blankets and slept soundly through the night. Then one day, we had the brilliant idea to make a change to this efficient system: crate training. We gave each of the puppies their own metal crate. After we finished dinner, we put the puppies to bed in those strange dark metal boxes without any indoctrination. Oblivious to the chaos we were wreaking, we went back into the house to watch TV. You have never heard such a commotion. The puppies screamed and cried in protest. Finally, after two hours, our ears couldn't take it any longer. We gave in and put them back in the big pen. They whimpered for about three minutes and then conked out ... five little heartbeats back together again. The next night, we tried again. They fussed and screamed for about thirty minutes and then settled down. After that, it was smooth sailing.

Three months of rapidly growing puppies was all we could stand. Soon they went to new homes. Our friend John came over first. The Westie book suggested we apply a puppy behavior test to each dog. The six tests included:

COME (attraction to people)

STROKING (attitude toward social activities)

FOLLOWING (desire to stay in a social environment)

RESTRAINT (acceptance of human dominance)

RETRIEVING (concentration and desire to please)

PINCH (pain tolerance and forgiveness)

I read the instructions for each test. John tested each puppy while I recorded the scores. I could see John wanted Woodrow ... they just clicked. Woody scored 100% on every test. (He was a little hoarse because he barked the loudest and the longest during the crate initiation evenings. This may have made a difference in my enthusiasm for giving him good scores.) When all was said and done, Linda, the owner of the sire, picked Agatha and named her Lucky because she was born on Friday the 13th. Woody went home with John. Rutledge went to a farm in Astoria to live an idyllic life with a variety of house pets. We kept happy-go-lucky Hector and a handsome pup named Dietrich. Dietrich went on to get his American-Canadian championship thanks to Linda's tutelage and handling.

Dietrich

At first, the metal crates were stacked two and three high. Hector, a big chunk of a dog, was always in the top crate. Every night, he would stand in front of the crates, face me, and wait to be picked up and stuffed into his crate. As each puppy found a new home, the arrangement of the crates changed. Soon, all the crates were at floor level. When I told the Westies to go to bed, Tori walked into her crate, Dietrich walked into his, but mild-mannered Hector stood there belligerently, refusing to enter the crate, actually turning his back to the crate. I told him to go to bed a second time, but he remained determined to disobey my order. It was so unlike him. It finally dawned on me: he didn't know how to go into a crate. He'd always been picked up and placed into the crate. Laughing, I turned him around facing the entrance and gave him a little nudge. He was more than happy to go in.

Dogs ... gotta love 'em!

Connie, a lovely friend who often came to my tea parties with her granddaughters, thought the sun rose and set over Hector ... and he thought the same about her. When we were ready to find him a home, she and husband Gary snapped him up. He had a good life.

JESSICA

Our friends, Doug and Charlie, had a litter of kittens. They were all white. Since we were raising little white frou-frou dogs, I thought it would be nice to have a white kitty. Enter Jessica. Although I am very allergic to cats, we made it work. Jessie turned out to be a tabby kitten and darkened up pretty rapidly over her first couple of months. During those months, I called her with a sing-song voice ... "Jessie" ... and she would come trotting to me ... "Mew." Who knew you could train cats to come on command?

Our little "come-on-command" worked out to be quite useful. When Jessie was about six years old, we hosted a fortieth birthday party at Two Ponds for Carol of Bruce-and-Carol, Harry's friends from way back. We didn't know any of their friends and they had a lot of them. Everyone was down on the patio and the terraces. I was coming out the front door after going into the house for something, when I noticed Jessie coming up through the ivy from the gully. She had something dangling from her chops ... and it was moving! AACK! "Jessie," I said in my sing-song voice trying to keep control of my horror, "Jessie!" She had been on a beeline for the patio to show off her new catch to all the people. Fortunately, she happily turned to the left and came right toward me. After a few pauses, replete with deliberate crunches, she set her newly demised catch before me. I used my gardening gloves to give it a well-directed fling back into the gully. Everyone was happy (or none-the-wiser) ... except the mole.

When Jess was about twelve, she disappeared. We had frequent sightings of coyotes, raccoons, bigger-than-house-cat cats, hawks, and larger birds. We knew what to expect since we had bought a house above a gully. A disappearing cat could mean only one thing. I was so sad to lose our kitty. But no corpse meant hope. I called her every time I went outdoors. "Jessie ... Jessie!" No response. Hope dwindled by a full percentage point with every failure until we were down to one percent. I kept the one percent alive and continued to call for her for days even though I knew she was gone. After about seven or eight days, just before bedtime, I leaned out the back door with my usual plea ... "Jessie?" ... "mew." What? ... maybe it was just my wishful thinking. I called again ... "mew" ... and again ... "Mew." As I walked toward the cul-de-sac, the response got stronger. By the light of the moon, I could barely see her on the roof of the neighbor's house. It would have been

Jessica

smart to alert the neighbor, but I wanted my kitty back. I ran home, grabbed a stepladder, rescued my kitty from the roof, re-grabbed the stepladder, and beat it out of there. I could have been shot (unlikely, but still). I was glad for the early cat training.

HOMEMADE BREAD

I was into bread-baking in a big way in the '80s. In 1985, someone suggested I enter my bread in the Clark County Fair. It sounded like a fun thing to do. I did my best and took the bread in on Friday morning, the first day of the fair. Harry's folks were visiting us at the time. Harry's mom and I went to the fair a week later to see if I had won anything. There were a lot of blue ribbons on a lot of entries, but my poor little loaf was nowhere to be found. After we had looked at every loaf, Mom found a little table off to the side with three strange lumps on display. My beautiful loaf of bread had turned green and fuzzy after a week exposed to the August weather. Nevertheless, it earned a blue ribbon And what's more, it earned a yellow rosette! The Washington Association of Wheat Growers had conducted a contest ... all the fair entries were contestants. It was quite a thrill. I took the rosette and the recipe to work and showed it off. I even told people the key ingredient that made my bread taste so spectacular. Mark, in a neighboring office, looked closely at the recipe and said slyly, "I wonder if the Washington Association of Wheat Growers know the secret ingredient for your award-winning bread is cornmeal?"

The Washington Association of Wheat Growers sponsored a contest for yeast bread entries in the 1985 Clark county Fair.   This bread took first place ... Enjoy!   Kathy 8/3/85

Whole Wheat Bread

1/2 cup	Cornmeal	1 pkg	Yeast	1/2 cup	Rye Flour
1/3 cup	Honey	1/2 cup	Warm Water	2 cups	Whole Wheat Flour
1 Tbsp	Sea Salt	1/4 tsp	Honey	3-4 cups	Unbleached White Flour
2 cups	Boiling Water				
1/4 cup	Oil				Cornmeal

Combine the 1st five ingredients; Cool to lukewarm.

Dissolve yeast in warm water with honey; Add to cornmeal mixture. Add flour in order shown until dough is fairly stiff. Knead on floured surface until smooth and elastic. Place in oiled bowl, covered, and let rise in a warm place until doubled in bulk (1 hr).

Knead and shape into 2-3 loaves. Place on an oiled baking sheet or a baker's stone sprinkled with cornmeal. Slice top of each loaf several times for decoration. Cover with a clean towel and let loaves rise in a warm place until doubled (1 hr).

Bake at 350°F for 35 minutes.

Adapted from a recipe for "Early Colonial Bread" from The Whole Grain Bake Book, by Gail Worstman.

PART TWO

OUR YEARS AT TWO PONDS

1986–2015

Hoity-toity people name their property. We got on the bandwagon. We tried to think of something original. Since we're only moderately hoity-toity people, we decided the name should have something to do with the fact we have two ponds on our property. I was hungry at the time and suggested we use some bashed-up French and call it "Pon Deux." Harry wasn't into French and blurted out "Two Ponds." No marriage should have to hang in the balance over such a simple issue … I caved. It was settled … we lived at Two Ponds … but I wasn't crazy about the name and stuck it in a drawer for more than thirty years. And now it has seen the light of day!

1986

" And This one says ... Mer...ry... Christ... mas... To ... "

The message included in the Christmas card:

It's been six months since we moved to our new home. Harry has been busy with his latest toy ... a chipper/shredder. The forest is now under control and the property line is taking on definition. Our next project is building the fence. We plan to build several concrete-block posts with board fencing between the posts. We'll make the concrete blocks by ourselves. If the weather cooperates, we should have a substantial fence in place by mid-'87. All we need to do now is find a little cement mixer.

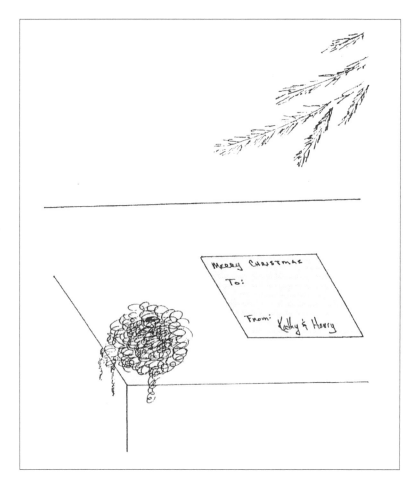

Bizi had a litter of Boxer-pup (not a typo) in mid-September ... only one ... but what an absolutely fine little mountain climber. When she was just weaned at 5½ weeks old, she climbed out of her three-foot high pen ... the last step must have been a doozie. She had a wonderful time exploring the kitchen that day and ate like a pig for the next day and a half. I have a picture of her doing it again at 6½ weeks.

— FORCING BULBS —

I found a nice little article in the 10/86 issue of Better Homes & Gardens. If you do this before Christmas, you can have your own indoor blooms (the hard way) by Easter.

1. Plant bulbs in a pot of soil with good drainage (Don't let them touch each other or the side of the pot.) Water thoroughly!
2. Place in refridgerator for 8-10 weeks. Keep the pot moist.
3. Check for growth about Valentine's Day: When stems are 1-2 inches high, move to a bright 60-70° area.
4. When the buds finally form, enjoy them in any room!

Priscilla and Freddie, from Tori's second litter, are seven months old. They'll have their first dog show on December 14. Whether they win or not, I know Priss will have a good time talking to the judge!

I've taken up oil painting this year. Comments from art critics regarding my first two paintings ranged from "very nice, and such depth" to "nice, but not much depth." That gave me a pretty good idea of how I was doing. My art instructor says I have to paint ninety paintings before I'm a bona fide artist ...I have 82 to go!

Have an extra-special holiday season!

TORI'S SECOND LITTER

Early in our fifth year, May to be exact, Tori had a second litter of six pups. Just when I thought we'd be living on 107th Street forever, Harry, who had been eager to have another reason to use his Troy-Bilt tiller, up and moved us 23 blocks east to a "little house with possibilities" and two ponds. We had nine dogs and no fence! I was in the middle of interviewing potential dog owners (the puppies were exactly six weeks old). They had to come for a one-hour interview in early June and then another one-hour interview when they picked up their little puppy. Two puppies went to their new homes on the day before and the day of the move! (Could it have been more hectic?)

Tori was an exceptional mother. She was good to her puppies, but when a potential owner came, she buffed the little puppy around acting like a bully. This behavior occurred consistently at every final interview. It was as if she was showing the new owner the puppy wasn't fragile and needed discipline from the git-go. (I've misread a lot of signals, but I think I got this one right.)

Beresford and McGuyver went to their new homes during the move! Jonathan and Wadsworth went to their new homes a month later. We kept Winnifred (Freddie Lu) and Priscilla to see how they would grow up. Wadsworth couldn't have gone to a better home: When Bob and Anita were looking at the puppies during their first interview, I told them how I could always feel Wadsworth before he was born because he was such a huge pup. Bob's heart melted. Wadsworth was renamed MacGregor when they took him home. He never failed to send me pictures of himself sitting on Santa's lap! In fact, he trained Bob and Anita so well they still send me Christmas pictures of their puppy on Santa's lap ... every year ... 36 years!

Within three weeks, when we were still getting settled, the Fourth of July fireworks scared our old Airedale, Jude. She ran off in a confused state and managed to find her way back to the old house ... she had traversed more than two miles of residential area, crossing

Highway 99 and going under Interstate5. How did she know where to go? It still amazes me.

The new owner of the house called me. When I arrived to pick her up, I was stunned to see the backyard had been totally transformed ... lawn everywhere and absolutely no garden area! However, there was the lovely young photinia hedge just inside the fence line: It had been invisible during our gardening efforts and was now strikingly showcased against a green lawn! Different strokes for different folks. Nevertheless, I was pleased with the result.

Unfortunately, the long and wild run took the wind out of Jude's already weakened sails, and we had to say goodbye to our loyal friend three weeks later.

In May 1986, I wrote a letter to two hundred of our closest friends, saying:

Happy Days are here again! Tori had six pups ... four males and two females ... on Sunday morning, May 4, 1986.

We're all old hands at this, nevertheless, Tori, Harry, and I were exhausted on Sunday. We had waited seven hours for the first one. Naturally we were a little anxious when the second came just five minutes later ... at 2:35 in the wee hours of the morning. The rest came in a rhythmic pattern at 4:15, 5:05, 5:45, and 6:15. They're all healthy and, except when Mama takes a break, they're all quite happy, too. We don't have a runt this time ... we have five big pups and a giant.

Tori's 2ⁿᵈ Litter

Harry and I put earnest money down on a sweet little home with lots of character and two large ponds. There's a separate one-bedroom cottage about twenty yards away, which we plan to turn into a full-fledged kennel over the next several years. The house is a

30-year-old concrete structure and we're still just four miles from work. With any luck, we'll be settled by the 4th of July. We've been looking for about three years and we both have very positive vibes about this house.

I got the job I was bidding on ... Section Chief of Scheduling ... supervising the group I started with in 1970. All in all, I'll be looking forward to the stress of the holidays because it'll be a piece of cake compared to life for the next few months.

We moved in on June 15, and Harry announced that the four years we lived in our first house was the longest he had lived anywhere. That was a scary thought for a deep-rooted settler like me.

In July, I sent out another letter to the same two hundred of our closest friends, saying:

For now, it's a white masonry house with red trim and a moss-green roof ... but we're working on the roof.

The view out the front room window started out good and keeps getting better: two home-built natural-stream-fed ponds. Harry's been clearing the banks with a gas-powered Weed Eater, some limb snippers, and a chain saw. Someday, we hope to have floating decks at odd intervals. Harry's been going out in a rowboat with Dietrich (ten-month-old Westie) clearing trash from the top of the pond with a pool net. It's a very pleasant atmosphere. We are enjoying the serenity of country life ... right in the city!

The view from the back of the house ... from the kitchen ... is an enclosed porch area with a lot of indirect sunlight. The backyard is in lawn and is surrounded by a mini-forest. Harry has carpeted the paths so we can all walk back there without getting our shoes or paws dirty!

We have some fun things planned for the next five years like a two-story greenhouse to provide an indoor path from the main floor to the basement, and a garage and kennel area within view of the dining room and greenhouse so we know what our little treasures are doing. We've had no major unexpected surprises, but we'll have to start with a roof and a fence for now.

We sent Bizi up to the Seattle area to be bred. You can just imagine what we'll be doing on our fourth anniversary ... we'll have boxers and Westies all over the place.

THE ROOF

The roof was actually a slightly faded red, but we were told it was a bar-tile roof. I enjoyed telling my friends we had a bar-tile roof. Every time I said it, my left eyebrow raised about a quarter inch (looking very much like Paulette's left eyebrow). Other people had tile roofs ... we had a *bar*-tile roof. It never occurred to me to check and see what that meant.

The roof was covered in moss, Harry went up to check it out ... our precious bar-tile roof ... and stuck his foot right through one of the tiles. It turned out bar-tile retains moisture, consequently it lasts only half as long as regular tile. We had to deal with roof replacement immediately. In the future, whenever I mentioned the bar-tile roof, it was my left nostril, not my left eyebrow, that raised about a quarter inch.

DREAMS

The dream of having a large two-story glass structure on the south-facing wall never materialized. Neither of us wanted to be in charge of window cleaning. A fence surrounding the property came and went. We had the trees thinned and cut into fireplace wood during our first year. It was a lot of wood. We stacked it along the east property line. Instantly, we had a cord-wood fence about three feet high ... enough to keep the Westies on our property. Over the next few years, we burned our fence, a couple of logs at a time. By the time it was gone, the dogs had learned to stay in the yard.

BOXER PUPPY

Bizi Bodi was pregnant. The book said the gestation period was 62–65 days. Whelping Westies was pretty exciting. I thought I'd better not miss whelping the boxer puppies. I did the math and sat up with Bizi … all night of the 62nd day … nothing. I was a little tired. I sat up with her the next night … all night of the 63rd day … nothing. I was more tired. I sat up with her the next night … dozing all night of the 64th day … nothing. I was a wreck. I gave up and slept through the following night. When I got up in the morning, our sweet little boxer was looking up at me

Bizi Bodi

with a guilty look on her face. There in front of her was a little brown lizard about nine inches long. No placenta, no cord, no mess. I put my glasses on and discovered the lizard was actually a beautiful fawn-colored female with a black mask. We named her Missie. I told Bizi what a good job she had done. She started beaming immediately.

I was surprised Bizi had only one pup, but what a pip of a pup. She had mountaineering blood in her veins. Even though she had the run of an eight-foot-square area in the kitchen, she wanted to explore the world. At the astonishingly early age of six weeks, she climbed up and over the thirty-inch fencing and began exploring the house. Bizi knew the rules and stayed in the pen. I wondered if Missie would have been able to get back in the pen when she got hungry.

Missie

1987

Priscilla (Color the star a bright yellow)

I took an art class from a woman who suggested adding one spot of color to a Christmas card drawing to give it a little drama. It resonated with me. I tried to think it through so it wouldn't be a tedious project. 1987 was the best year ... 1997 (gold spray paint) was the absolute worst!

The message inserted in the Christmas card:

Happy Holidays to you!

We decided to see the world this year. We started with a trailer trip to Lake Louise, Banff, and Jasper ... just the two of us ... and a boxer and four little white dogs. The Canadian Rockies were awesome ... inspiring. I hope to capture the feelings on canvas in 1988.

Dietrich impressed us all by acing his American Championship this summer. One more trip to Canada and he should have his Canadian Championship as well.

Tori has had a date with Laird and is expecting another litter of treasures by mid-December. They'll have their eyes and mouths open by Christmas. Freddie and Priss are both expecting about Super Bowl time. Hurray for life!

Have a good year!

Designer Dogs By Kate 1987

WEST HIGHLAND WHITE TERRIER

MUST REBOOT

The Westies were driving me crazy. They were getting up with the sun ... waking me earlier and earlier each day. Lake Louise, Banff, and Jasper are in the province of Alberta. It is one time zone over. I don't know how or why it happened, but the dogs all rebooted during the trip. By the time we got back to our own time zone, we were all back on the same schedule!

MORE HOMEMADE BREAD

My passion for baking bread continued. I got pretty excited when Marg's birthday rolled around. We worked in the same office at the time. I baked a nice free-form loaf in the form of an infinity symbol (a figure eight). Mornings in the office were especially hectic with everyone looking into what had happened the night before and adjusting their duties accordingly. (Our offices managed water flow to meet Northwest energy needs: Water in the largest Northwest rivers was used to generate enough electricity to meet half of the energy needs. We worked closely with public and private utilities who served the other half of the energy needs.) Even though everyone was pretty busy, I went around to the offices and dragged people over to the central area. Everyone stopped what they were doing, gathered around, pulled a fistful of bread from the large loaf, and waited patiently, as directed. The duty scheduler had an atomic clock on the console. We used it to count down the seconds. At eight seconds after the specified minute, we all shoved our bread in our mouths so each of us could say, "I ate an eight at 8:-0-8:-0-8 on 8/8/88!" It doesn't get much better than that!

TORI'S THIRD LITTER

On December 4, Tori whelped her third litter: five beautiful pups. Westies usually have about three puppies per litter. Tori was averaging more than five! The woman who raised her was into animal husbandry. She knew her genes! These pups were eventually named MacDuff, Murdock, Charles, Laddie MacFarland, and Jonnie Bo. With all the stress of the holidays coming at the same time as Tori's third litter, I left most of the naming to the new owners. Bonnie Jo was one of the new owners … I was so confused.

When the puppies were born, I gave them nicknames: Tinker, Murdock, Cully, Farley, and Lily-Ann. Tinker was my favorite. As always, when there was a new litter, I weighed the puppies every eight hours to make sure they were going in the right direction …

Tinker wasn't. He was losing weight. The book said if he lost too much weight, he wouldn't be able to suckle. I gave him first dibs at every feeding, but he was lackluster. I weighed all the pups every four hours and watched Tinker's numbers drop. It was very discouraging. He was only 167 grams at birth. When he dropped to 137 grams, 28 hours later, I took action: I got a wee little eye-dropper and put a teaspoon of formula in it. Pressing him against my chest, I gently squeezed his little mouth open with the finger and thumb of my left hand. Squeezing out a few drops with my right hand, I was glad for gravity, my friend. Drop by drop over the next two days, little Tinker regained his birth weight and started growing. Tori took care of the others like a pro. After a week, Tinker was ready

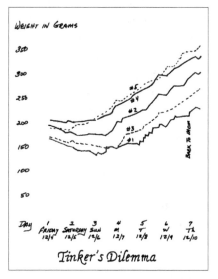

Tinker's Dilemma

to rejoin his littermates. He jostled his way to a spigot and did what came naturally … a very good sight! A month later, he was the third heaviest.

With the stress of Christmas and Tinker's feeding routines out of the way, I had time to relax and enjoy watching the pups. I recorded their antics as they grew from 2½ to 6 weeks:

12/21 – Tinker and Cully did not like being on their backs. Farley and Lily-Ann settled right down when they had a little tummy rubbing. Tori was standing up to nurse the pups.

12/22 – Tori sneaked out of the whelping box again through the door flap.

12/23 – Murdock was sitting up. We put sturdy boxes outside the wooden whelping box to make it easier for Tori to get in and out.

12/24 – The puppies started to sound like seagulls. I took a three-day break for Christmas fussing.

12/28 – Lily-Ann started barking, growling, and pouncing (on nothing).

12/29 – Dinner was at 6 p.m. One half-hour later, they were all walking about pretty slowly with droopy eyes, looking for a place to crash. Everyone ended up on the heating pad. There was some gentle playing as Tinker chewed Cully and then Lily-Ann. Murdock went in for the kill on Tinker's rear leg. When they piled up, Tinker climbed on top of Farley and Lily-Ann. Finally, they all ended up in a daisy shape with noses in the middle … five little sausages, all conked-out.

12/30 – Farley attacked Cully, but Cully held his ground. Farley attacked Tinker, but Tinker lifted his paw to keep him at bay. Farley and Lily-Ann gave guttural growls. Farley strutted his stuff with his tail held erect. Tinker liked biting others on the nose … especially Cully.

1/1 – Tinker bit Farley on the nose. Lily-Ann was teething on the ledge. Farley was teething on anything … like Lily-Ann's leg and ear, or Cully's ear and neck.

1/3 – Farley attacked Lily-Ann and bit her on the ear. Lily-Ann attacked Murdock and bit him on the ear. Cully cuddled with Farley and bit his nose. Murdock wrestled with Farley and got a nose-hold. Cully pretended to be a bunny.

1/4 – Farley climbed on Tinker's back, but Tinker wouldn't cry "uncle." Farley went for Murdock … Murdock bit his ear. Lily-Ann climbed on Tinker … he took her on … they danced in a circle, playing bite-the-other-guy's-tail. Cully ran up and attacked Farley like a boxer. Cully got a double dose of discipline from Tori.

Murdock tried very hard to reach up and clean Tori's beard (after dinner). Lily-Ann got disciplined from Tori's front end so she went back to a spigot for a drink. Murdock rolled over and played dead right in front of Tori. Farley found out you don't have to work so hard if you roll over on your back and chew your own leg. Tinker and Farley were tussling again: Brains and Brawn.

1/5 – Cully got the better of Murdock. Farley dropped a paper towel into the bed area and everyone closed in to play with it. Tinker instinctively knew the shortest distance between two points is a straight line … even if it's right through the water dish.

1/6 – Murdock's ears went up. Murdock (the smallest) took on Lily-Ann (the biggest) and succeeded. Tinker got up on the cases with Tori … when the food was placed in the pen, he took a header off the cases to get his fair share. At times, Tori was still nursing her fat little brood. They lay on the floor and suckled vehemently while she stood there eating her dinner. Cully was a real pip … he growled when someone played with him. Murdock and Farley played together; Tinker and Lily-Ann played together. Tori looked like she had just about had it with puppies … their teeth had started coming in. I put soft puppy chow in the pen which they gobbled up before the next feeding.

1/14 – Tinker stood on a slope to pee as if to lift his leg … unfortunately, it was the front leg he lifted.

In the middle of January, the puppies started going to their new homes. Charlie (aka Cully) spent his first eighteen months with a family who later had a change of circumstances and asked me to place him in another home. I had a great home in mind: Bob and Anita were ready for another puppy to join MacGregor (nee Wadsworth). Charlie won the jackpot. A few years later, MacGregor and Charlie came for a weekend visit in the spring. We had five Westies of our own. At one point, Jessie-Kitty ran through the backyard and all the Westies started chasing her … but they didn't chase her like a pack, they were all lined up like a train. Jessie was the engine running just fast enough to stay ahead of our five Westies, MacGregor, and Charlie (the caboose). It was a pretty sight seeing all those little white frou-frou dogs against the rich green color of the lawn. And then ... Charlie expelled a lungful of air with every gallop. He sounded like a goose! ... "Uh-Uh-Uh-Uh-Uh." It startled everyone ... Jessie and the Westies ... the whole train stopped and turned to look at Charlie. The game of "Get Jessie" had morphed into "What's Up with Charlie?"

Bizi Bodi – Poof

Bizi Bodi, our gentle little boxer, loved to go everywhere with Harry. He would take her to the office with him. She would curl up under his desk and take a nap: She curled into a tight U-shape, her head and tail both facing out. So one day, Bizi Bodi was napping and guarding, while Harry was selling insurance to a customer. It was a cold, windy, winter day. Harry's office was at the very back of the building next to the outside door. That night Harry came home and said, "Something's wrong with Bizi."

"What do you mean?"

"Well ... she has gas really bad. It was so bad my eyes were burning while I was talking with a customer, and there was no way I could open the back door because it was so cold and windy outside."

"Oh!" I responded, thoughtfully.

(I had read about fleas. Yeast was said to be a really good deterrent for fleas ...and I wanted to deter fleas. I got a little brewer's yeast and started sprinkling it on all the dogs' food. A little on Monday, a little on Tuesday, and so forth. Well, as it turned out, Boxers are prone to flatulence and Harry took the brunt of it. Oops. I immediately stopped sprinkling yeast on her food, and she soon recovered. A failed experiment! What was done was done. And I was done ...no sense troubling Harry with the details. It will go with me to my grave.)

1988

(Color the fire orange and yellow)

FREDDIE'S FIRST LITTER: PUPPIES EVERYWHERE

In January, the puppies from Tori's third litter were ready to go to their new homes ... but not before Freddie Lu had her first litter.

We had puppies everywhere. Well, to be honest, Tori had a penful of five puppies and Freddie had a whelping box of five puppies. Everything was under control, but there were so many! (Priscilla had had a false pregnancy. I was disappointed but grateful we didn't have even more puppies.)

...FOR A SAFE AND HAPPY HOLIDAY SEASON

Having travelled to the Grand Canyon this year, we were not content to be truly inspired from the top. We took the mule train down the cliffs. (Others had lived, maybe we would too.) They told us to point our mule's head to the outside each time we stopped...if it can see the canyon, it won't back off the path to the depths below...but I swear no one said the whole mule would follow. Do you know how far out over the edge of the Grand Canyon a mule (larger in some cases than a horse!) sticks out?! It was a little disconcerting to say the least. But the real thrill occurs when you accidently find yourself about 10 feet too far back in the train and your mule TROTS down the cliff to catch up!

We kept a little puppy, Sara, from Tori's last litter. Now we're experiencing the thrills of teething, housebreaking and training all over again...and soon we'll become Dog Show People...all over again.

Make it a Happy New Year...

Tori was able to manage her five ... Tinker had been suckling for weeks. But Freddie was a totally different mother. I rarely saw her in the whelping box with the puppies. I was concerned she was abandoning them. Weigh-ins were an eye-opener for me. Each of her pups was growing at a steady acceptable rate. Evidently, she just liked her peace and quiet in the mornings.

Here's a recipe I found for a healthful
alternative to a sweet-stuffed squash...I
hope you like onions, they MAKE the dish!

     2 medium acorn squash, halved & seeded
     2 tablespoons "butter"
     2 cups finely chopped onions
     1 cup cooked brown rice
   1.5 cups shredded cheddar cheese
     2 tablespoon minced fresh parsley

     Spread the cut sides of the squash with
1 tablespoon the of butter. Place the squash
cut side down, in a 9x13-inch baking dish. Bake
at 400 F. for 30 minutes. Meanwhile, saute' the
onions in the remaining tablespoon of butter
until tender. Combine with the rice, 1 cup of
the cheese and the parsley.
     Turn the squash cut side up. Fill each
with the onion mixture. Sprinkle with the remaining
cheese. Bake another 30 minutes at 350 F.
     Serves 4 as a main dish.   *Kathy*

One of the puppies from Freddie's litter went to a man named
John. He called to interview me! Cheeky! He wanted a female
before she was six weeks old ... I said she absolutely wouldn't be
available until she was six weeks old. He reluctantly agreed and
said he wanted puppy number two and would fly from Chandler,
Arizona, to Vancouver to pick her up at 6:30 a.m. on March 8. It
was strangely detailed, especially the part about him coming well
before Harry normally woke up, but all the responses I got from
him indicated he would take good care of her. She was exactly six
weeks old when he arrived. He brought a little lunch-box-sized
crate suitable for storing a small dog under the seat of a plane.

When he unzipped his jacket, I discovered he was a commercial pilot on a short layover. He named her Lady. It was a very good fit.

Three of Lady's littermates were named by their new owners: Lady, Kenyon McDudley, and Alfred MacArthur. No thanks to me, the firstborn never had a name.

Bizi, JIVE!

Bizi Bodi was such a lovely little boxer, but with all the Westies she wasn't getting the attention she deserved. Harry, my Man-of-Few-Words, may not say much, but he does listen to what people say. He knew Dick liked Boxers. We asked if they would like to adopt Bizi. Dick and Carol were ecstatic. (I worked with Dick; years later Carol brought her granddaughters to my tea parties.) When they came over in January, I ran through all the details like what she ate and how often and gave him a list of the commands she knew: Sit, Down, Off, Settle, Give.

I told Dick she would get a ball, bring it over, and give it to him on command. It was just too much for Dick. He had been assaulted with all sorts of information and was still reeling from the thought of taking Bizi home forever. But I was right there to help him and make sure he understood the commands. We rolled the ball away and Bizi went after it, grabbed it, and brought it back to Dick. He tried to get the ball out of her mouth, but she wouldn't let go. She didn't have many teeth, but she did have a good lock on the ball. He tried again, but he just couldn't get it out. I told him it wasn't a problem and spelled out the command for him: "Just say G-I-V-E." Dick immediately said "JIVE!" Bizi didn't do anything, but Carol and I just roared.

Bizi had a cute little way of dancing around in a circle when she was outside … it became memorialized as her Jive.

Bizi, DOWN

They took her home and introduced her to their other midsize dog, Lady. One of their rules was dogs do not get on the furniture.

Bizi, not knowing the rules of the new house, got up on the sofa. Knowing she was well-trained, Dick said, "Bizi, DOWN!" Wanting to please Dick, Bizi dropped down on the sofa pretty as a picture. Dick and Carol looked at each other in dismay.

The next time I talked to Carol, she said the Bizi wasn't as well-trained as they thought because she stayed on the sofa when they told her DOWN.

"What did she do?" I asked.

"She dropped down."

"Well … that's what she is supposed to do when you say DOWN. Did you by any chance use the command OFF?"

"Oops," she said. I could almost hear a sheepish grin on the other end of the phone.

THE GRAND CANYON

We took the Mule Trip to a ledge halfway down into the Grand Canyon. All the way down the mule trail and all the way back up, there was only one thing I saw. That was the picture that should have been on the Christmas card. It's a classic. Oh sure, once in a while the mule train would stop, and my mule, Spud, would instinc-tively turn 90 degrees … perpendicular to the path, just like the mule-wrangler said he would. Yes, it's disconcerting, but my whole view changed and I could actually see the features of the Grand Canyon. And then the mule train would start up again and I'd go right back to the view I'd had for the previous fifteen minutes. Many people have taken absolutely amazing pictures of the Grand Canyon, but here's the only thing I remember from our mule trip.

Spud

TORI'S FOURTH LITTER

In the summer, Tori had her last litter: Ever-So-Clever, Sparky McNab, Sara Gee, and Cricket. Cricket was my favorite. She dove into the pond on her first walk outdoors and scrambled back up the rocks before I could get concerned ... the owner of the sire picked her. Sara was a lovely little thing ... we kept her.

JOYCE

It was a very busy year. I had taken on more responsibility at work. With puppies and interviews all over the place, I was feeling a little worn out. We were settled from the move but needed to address division of duties in our new location. Harry easily volunteered to do the vacuuming and dusting. I would keep the laundry and the cooking. Wow, I couldn't believe how easy it was. I found myself wishing we had had the conversation years ago! Once the puppies were all in the clear, I stopped coming home at noon ... except for one day. I arrived unexpectedly at noon to find a strange car in front of our house. Since we're hidden far back from the road, it seemed mighty peculiar. I was wearing a heavy broad-brimmed charcoal-gray wool hat, with a matching three-quarter-length jacket over a long black skirt. There was a foe in my house ... I went to meet the foe. The house wasn't much to look at, but it was ours. When I entered, I found a woman with her back to me chatting on the phone in the front room. I narrowed my eyes, straightened my spine, filled the doorway with a dark foreboding presence, and glared. The woman looked around, startled, put down the phone and started talking. "Are-you-kathy-harry-hired-me-to-do-the-vacuuming-and-the-dusting-he-said-you-wouldn't-be-home-at-noon-it-was-supposed-to-be-a-surprise-my-name-is-joyce- ..." She didn't stop for fifteen minutes! All was well in my world again.

Harry ... gotta love 'im!

1989

(Color the leaves green and berries red)

HI!

After 3 years, we finally got into landscaping. We had a bulldozer tear up our front slope. Five terraces took shape in just a week! But it took us 3 months to finish them...with 350' of retaining walls. Now they're covered with lawn...Harry can mow it with a ride-on mower in just 45 minutes. We were amazed when our dozer friend came back three months later and told us he had *never* done terraces before!

In September, we started our vacation at Yellowstone and Jackson Hole about the time the pre-conference talks were taking place. We went to Albuquerque, for the 8-day Hot Air Balloon Fiesta. We got up at 5:00 am to see the Mass Ascension of hundreds of Hot Air Balloons. FANTASTIC! After 3 hours, we had seen it all! We zipped home via the wind farms of the SW. We stopped only for rest stops and World Series playoffs!

Check the back of this card for a treat. Have a warm holiday season!

All the best,

Kathy

HAPPY

WINTER

DAYS!

Kathy & Harry Hoffman

FREDDIE'S SECOND LITTER

In January, Freddie had her last litter: Lucy Ann, Black Bart, Jeannie, and Molly. When the pups were old enough to mill around and explore in the pen, I put my hand in. Three little puppies started playing with my fingers, Molly bared her teeth (well, she would have if she'd had any) and clamped on to my wrist. I knew she was the one. This was the dog I would take to the ring for her championship! When she was six months old, I took her to some conformation classes and was sad to find out she had a problem with her knee and couldn't be shown. It was just as well … her initial feistiness turned out to be just plain crankiness. Cranky or not, she was one of the family.

We had five Westies counting Sara. Whenever I took them out for a walk, I used one leash and three splitters. Sara was always in the lead, Freddie and Molly were in the middle, Dietrich and Tori in the back. After a while, I'd say, "Take a left" or "Go right," and Sara complied. She was a good lead dog. I tried mixing them up one day … they were out of their normal positions … chaos … it was like they had all forgotten how to walk!

Here's a recipe adapted from a
"doggie" friend's file:

GARLIC CHICKEN

2 bulbs Garlic
1 cut-up Fryer
1 bottle Dark Beer

Separate Garlic into cloves.
Place garlic in a deep narrow
    baking dish.
Layer the chicken on top.
Salt & Pepper to taste.
Pour beer over top. (Chicken
    should be almost covered.)
Bake 1/2 hour in 450-oven, then
    1 hour in 350-oven,
                basting twice.

Thanks to Kitty Benoit!

WEST HIGHLAND WHITE TERRIER
(206) 573-6909

HOT AIR BALLOON FIESTA

We're not morning people, so getting up and being somewhere at
5:00 a.m. is not normal for us. But
we did get up because someone told
us not to miss the Hot Air Balloon
Fiesta, which just happened to be
taking place when we were passing
through Albuquerque. We had breakfast before sunrise, left the dogs in
the trailer, and arrived at the specified
location in the dark. Imagine our disappointment when all we found was
an empty field and no cars for miles.
One of us, probably me, must have
gotten the directions wrong. Still
trying to make sense of things in our
early-morning fugue, we noticed a
truck drive up. It passed us and went
to the middle of the field. A couple of
minutes later, another truck and some
cars arrived. It was almost a non-
event because I was sure we were in
the wrong place. Within fifteen minutes, dozens of cars and trucks were
in orderly placements, balloons and
baskets were being unloaded, and
the hissing sound of balloons being
raised was all around us. Many of
the balloons were in the air before
the sun came up. It was fascinating
to see how the inflation flames lit up
the entire balloon. They looked like
giant fireflies, aglow for a few seconds while the flames were in
operation, then disappearing into the darkness. After the sun came

up, there were sooo many balloons drifting in the air. It made me wonder why I ever doubted myself.

I checked stats years later: In March 2022, more than 900,000 visitors and 500 balloons participated during a nine-day period. Albuquerque is known as the Ballooning Capital of the World … who knew!

TERRACES

When we put in the terraces, I had wonderful ideas of rock gardens acting as retaining walls. Our good friend, Bill Oman, came over. I took him out to see the terraces and encouraged him to see the vision. I made grand sweeping gestures and told him how we were going to bring in twelve-inch boulders and place them throughout. I was so eloquent I amazed myself! Pretty soon, I realized Bill was simply not listening to my grand plans. He had plans of his own. He told Harry we needed to dig postholes and sink four-by-four posts into the ground every four feet. And what's more, he offered to help dig the postholes. I knew when to keep my mouth shut. Before I knew it, Bill and Harry had dug 98 postholes in the terraces and two postholes up by the mailbox. There was no grand plan, just post-holes in a line, four feet apart. When they were finished and had

cemented the posts in the ground, I decided we needed a pathway through the ter-races, down to the road. It could have been a disaster, but it wasn't. The holes lined up perfectly for a diagonal path … as if it was planned. Sometimes things work out … it's a good thing!

Molly

1990

(Color the tongue pink)

The message inside the Christmas card:

HAPPY HOLIDAYS TO YOU

We had a fairly quiet at-home type of year. I started the year by landscaping the terraces. We have grass on each level, but we wanted new flower borders at the top and bottom of each retaining wall. With 350 feet of retaining walls, that's 700 feet of flower borders. It took two months to finish the work and the weather was perfect for it.

In July, Harry built a small 3 x 7-foot dock extending into the Lower Pond. He put an irrigation pump on it and we had water …for the yard. (The dock might be a great place to sunbathe, if you're not prone to rolling over.) Then he spent most of the fall working on his model tugboat. Shortly after he had it working on the pond, he started building a thirty-inch sailboat with a 44-inch mast. If he starts one more model boat, he'll have to add a moorage to the dock!

As we started to get ready for the holidays, we realized we had a new challenge on our hands: How can we arrange the living room to accommodate a six-foot tree in the center of the room while still maintaining room for five active Westies to play? We did it with a narrow holly tree set in a brick-laden base. Later, while I was putting together a decorative basket of presents, Tori tried to jump into the basket to take a nap …I caught her just in time!

HOLLY CHRISTMAS TREE

There was a little more to the story, but I didn't realize it until I started taking down the Christmas decorations … the lights didn't come off as easily as they went on … my hands were full of holly-pricks by the time I was finished. And it wasn't even a very big tree. It was our last traditional Christmas tree! All the decorations graced the top of the pool table in future years.

Have A
Warm
&
Safe
Season !

Kathy & Harry Hoffman

LOOKING FOR YELLOW

I had grand plans of sweeping lengths of marigolds at the top and bottom of each of the retaining walls ... a massive splash of yellow. That dream died a slow death when I planted the seeds a little too early. It seems I was not the only one looking for the seeds to grow. I had a fine crop of slugs watching the progress with me ... they won. I have always been grateful Bill didn't let me go ahead with the rockery idea ... the weeds, alone, would have swallowed me whole!

The planting area at the top of the retaining walls was eventually replaced with grass. Thirty years after the marigold fiasco, the bases of the retaining walls were planted with Creeping Jenny ... I got my yellow! And who cares if it creeps into the lawn!

Here's a copy of my favorite cake recipe.
It's easy and festive looking...(but it's
not chocolate, sorry.)

DUMP CAKE

Mix in a 13x9x2 cake pan:
      One 20 oz can Crushed Pineapple
      One 20 oz can Raspberry Pie Filling
Sprinkle with mixture of
      1 1/4 cup Sugar
      2 1/2 cup Krusteaz Baking Mix
Cover with
      1 cup nuts
Melt and pour evenly over cake:
      1 cube Margarine
      1/2 teaspoon vanilla

Bake at 325°F for 1 hour.

For a variety in the Fall, try Lemon Pie
Filling and fresh apples...with some
cinnamon in the topping, you can't miss!

KATE

'90

WEST HIGHLAND WHITE TERRIER
(206) 573-6909

WOULD YOU LOOK AT THAT!!

The little house served us well for raising puppies. About thirty feet behind the house, tucked in a stand of fir trees, was a three-sided lean-to made from peeler cores. Old Bill Ross, the first owner, was thrifty as the dickens. He worked in concrete and brought home leftovers. We never knew if removing a concrete

The Little House

pad would take an hour or a week. We soon found out the blocks in our concrete-block structures might be hollow or might be filled with concrete. He must have had access to plywood fabrication as well, because he brought home remnants called peeler cores: four-foot logs with a five-inch diameter. He stood the peeler cores in a trench on three sides of an 8 x 8-foot square. Then he stood another row of peeler cores on top of the first and held them together with a horizontal 1 x 6 board all along the seam. He put a roof on the top. We stored our outdoor equipment in the little lean-to. It wasn't important to know how the lean-to was constructed as long as it was sturdy … which it was … unless it became necessary to remove it … which it did.

One hot day, I saw bees or flies or something swarming from the peeler-core lean-to roof to the eaves of the little house. "Would you look at that," I mused. A few hot days later, I noticed another swarm. On the off-chance bugs don't just swarm when I'm looking, I decided to investigate. They looked like humongous flying ants with enormous wings. (I later discovered they were a select type of termites … those looking to start their own colony.) Well, I knew that couldn't be good! We solved the problem by dismantling the little house … and it became necessary to remove the source of the problem: the peeler-core lean-to. Harry was not involved in that venture.

I had put it off for a few days, but termites are not to be trifled with. Being somewhat of a carpentry aficionado, and having great confidence in my skills (even if untested), I instinctively knew I needed to implode the lean-to with a sledgehammer. How hard could it be? I got out my new best friend, the nail-puller. In minutes, the 1 x 6 boards girding the outside of the structure were gone. A few good whacks and it would be a done deal. I gave it a good one, but nothing happened. Oops, there were 1 x 6 girders inside the structure, too … reinforcing the middle and the top. My project was not going well. Over the next 45 minutes, I practiced darting: enter the structure, deliver a mighty whack, and dart out before anything could fall … on me.

The Lean-To

Well, it came down eventually and I still had energy, so I went on to other things like getting rid of the peeler cores. I offered them to Morrie who thought it might be good to burn them in his outdoor woodstove. Morrie frequently wore coveralls. He came over with his pickup, walked over to the lean-to, picked up three good-looking logs, and started carrying them back to the truck. Just before he reached his pickup, they exploded out of his arms and started bouncing down our driveway toward the gully. I wasn't sure what was happening, but I was pretty sure an exorcism wasn't needed. Morrie was dancing all around and yelping … they were inside his coveralls and they were angry. Evidently, termites can move fast and can bite. Graciously, Morrie stayed long enough to help me dispose of the peeler cores … in the landscaping … well-away from the house.

As for the road, every time the logs bounced on the road, a mini-colony of termites bounced off. I used bug-spray until I couldn't see any more movement and then relaxed. I noticed one dead leaf in the middle of the road. Lifting it, I saw three termites looking directly at me. They are smart little devils.

WISTERIA

When the little house was torn down, the garden had to go, as well. There was a young wisteria plant in the garden. It had never bloomed, but I didn't want to lose it. I took it and transplanted it way down on the peninsula at the base of a dead fir tree, thinking how nice it would be when it grew up and around and in and about the fir tree. I was good at envisioning things ... I envisioned a beautiful mass of lavender chains of flowers. I was getting giddy just thinking of it. Harry's not really into that, so I didn't even consider telling him.

Fast-forward a couple of years: Harry sat outside on the patio each day to enjoy the view and the fresh air until, one day, he came running in franticly saying, "I can't be out there; I can't be out there! There's something out there!"

Now, it's not like Harry to be afraid of an animal, so I was wondering what in the world could be out there. Pretty soon it became clear to me he was allergic to something that had just gone into bloom. I told him I didn't plant anything. There was nothing new out there, except maybe the wisteria vine from a couple of years ago, but it was way down on the peninsula. There was nothing more to be said. He had long given up on thinking of me as innocent ... we both realized that I had to be the culprit. I dug up the wisteria and transported it all the way up to the other end of the property by the gate. Harry had been on a rampage with a chain saw, leaving a twenty-foot-high stump where a lush maple had once been. I started getting a little giddy again as I envisioned the wisteria growing up the maple stump and around and in and about the new branches that would eventually sprout. It would be a beautiful mass of lavender chains of flowers. I could hardly wait. I babied that little vine and trained it up the maple tree for a couple of years, until it finally took hold ... and then the wind blew the tree down smashing Dorothy's trellis ... oh well. I was just glad I didn't have any violent allergies.

1991

(Color the ornaments gold)

DUMPED

Someone dumped an un-fixed German Shepherd in the neighbor-hood. He was bigger by far than any of the dogs we had. He came in from the cul-de-sac and started checking out Tori, my little white frou-frou dog. That was a little scary. I didn't want anything to happen to my little Westie … or the other three Westie females who hadn't been spayed! I was able to get a leash on him and put him in the pen. At least he was corralled until Harry and I could figure out what to do.

In January, we adopted a beautiful 10-month old German Shepherd and named him Bo. He wanted a home so badly that he did everything Harry asked him to do. Harry bought a dog-cart (like a pony-cart): He's training Bo to pull him around in the cart. (What a kick!). The little dogs were slow in accepting this big strange dog...until the night he rescued Tori (from the clutches of a raccoon who was trying to drown her). Now all the dogs are good buddies.

I've finally made the list of those who've had major surgery... fortunately, the tumor behind my ear was benign. It was a very common operation. Now I'm sporting an 8-inch scar. According to my doctor, it should be hidden in the "folds in my neck". The hardest thing to accept was that I had folds in my neck that would hide such a huge scar!

In August, we started getting serious about adding on to our house: A new living room and a 3-car garage (remodelling the rest of the house is part of the 10-year plan). Whoever said that building your own house was maritally stressful was taking it far too seriously...though it's certainly a test of your communication skills. Our ideas of what the final product will look like are so different that we decided to move if we don't like the outcome. So far, so good.

I intended to say, "Harry, there is a strange dog outside in the pen and I am concerned he might harm our little Westies." True to our penchant for miscommunication, what Harry heard was "There's a new dog outside in the pen and we're keeping it." And so Harry went outside and started working with the German Shepherd. As he walked the dog, he found out the shepherd would cross over in front of him. Harry pretended to trip over the dog. After three times, the shepherd decided Harry was just too clumsy and walked by his side from then on.

Harry had me work with him. Harry said if the dog crossed over in front of me, I should just walk right into him, step on his feet, and apologize ... and if I apologized everything would be okay. And it was. The dog was a quick learner.

Have a Safe & Happy

Holiday Season !

Kathy & Harry Hoffman

We named him Bo. He was a wonderful dog. The vet said he was ten months old. He must have eaten some poor family out of house and home for ten months while he was growing. By the time he came to live with us, he was fully grown and eating a normal amount of food each day.

Dietrich wasn't too pleased. He tried to tell Bo we have rules and Bo was to follow them. Bo acknowledged Dietrich's rules. They were fine with him, but he really wasn't an accepted member of the pack, until one evening about a week after Bo arrived ...

It was already dark at 8:30 p.m. when Harry announced "last call." He let all the dogs out, as usual. But this time, all the terriers ran to the bottom of the hill, barking. Something was there! We couldn't tell what it was, but there was a big ruckus and then some screaming. Harry let Bo loose. Everything happened so quickly. Harry ran down the wet grassy slope as quickly as his Birkenstock sandals would allow. I had no glasses and no shoes ... I was useless. The Westies had discovered a raccoon. Tori was fearless ... she was the first one into the pond. The raccoon jumped on her

```
For Ted and Cheryl:  This is a pretty pumpkin pie.  The ingredients
are very similar to the more common custard form but with LESS SUGAR!

PUMPKIN CHIFFON PIE

Prepare:   1 baked pie shell
Pre-soak:  1 tablespoon gelatin      in      1/4 cup cold water

Beat:      3 egg yolks
Add:       1/2 cup sugar                 1 1/4 cups canned pumpkin
           1/2 cup milk                  1/4 teaspoon salt
           1/2 teaspoon cinnamon         1/2 teaspoon nutmeg
Cook and stir ingredients over, not in, hot water until thick.
Stir in soaked gelatin until dissolved.  Chill.

Whip until stiff
       but not dry:            3 egg whites
When pumpkin mixture
       begins to set, stir in:  1/2 cup sugar
Fold in egg whites.
Fill pie shell; chill to set.
```

Kate
'91

West Highland White Terrier
(206) 573-6909

back and was trying to drown her. The raccoon was at least as heavy as she was, and she was losing. It was so dark I couldn't see much of anything, but I heard Bo go into the water. He was going for the raccoon. While he was busy with his prey, Tori, with what little air she had left in her lungs, was walking toward the bank ... completely submerged. There was just enough light for Harry to see her and grab her collar, dragging her the rest of the way up to breathable air.

And that was it. Tori, the Grand Dame, had always held a place of honor in the pack. Bo had saved the Grand Dame: He was instantly accepted as a member of the pack. After that heroic gesture, he could do no wrong in anyone's eyes. The humans were grateful and the Westies were pleased to have a big guardian angel.

We could see he was a special dog. We contacted the police department and the guide dog people to see if they wanted him. To our great joy, they said they take only puppies. We advertised to see if anyone had lost him ... no responses. Again, we were elated! We were finally able to relax and enjoy the new addition to our family.

A few weeks later, Harry and I were talking about the first day Bo came onto the property. I told him I was surprised he wanted to keep Bo because we already had a lot of dogs. Harry said he thought because I had put Bo in the pen I wanted to keep him.

Communication ... gotta love it.

TOP DOG

Not too long after Bo found us, Harry went up to visit Morrie. Early on, Morrie had told us he was afraid of big dogs. An introduction was in order. The two men were standing there talking when Bo started wandering off. Harry called him back. Bo turned and looked at Harry, then continued exploring. Harry hollered, "No!" Bo wasn't really into belligerence. Even though Harry was wearing Birkenstocks and running on a sloped lawn, he was able to run Bo down and bite his ear until he yelped. That's all it took ... Harry was Top Dog, forevermore!

Bo

1992

(Color the stripes on the wings and fuselage red)

Happy Holiday Season to You!

The politicians were shouting for change so loudly that Harry and I decided to do our part. Harry quit smoking and drinking last Spring and then took up flying. He's a few sunny days away from getting his private pilot's license. In the meantime, I joined the Clark County YMCA Board and took up Tai Chi (a slow-motion martial art). Just to keep pace with each other, Harry started Tai Chi and I started flying. What fun!

Meanwhile, the inside phase of our remodeling project began last month, after a one-year layoff. The greenhouse is now finished and the basement is getting close. (It seems that a Christmas Tree flocked with sawdust would be the most appropriate decoration this year.) We'll put off re-doing the upstairs for another year.

The dogs have enjoyed the expanded house and the new deck, immensely. In fact, Molly stands guard and always lets me know if someone is approaching ... unlike Bozo who may or may not even notice intruders ... thus giving incontrovertible proof that *my dog Molly knows more about foreign policy than that Bozo!*

Have a Great Year!

BO LIKED BLACKBERRIES

In August, I broke out the sixteen-foot rowboat, piled into it with Bo, and carefully rowed around the Upper Pond. Bo was perched calmly in the front of the boat. I had only intended to take him for a little ride, but as we got closer to a blackberry patch, Bo stretched out his neck and started nibbling. We had great fun: I rowed right into the blackberry patch; Bo nibbled furiously but delicately. As the blackberry vines resisted, we drifted away. We rammed those vines over and over. I didn't get many berries, but it was a lot of fun to see Bo energetically joining in the hunt.

CART RIDES

Harry and Bo went everywhere together. One day, Harry took Bo for a drive. When he came home from the pet store, he had a small one-person cart and a harness. He told me he and the

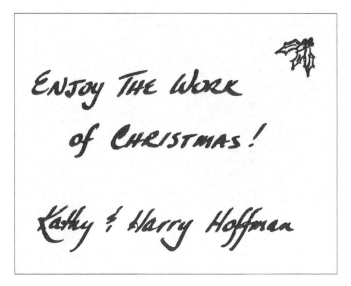

ENJOY THE WORK
of CHRISTMAS!

Kathy & Harry Hoffman

salesperson had selected the cart to fit the dog. I could not understand what it was for. The cart was too nice to hold branches so it certainly wouldn't be used for yard work. And it was big enough to hold only one person, so it couldn't be used for joyriding. Wrong! Harry and Bo worked together to figure out the intricacies of carting around our property. The next time I looked out, there was Harry with the biggest smile on his face and Bo, likewise. They were just trotting along together, Bo pulling Harry in the cart … together … sheer joy. It was a thing of beauty.

When we had visitors, Harry would get out the cart, harness Bo, help the visitor step into the cart and provide a nice little ride. We took the cart with us when we visited Harry's folks, Mom and Bill, in Yuma. Harry harnessed Bo and put a leash on him. Bill, in his late 70s, got in the cart and the three of them went on a merry little trek. Afterwards Harry noticed Bo licking his feet … the pavement was too hot and it wasn't even summer … no more cart rides in Yuma.

CHRISTMAS IS FOREVER

When the Song of the Angel is stilled,
When the Star in the sky is gone,
When the Kings and Princes are home,
When the Shepherds are back with their flocks,
  The work of Christmas begins:

    Find the Lost,
    Heal the Broken,
    Feed the Hungry,
    Rebuild the Nation,
    Release the Prisoners,
    Make Music in the Heart,
    Bring Peace among People.

        - Anonymous

KATE
'92

WEST HIGHLAND WHITE TERRIER
(206) 573-6909

DUMP TRUCK

Harry, Morrie, and Terry (also a State Farm Agent) went in on a big old dump truck. It wasn't much to look at and it didn't run, but it was theirs. They kept it over at Terry's farm. Morrie got a little bit of a cut because he was the mechanic. It wasn't long before Morrie got it up and running. The three of them used it for lots of big projects.

When we added a garage onto the house in 1991, there was a significant drop-off on the other side of the road and most of it was on our neighbor Gary's property. Backing out of the garage was downright scary. That old dump truck got a lot of exercise bringing in rock, gravel, and dirt to stabilize the road and the bank.

One day, Harry was using the dump truck to haul dirt over to the peninsula. The terraces and retaining walls were already in place. There was precious little room between the retaining wall of the bottom terrace and the bank of the pond. I didn't realize it was possible to take the truck over there

Dump Truck - Listing

... which is probably why Harry was using it while I was at work. Imagine a narrow grassy strip, a 60-degree bank, a four-foot drop to the water, a great big heavy dump truck, and a driver's door stuck shut. What could possibly go wrong?

It was dark when I got home so I didn't notice anything wrong. Harry had gotten a little too close to the edge of the pond. When I got up the next morning, I saw the dump truck facing the road but listing about twenty degrees ... the inoperable driver's door was on the pond side! Harry had to use the passenger door! If the truck had tilted much further, it might have rolled down the four-foot bank into the pond. Cheated death, again! ("The Scream" by Edvard Munch.)

ORANGE CUPCAKES

We have a group of friends who get together several times a year. We decided to have a potluck dinner close to Halloween. I signed up for a Halloween dessert. There was a recipe I really wanted to try: chocolate cupcakes made in carved-out oranges. I bought ten beautiful oranges, cut the tops off like you would for a pumpkin, and scooped out all of the innards.

I followed the directions to the letter, which was unusual for me, and checked back with the recipe several times after the event because I just couldn't believe what happened.

The recipe called for pouring one-half cup cake mix into each of the orange shells and baking the filled oranges for twenty minutes. It didn't seem long enough, but that's about right for cupcakes. I figured they knew what they were doing. They didn't.

I cooked the cupcakes as directed, put the orange lids back on the little "pumpkins," and took everything to the potluck. Everyone was standing around visiting, having drinks and hors d'oeuvres when Connie looked over at my pan of oranges. "What's this?" she asked.

I perked up and said, with a proud smile, "They are cupcakes for dessert." I lifted the lid so she could see inside one. She peered.

"They don't look done," she said simply and directly.

I looked in and, sure enough, they weren't done. Why in the world hadn't I checked them with a knife … what had I been thinking? I asked Carol if I had oven privileges. I did, but I had to wait until the main course was removed. She turned the oven on to 350 degrees and, while the others were filling their plates with the main course, I put my precious little oranges on to bake for a second twenty minutes.

We ate dinner, enjoying each other's company. When the alarm went off, I said, "Oh that's for me." I checked on the oranges … still fluid. I reset the timer for a third twenty minutes. The dinner was winding down. No problem. It wouldn't be bad to wait just a few minutes for the dessert. We continued to sit around the table for about ten minutes until the timer went off again. I ran into the kitchen to check on the dessert … not as fluid, but still runny! I set the timer for a fourth twenty minutes and went back to the dinner table.

It was not going well. Some people were getting surly. Connie announced, "I have a German chocolate cake in the refrigerator at home. I could run and get it." Although she lived close by, it was at least fifteen minutes one way … and of course everybody knew she would just stop at Albertson's and pick up a German chocolate cake.

No one left … we toughed it out. Finally, I checked and found they had set up. It was time. Marg helped me take the now-solid oranges from the pan and put them in dishes. Before long, everyone had been served. Nevertheless, there was an uncomfortable silence around the table. Everybody dug in and had a bite of the chocolate cupcake. The oppressive aura lingered until Marg casually said, "Umm, these are quite good." (She's a true leader!) With that, the tension was blasted away. Everybody started laughing and talking. We were back on track, having fun.

No wonder I don't like to follow recipes exactly!

1993

(Color the scarves pastel blue)

Merry Christmas!

Harry earned his private pilot's license and bought a plane this year. I'm still working on my pilot's license. I have to wait for good weather to fly to Roseburg or Pendleton as part of my training. Then, I should be ready to take the big TEST. (Lots of studying left to do, yet.)

Harry's knees finally started bothering him. He had one knee repaired in October and he's recuperating from an operation on the other knee, even as you read this. They were rebuilt to work like kangaroo knees! It was just what he needed to get out of doing the tile work in our newly remodeled home. *YOU READ CORRECTLY!* The project we started in 1989 is coming to a close, with tile floors in the living rooms, a magic breadboard, counters for tall people, and a ceiling of "wispy clouds in a summer sky".

One of Harry's happiest surprises was the patio outside the bedroom. It's a quiet little hide-away, sheltered from the rain by the upstairs deck. (Next, we'll move one of the apple trees to reclaim our view of the ponds.) Our martial arts commitment continued through the year and brought peace, discipline, and new friendships.

Peace to you, too!

Kathy & Harry

AJAX

Harry thought I liked birds because I had a canary when we met. He bought me a parrot when I was recovering from neck surgery. Ajax seemed nice enough ... not inclined to bite. As I was reclining on the sofa in my bathrobe, with dogs all around and my knees heaven-ward, Harry placed Ajax on my knee. As a family, we all sat there enjoying whatever was to be enjoyed in our unfinished living room. Peace reigned. Ajax, a little too peaceful, lost his footing and fell, unceremoniously, to the floor. Several black noses surrounded

> # Have a
> # Happy Holiday Season
> # and a
> # Great 1994!
>
> ## Kathy and Harry

him. He got up, fluffed his feathers, and started growling. It was the strangest sound, just like a dog grumbling. He must have been embarrassed. I laughed as I picked him up, replaced him on my knee, and talked him down. Eventually, his growls subsided. "GRR ... GRR ... Grr ... Grr ... grr ... grr ... rr ... r." Nobody messed with Ajax.

He was a nice, mid-sized Orange-Winged Amazon: bright colors set on a kelly-green base. Poor little Ajax wanted what he wanted. If he didn't get it, he would do what he learned. I guess his previous owners did most of their cooking in a microwave because Ajax would complain in a loud, shrill tone if he didn't get what he wanted ... *BEEP – BEEP – BEEP*! Harry was not pleased!

Here's a pleasant accident that turned out to be very healthy... A while back, I was making oatmeal cookies from the recipe on the Oatmeal package. After I put the first batch in the oven, I discovered I had left out *two-thirds* of the "shortening" ingredient. They turned out great!

LOW-FAT OATMEAL COOKIES

1/4 cup Canola oil	1 cup flour
1 cup brown sugar	1 tsp. salt
1/2 cup granulated sugar	1/2 tsp. soda
1/4 cup water	3 cups uncooked oats
1 tsp. vanilla	1/2 cup raisins or dates
1 egg	1/2 cup walnuts or pecans

Beat together: Oil, sugars, water, vanilla, egg.
Mix in: Flour, salt, soda.   Mix in: Oats, fruit, and nuts.
Drop mixture by spoonful onto ungreased cookie sheet.
Bake at 350°F for 15 minutes.   Cool on a paper sack.

KATE
'93

WEST HIGHLAND WHITE TERRIER
(206) 573-6909

I've heard "If you can't beat 'em, join 'em" so I invited Ajax to sing with me. We started with Christmas carols and regular piano music, but that bird had lungs and range. Eventually, we settled on Rodgers and Hammerstein tunes. Our specialty was "I Could Have Danced All Night" from *My Fair Lady*. I sang up the scale to the high note … Ajax kept pace. I sang softly and then at full volume … Ajax kept pace. Finally, I went back up the scale to the high note and began bending my notes ... like you would if your voice was a dustrag and you were dusting a small picture hanging in the hallway ... *I could have danced all ni-uh-i-uh-ight!* ... and still, he kept pace. We bonded at the piano. Meanwhile, Harry ... three hundred yards away ... down by the pond ... could hear us clearly. We had found our niche!

BPA ARTICLE

The following article appeared in the March 1993 issue of the *BPA Circuit*, an internal BPA publication.

HOFFMAN'S SOLD ON SOLOING

by Kathy Hoffman

(Editor's note: Kathy Hoffman, a hydraulic engineer on a detail to the Power Sales staff of the Lower Columbia area, is known for her eccentric sense of humor. Friends know she's prone to occasional Flights of Fancy–flights which have become far more frequent with the undertaking of her new hobby.)

I had never had a burning desire to fly an airplane. At least not until last fall, when my husband started taking lessons. At that point, I figured "Why not?" then "Why?" since I was more apprehensive than I'd ever been. But after four months of lessons, I was a changed woman: I was ready to solo. I just had to prove it to my instructor, Brad Vrilakis.

My assignment was to make three takeoffs and landings from the airport at Scappoose, Oregon. The first two were to be "touch-and-go" landings ... on the last one, I would come to a full stop. Brad would watch from the ground. His famous last words for me before takeoff were a flight instructor's peculiar interpretation of scripture: "Keep thine airspeed high, lest the Earth rise up to smite thee!" And then he smiled and left!

I could feel a twinge of excitement building as I ran through the standard checking procedure. "Cabin doors closed and latched?" Yes. "Flight instruments set?" Let's see: AT-titude Indicator: set for straight and level flight. AL-titude Indicator: set for … Oh no! It read 220 feet too low for the airport elevation. I changed it quickly, but something still felt wrong. Then I realized I had just set it for the field elevation of my home airport in Vancouver, Washington, but I was about to depart from Scappoose, Oregon. I changed it back just as quickly. The rest of the preflight check went smoothly.

I taxied to the beginning of the runway. This was it! I announced my departure using that deep husky voice all *real* pilots have. The voice you practice while weeding the garden all the while wishing you were up in the air transmitting on frequency 122.8 because you sound so good … like a *real* pilot! And I took off.

I had been warned the plane would perform a lot differently when there's only one person in it instead of two. So, I braced myself for a wild, bucking struggle of a ride as I rolled down the runway. I anxiously eased back on the controls and the plane rose into the beautiful blue sky, smooth as glass. It was almost a disappointment.

Once up there, all the standard things happened. I climbed to the prescribed altitude and circled the airfield with the precision *only* a solo student can master. Then I came in for a perfect–or "greased," as *real* pilots say–landing.

Oops! I was a little high and "wobbly" (a highly descriptive word I wish *real* pilots would use). So I decided to do a go-around: carburetor heat off, full throttle, raise the flaps a little at a time. I prepared to announce my intentions to all of the Portland-Vancouver-Astoria-Kelso area. *Oh no! The flaps! I raised them too fast. The airplane was sinking*! As the airplane bounced unceremoniously on the runway on one wheel, I released an almost inaudible expletive. I was relieved to be up in the air again. Now, back to my transmission. *Oh no!* During the entire "bounce and go" the mic button had been depressed … though not as depressed as I was once I realized it. (Maybe that expletive had just sounded like static. It certainly wasn't a *real* pilot's word!)

Whew! One down, two to go. I was starting to feel pretty good about these solo takeoffs now. I was airborne again. The second pass was going a lot smoother.

As I was about to turn parallel to the runway, a little red airplane came into the traffic pattern next to me. He was a lot closer than I'd ever experienced, so I knew I'd better keep him in sight. I banked left as usual, then looked for him, but he was *gone*. Where was he? What was that radio call sign he used? I flew on, but where was he?

It was time to radio my intentions to turn left. Then I heard: "Scappoose airspace, blah-blah-blah-blah-Victor, turning base, runway one-five." It was like *he was occupying the same physical space as I was!* I extended my straight flight, looked back, but still didn't see him. I kept flying straight for at least a mile. I knew it was overkill, but it seemed a lot safer than turning just yet. As I finally radioed my intentions, I secretly vowed *never* to go through something like that again without contacting the other plane. All through my training, I'd heard war stories of people who froze on the radio and wouldn't fully communicate their problem. Now, alone in the cockpit, I sheepishly realized I'd just contributed another story to the lore.

But back to the task at hand: "Scappoose airspace, Cessna zero-five-eight on short final for runway one-five, touch-and-go." The last two landings were uneventful. I taxied back to Brad. He came running up to the plane, all smiles, giving me the thumbs-up sign. He burst into the plane and gave me a huge hearty handshake, saying "Congratulations!" I felt great!

And off we went. I had done what I had come to do and we were flying home. My hands were relaxed. *I was a real pilot!* I knew it and my instructor knew it. We made *real*-pilot small talk on the way back. Everything was great.

As we approached the Clark County Airport, I descended to the prescribed pattern altitude, made a perfect radio transmission and paralleled the runway. Things were going great. Just as I throttled back to make my turns for my final landing of the day, I realized I was too low … not in danger, but not where I should have been. I hoped I could adjust for it before Brad pointed it out.

No such luck. I had overcorrected and was off course. Brad took the controls, pulled us back on-line and mumbled, "Travesty!" followed by "Every solo pilot I've ever had did that!" and more. Duly humbled, I landed the plane, taxied down the runway, and pulled up to the pump as usual. Brad went into the office to record the flight and I set out to refuel the plane. But the experience had refueled my psyche as well. I had a smile plastered all over my face that just wouldn't quit! A real pilot's smile!

Brad

MORE ON FLYING

Harry went on to get his pilot's license and suggested I take the rest of my training in our new plane … a Tri-Pacer. Unfortunately, Brad was not certified to teach in a Tri-Pacer. I found a certified pilot who really didn't want to teach. That lasted a few weeks. Then I found another certified pilot who was too much like me for my own comfort. For example, he asked me how I was going to fly to Tillamook. I told him I planned to come up to altitude and follow the airway from Portland to Tillamook. It made sense to me, and I was proud of myself for using the words correctly. Then he clarified my intention was to fly where other airplanes fly. Suddenly, it didn't make any sense at all.

The more I thought about flying, the more I realized I was mortal. Annual maintenance schedules and weather combined with my waning desire to become a pilot. Eventually, I decided to hang up my earphones for good … but not until I took a flight with Harry …

The last time I went up with my instructor, I learned it could hurt the struts if one landed too hard (my instructor had good reason to share this tidbit with me after I made a hard landing). Armed with this specific piece of information, and my limited knowledge of flying, I went up with Harry. We had a nice flight over to Scappoose. Harry was all lined up and coming in for a nice peaceful landing at the airfield. He was doing everything correctly. I, on the other hand, kept thinking about the struts. The closer we got to the ground the more anxious I became. Finally, just as Harry was about to cut the engine, I exploded with, "WATCH OUT FOR THE STRUTS!" Harry's peaceful bubble popped. Although shaken, he made a decent landing, but I was definitely low on the list of his favorite passengers.

1994

Boris helps himself to Ajax's stocking stuffers

(Color the tail feathers red)

Merry Christmas!

Although we've been out of the breeding business for several years, we went from three pets to six in just one month! One of our little puppies came back home after five years and is now nicely settled in the pack. The other two pets are parrots: Harry's parrot (pictured) still doesn't have a real name. (Do you have a suggestion?) He is a smart little African Gray that was hand-fed from birth. Harry got him when he was freshly weaned. He adores Harry (and tolerates me).

Ajax, my 3-year old Orange-Winged Amazon, is the exact opposite of Harry's little bird. He's larger, more colorful and very gentle. He may not be as smart as the little one, but he can really sing (chirp, whistle, screech and shriek). He's especially fond of Christmas carols. His all-time favorite is "O Holy Night" ... sung with a flair! I'm also getting him interested in singing "Silent Night" (like you've never heard it before).

I had a little scare in mid-summer that turned out to be benign, but the Doctor said no lifting, pushing or pulling for several months. Consequently, I spent August and September enjoying the sunshine, flowers and birds. Next year, the focus will be back on landscaping the front yard.

Harry's still flying at least once each week, mostly in the Vancouver area. So look for him if you see a small plane over Vancouver Lake.

All the best! *Kate*

Have a
Safe and Happy
Christmas!

Kathy & Harry Hoffman

Bo

Tori

Molly

Chatterbox

Ajax &

?? Harry's Bird ??

BUCKWHEAT

One Saturday, we left to go to breakfast. I was driving. We went out by way of the easement. Within one hundred feet, I started sneezing. After another two hundred feet, I was sneezing uncontrollably! I got it under control enough to be able to go back home and wash my face.

"What in the world is wrong?" I asked Harry.

Harry, being no stranger to allergies, said, "Maybe you're allergic to the buckwheat."

SPRINKLED SWISS PARROT
(Serves 4)

4 chicken breast halves (1.5 pounds)
skinned, boned, cubed

Salt (optional)

2 tablespoons mustard, flavored

3 green onions

1/2 cup Swiss cheese, shredded

Paprika

Place chicken in shallow baking pan
sprayed with vegetable cooking spray.
Sprinkle lightly with salt. Brush mustard
over chicken. Slice onions; sprinkle over
chicken. Sprinkle evenly with cheese.
Sprinkle lightly with paprika. Bake at 350°
for 40 to 50 minutes or until
chicken is cooked through.

KATE
'94

WEST HIGHLAND WHITE TERRIER
(206) 573-6909

"Oh, that can't be right!" I countered, dismissively. (We had planted a cover crop of buckwheat over the winter. We were very excited about how rich the soil would be when we tilled it in.) Just to prove him wrong, I jumped out of the car by the buckwheat crop, bent over from the waist, and took a great big snootful of air. Buckwheat pollen. The air was heavy with it. It got into every corner of my sinuses. My head detonated. It was like I was seeing stars everywhere. I started sneezing, non-stop. I guess Harry was right.

Woo-hoo! I hit the big time. I had a violent allergy!

CHATTERBOX

In the summer of '93, John, the pilot from Chandler, was going overseas for an extended period of time. He wanted us to place his Lady as well as another Westie, Max. And he wanted them placed in the same home. It took a year and three homes before we realized it wouldn't work. Max stayed with the third home, and Lady came back to us. She was traumatized by all the unsettling living arrangements … her little mouth chattered non-stop with no sound escaping. We called her Chatterbox. After three weeks with us, she never chattered again, but the name stuck with her. She was very sweet and liked living in a peaceful house.

REINCARNATION

Harry's folks, Mom and Bill, would come and visit every summer. We played dominoes and the darndest things would be said while we were focusing on our game. One day, out of the blue, Bill said "If there is such a thing as reincarnation, I want to come back as one of Harry's dogs."

Harry & Solo

1995

(Color the apple red)

BORIS

Harry's baby bird finally got a name … Boris. We were pretty sure he was a male, but if we were wrong, we could just change his name to Doris. How hard could it be!

Boris picked up words quite well from repetition. His first word was "OUCH!" It came through clearly in my voice. Next, he learned to laugh. The little stinker managed to put the two together. Whenever I would change his food dish, he would lunge for me. Usually, I'd withdraw my hand quickly enough as he would say "OUCH … ha-ha-ha!" It was demeaning to hear the little pause before the laugh. And I couldn't retaliate because anything I might say would come back to haunt me!

Merry Christmas to You!

This year we went halvsies on an antique backhoe with our neighbors. Harry has really developed "the touch" for moving earth. Between Harry and our neighbor, our backyards (which face each other) are becoming a lovely parkland. Now when we go to the Japanese Gardens, or the Butchart Gardens, we don't come home feeling intimidated. We've put a lot of their concepts to work for us, especially with the espaliered apple trees. (Pictured on front)

Harry drained the pond to the bottom. He plans to have it down for 6 months. Instead of looking at slimy pond sides, we've decided to look at rocks. We put a deposit on 59! tons of boulders for pond and yard. (If you are keeping track of the number of times we've said we were going to start on our front yard, you can stop counting ... this is it!)

He got adept at saying another phrase. Every morning, I would rush him from his evening cage in the front room to his daytime cage in the sunporch. We'd stop over the wastebasket, he'd immediately do what had to be done, I'd say, "That's a good one," and into his cage he would go. Every morning! Repetition!

Then one day, friends Marg and Roger came to visit. We were sitting in the front room. Boris was with us, on his perch. We were chatting peacefully and then Roger told a joke. The rest of us started laughing. As if on cue, Boris said, clear as a bell, "Ha-ha-ha ... that's a good one." We were all stunned. How in the world did he know how to respond to a joke?

Over the next couple of days, I started to realize what must have happened: Boris had been resting peacefully on his perch listening to the flow of the conversation. When we laughed, he reacted ... "Ha-ha-ha." His reaction stirred up his little system causing him to drop "a little something" to the tray below, which caused him to remember and utter the words from his morning ritual ... "That's a good one!"

Birds ... gotta love 'em.

Just remember, if you get a little down because of all the stress and fuss surrounding the Christmas season, it could be worse ... you could spend your Sunday mornings listening to a little one-pound talking machine (also pictured) saying:
"... oooooh ... wanna go out? ... tori, Tori, TORI! ... let's go ... ouch ... pretty birrrd ... ho, ho, ho ... harry ... puurrrrr ... phweet ... HARRY! .... ha, ha, ha, ha ... hullo"

Dear Friends ... Good Memories ... Thinking fondly of you this Winter.

Have a Safe and Happy Holiday Season!

With Love, Kathy and Harry Hoffman

WORKING AT BPA

What a wonderful time to be working for BPA. Those who were up for a challenge and for a change got a chance to fulfill their desires. Others, who chose to continue working where they were, found additional opportunities and challenges. People blossomed all over the agency! Management modified our standards for being "right" ... lowering them from 100% to 90%. It brought on an explosion of creativity, eagerness, and participation. "Teamwork" and "Cooperation" were no longer buzzwords ... they were the everyday course of business.

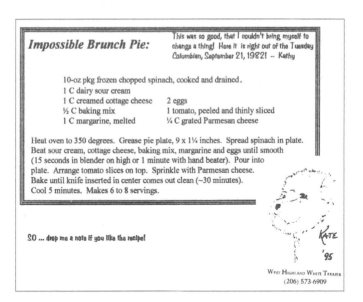

Impossible Brunch Pie:

10-oz pkg frozen chopped spinach, cooked and drained.
1 C dairy sour cream
1 C creamed cottage cheese   2 eggs
½ C baking mix   1 tomato, peeled and thinly sliced
1 C margarine, melted   ¼ C grated Parmesan cheese

Heat oven to 350 degrees. Grease pie plate, 9 x 1¼ inches. Spread spinach in plate. Beat sour cream, cottage cheese, baking mix, margarine and eggs until smooth (15 seconds in blender on high or 1 minute with hand beater). Pour into plate. Arrange tomato slices on top. Sprinkle with Parmesan cheese. Bake until knife inserted in center comes out clean (~30 minutes). Cool 5 minutes. Makes 6 to 8 servings.

SO ... drop me a note if you like the recipe!

KATE '95

WEST HIGHLAND WHITE TERRIER
(206) 573-6909

WHAT ABOUT BOB?

Back in 1975, when I met Marg at BPA in Vancouver, we immediately became fast friends. Bob was working in the same group.

Marg was the first to leave. She finished college and started up the corporate ladder, making it all the way to the top ... an honest trek. I thought that sounded pretty good so I followed suit in 1990, after twenty years with BPA. The first rung of my corporate ladder had been nice and sturdy. But when I put my weight on the second rung, first-line supervision, my ladder cracked right in two. Wrong ladder! I scrambled for a footstool and found technical analysis to be a much better fit for me than supervision or management.

We had both done very well in our separate fields. By the mid'90s, when we were working in Portland, we often got invited to stay late. Carpooling was a lifesaver. BPA said if we had three people in the carpool, we could park in the basement. Enter Bob ... who, by that time, also worked in Portland.

Bob was very patient with our schedules whenever we had to work late. One day, I called and told him Marg had to work late. We both went about our business waiting for Marg to finish. She was in a high-level meeting. I was very interested in the topic at the time. When the meeting was over, she called me. I grabbed my things and met her. She started telling me everything that happened. We chatted excitedly as we went down to the car ... we chatted excitedly on the freeway, which was not crowded due to the late hour, and ... we chatted excitedly all the way to the parking lot of the church from whence we carpooled. As we pulled into the parking lot, I slammed on the brakes and we both threw our hands to our faces, like something from Munch's painting "The Scream," as we exclaimed ... still excitedly ... "Bob!"

I recovered first. "You go home and call Bob. Tell him it's time to go down to the car. I'll race back and meet him in the basement."

Well, one doesn't mess with a lifetime of honesty: Marg raced home, called Bob, and 'fessed up. It took me another ten minutes to get back to the office where I sheepishly picked him up.

MOTHER NATURE FOR THE WIN?

Fifty-nine tons of boulders, professionally set along the road side of the Lower Pond and on the dike: A thing of beauty. We made a decision to drain the pond each fall and enjoy our view of our new boulders throughout the winter. How great would that be! Any weeds wanting to grow on the side of the pond would be frozen. We had thought of everything ... except gravity. We raised the pond in the spring and lowered it the next fall. Without the pressure of the pond water keeping the rocks in place, they slid down the silty side of the pond coming to rest about four feet lower than the road. Our eyes popped open, and Harry was off and running with the dump truck to get even more rocks ... smaller than the boulders ... rocks he could put in place by himself ... to protect the integrity of our road! They stayed put. Mother Nature got a point for giving us the challenge, but we salvaged the day with the smaller rocks ... it was a tie.

1996

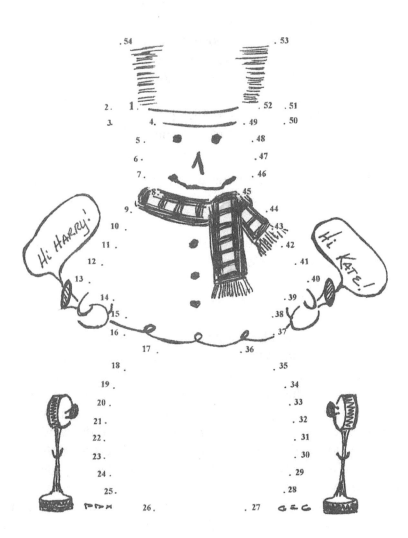

(Color the scarf green)

HERE'S A SHOCKING REPORT,
BETTER SIT DOWN IN A CHAIR
KATE WENT TO SPOKANE,
BUT HARRY ISN'T THERE.
SOMEBODY MUST BE BE HAPPY
WITH THAT EXTRA FARE.
IT'S A-T-&-T
AND SOUTHWEST AIR!

LAST YEAR WE TOLD YOU
WE LAID MANY A BOULDER
ON THE BANKS OF THE POND:
KINDA PILED-UP ON THE SHOULDER.
THIS YEAR, THERE'S BEEN A LOT OF RAIN.
WE LOOKED OUT WITH A FROWN:
(AACK) THE BANKS ERODED
AND THE ROCKS SLID DOWN.

IT FORCES US TO ORGANIZE,
AND GET OUT OF THE WEATHER.
SO WE CAN CUDDLE UP AT NIGHT
AND SPEND SOME TIME TOGETHER.
AS YOU CAN SEE, WE'RE HAPPY,
AND WHEN ALL IS SAID AND DONE,
WE WISH YOU MERRY CHRISTMAS!
NOW GO AND HAVE SOME FUN!

MOVING TO SPOKANE?

Everything changed at BPA this year. I was working with a wonderful team of people across the agency. The whole agency was at the top of its game. Our leadership decided to make a massive change ... even though everything was working well.

What were they thinking? We were all thrown into turmoil. My boss Rick was transferred to Spokane. He wanted to take me with him ... and I wanted to go. Harry and I had talk after talk. Harry's State Farm Insurance agency was running smoothly. He was at the top of his game. We talked about moving the Airstream to Spokane so I could commute. We talked about moving. We talked about keeping the agency in Vancouver and getting an apartment in Spokane. Every time we turned around, the problem was staring us in the face, but we knew we didn't have enough information, so we waited and toughed it out.

Peanut Butter Pie

Serves 12 !

This is great for the holidays because it can be made ahead. It can be a spacesaver if you're serving a crowd of people. It's sooo rich that a little goes a long way.

Crust

> 11 graham crackers
> 1/4 cup sugar
> 1/4 cup margarine

Mix well and press into 9" pie plate. Bake @ 375 degrees for 10 minutes. Cool.

Filling

> 1 package cream cheese (8oz)
> 1 cup peanut butter, creamy
> 1 cup sugar
> 1 cup margarine, softened
> 1 tsp vanilla
> 1 cup Cool Whip, softened

Beat cream cheese, peanut butter, sugar, margarine, and vanilla until smooth. Fold in Cool Whip. Spoon into crust. Garnish as desired.

Kate
'96

West Highland White Terrier
(206) 573-6909

In the end, I went with Rick to Spokane and he "forced" me to attend two meetings in his place in Portland every week. One was on Friday afternoon, the other was early Monday morning. I "had" to fly back to Portland every Thursday or Friday. What a Godsend: I got to spend weekends with my husband in Vancouver. After four months, another opportunity arose: Rick loaned me to the Portland office to work on a huge project ... one of the high points of my career. And I was back in town with my husband! There, I finished my 28-year career with BPA. Go out when you're at the top of your game!

POSTCARDS FROM SPOKANE

When I'm homesick, I write. I mass-mailed four postcards to people back home during my short stint in Spokane.

October 1996: I'm on my way to Spokane. Two weeks ago, I made a practice run … just reporting there to work, rather than reporting in Portland. My goal was to try as many new experiences as possible … and to make as many mistakes as possible while traveling light in good weather. There wasn't much difference between Portland and Spokane, except:

The BPA plane was one and one-half hours late leaving Portland due to maintenance problems. *** We flew in to Felts Field, not the commercial airport. They aren't set up for people arriving unmet. I hitched a ride with a crew from the transmission department to within one-half mile of the office. Later, I found out the one-half mile went right through the drug-panhandler-red-light district. I was glad I went through there at 10:00 a.m. *** The lady panhandler I met was the former girlfriend of the infamous South Hill rapist (way before my time). *** I was almost the only one still working on the whole floor that night, except the janitor and one other lady … it was only 6:00 p.m. *** There were two false fire alarms at the hotel: 11:17 p.m. and 12:42 a.m. I was glad I had packed my nightie at the last minute. *** The beautiful new architectural wonder within walking distance of the office is actually the city jail. *** My flight home was delayed indefinitely.

On the brighter side, we celebrated October birthdays with cake and pie on the day I arrived, and the travel agency BPA works through was able to easily get me all squared away with a seat on a different plane.

November 1996: Hello again. Things are starting to come together for me. I've made three more trips to Spokane and still have a steep learning curve. I'm constantly struggling to remember where my next change of clothes is located. The highlights of those trips include: The flu ... if you're going to have the flu in Spokane, it's good to stock up on Alka-Seltzer Plus and all the assorted medicines in advance. (I scored a perfect 10!) *** If Spokane looks sunny and warm, there might be ice in the puddles ... wear boots. (I scored a perfect zero!) *** On Halloween, it's okay to ride the bus even if the driver has long stringy hair and a camouflage jacket. *** Motels are colder than hotels. Check out the digs before making a reservation. *** The nicest dinner in downtown Spokane can be found at Ankeny's on the top of the Ridpath Hotel. *** Even in the worst ice storm, Spokane can be a beautiful place. We had the most spectacular silver thaw I've ever seen ... the smallest branches were more than one inch in diameter with ice; huge trees snapped at about fifteen feet above ground. It was reminiscent of the aftermath of Mount St. Helen's eruption blowing down trees like toothpicks. *** You can get pretty tired flying to Spokane in the morning, but the view of the snow-covered land, airport, roads, and houses from 26,000 feet during the sunrise is a sight to behold.

My winter lodging decisions were made based on who has shuttles to and from the Spokane airport and how reliable they are. Bus travel is very easy and the drivers are peaches. I think I'm completely over my dread of eating alone now.

December 1996: Hello a third time. This time it really hurts to write. As most of you know, I can be a very organized person. For example, by Thanksgiving, I realized if I wanted to get home with the minimum of fuss at Christmas, it would be good to make my reservation well in advance. In anticipation of a holiday rush, I even arranged to take the earlier flight home. Pretty good, huh? Well, it's always good to practice, so I took the earlier flight in the first part of December. Result: It felt too early. Then as time went on, I got used to the routine of taking the 4:50 afternoon flight home. On the Thursday before Christmas, just before another mammoth snowstorm hit the city, I proudly showed up in plenty of time for the 4:50 flight and checked in early at the counter. They asked if I'd recently changed my reservation. I broke out in a cold sweat feeling like I was starting to live my worst nightmare! I had scheduled a 2:50 flight on Southwest Airlines and I missed it! I called the travel agent to get an alternate flight on Alaska. Fortunately, they had one seat available and fixed everything for me ... all I had to do was get a ticket at the ticket counter. The Alaska ticket counter line was about 100 feet long (about thirty minutes long and I had only thirty minutes to spare). Another lady in line told me to check to see if I was in the right line. The ticketer said, "Sorry ma'am, you need to be in the Horizon line, not the Alaska line." The Horizon line was only six people deep, but every one of them had a five-minute problem. As Marg's Roger always said, "Do the math!" I finally made it through the line only to find the security line was one hundred feet long. Southwest Airlines was about ten minutes away from announcing who made it on standby. My heart was pounding as I worked my way politely forward in the line. People in Spokane are very congenial. Once through security, I all but ran to my flight and made it. When I got to Portland and returned the unused Horizon ticket, I vowed to confirm my reservation status early in the day, for future flights.

March 1997: I had planned to send this card before Valentine's Day, but got a little busy, so now you know how late I am. I went to the Spokane Opera House recently to see Robert Goulet in *Man of La Mancha*. It was wonderful. My friend from work and I had a good time. She suggested we go backstage to get his autograph. We braved the winter weather without our jackets and had fun standing outside the stage door like groupies. We were finally invited in and found him to be a very gracious host.

Marg's Roger, a dear friend, lost his eleven-year struggle with cancer on President's Day. Those of us who knew him were the lucky ones!

On a happier note. Harry and I put a down payment on some retirement property in a gated community at Lakeside on the Oregon coast. One of the requirements is that any dwelling be a manufactured home. We've been out looking a lot. There are lots of choices out there!

I've got a new work assignment. After working out of Spokane for the last several months, I've accepted a transfer to Portland for a year to work on the Northwest power industries' Subscription process. It's a plum assignment, and it really will be nice to be home more often ... although Harry and I may miss our marathon phone calls. Looks like flexibility is the name of any game for the next few years!

AJAX

Sadly, Ajax, my Orange-Winged Amazon, continued to express his displeasure by reciting the microwave song: *BEEP – BEEP – BEEP!* When I was in Spokane, Harry was in charge of Ajax. The handwriting was on the wall ... Ajax was in countdown mode. After one beep too many, Harry and I agreed Doug and Charlie would become his new owners. Charlie recalled the fun they had with their previous Orange-Winged Amazon ... she and their two girls wanted Ajax in the worst way ... Doug didn't ... Ajax bonded with Doug. It wasn't a match made in heaven, but Ajax had many great years with them under a new name: Sweet Pea. They had a grape arbor out back, which became his favorite haunt. He was a happy bird, indeed.

Years later, when he became a little too much for them to handle, he enjoyed a new home with a bicycle-riding hair stylist. He would perch on the handlebars and enjoy the breeze (reminiscent of flying). He was good at housework and perched on the handle while she was vacuuming. I don't think any of his new owners minded the microwave song. He was actually a nicer bird than Boris, but for that one little quirk.

1997

(Color the tree gold)

BORIS LEARNS TO FLY

Boris learned how to fly ... *before he learned how to land!*

Pretty Tricky: Boris learned tricks quickly. He was great at talking and could say our names clearly. Repetition is the best way to accidentally train a bird. Every night, I called for Harry to come to dinner. Boris would always get a little tidbit. Consequently, whenever Boris wanted food, he would say: "Harry ... HAR-ry!" His best trick was squawking at full pitch while Harry pretended to wring his little neck. That is, it *was* his best trick until Harry taught him how to fly a little at a time. He progressed from arm to arm ... to a perch ... to the end of the room ... to the back bedroom ... always with a downward trajectory. Then on a Saturday evening in August, with a houseful of company, he flew ... up! Up to a wall decoration, ten feet above the floor. Then farther up to the fan (thankfully, it was off). In retrospect, we should have clipped his wings that night.

Up-Up-and-Away: The next day, Harry and I were enjoying a breezy August afternoon with his brother Jon. The guys had just finished working on the barn. The dogs were lying in the shade. Boris was perched in the dwarf apple tree. One of the dogs moved suddenly.

The Happiest of Holidays to You!

We reached the end of an era just after New Year's when Tori died. She was our first Westie and a dedicated Mother and Grandma. She was also a good little buddy. Tori reminded me of a little quote by Edith Wharton:

> MY LITTLE OLD DOG ...
> A HEARTBEAT AT MY FEET.

Harry and his brother Jon (a building contractor) are constructing a barn where the garden used to be. The entry threatens the front yard so we're looking for ways to make the driveway look like lawn and flower bed ... but act like a driveway. Jon usually brings his border collies giving Bo a chance to play instead of pulling guard duty all day.

I accepted a temporary job back in Portland. I've been back since Spring. It's nice to be with my family, but when I return to Spokane, I'll enjoy that dry climate once again!

Have a very Merry Christmas,

Harry & Kathy Hoffman

Boris fell off the branch, flapped his wings and went sailing down the terraces. Suddenly a gust of wind caught him lifting him about twenty feet into the air. The next thing we knew, he was thirty or forty feet up in a maple, southwest of the house, across the gully! We hollered and chirped ... we whistled and waved ... nothing worked. He was stuck. To him, the world looked vastly different than ever before. We could see and hear him. He wanted to come back. It was unbelievably frustrating for all of us.

The Vigil: After a half-hour, he dove off the limb heading toward the deck. As he got close, he flared and flapped. Another gust of wind caught him, swooping him up, across the yard, and into a fir tree, east of the house. He was well above the roofline of the house. He was almost completely hidden in a bough, but we could hear him whistling to us. His whistles were not happy ones.

For three hours, we kept a constant vigil with binoculars. Finally, he walked out in the open, teetered on the edge of the bough, and dove off again. He was getting used to the gusts, but he still didn't know how to get down. It was getting dark. He was flying about twenty feet above the house and circled it twice before zipping into our neighbor Gary's fir to the northwest of the house. Suddenly, I saw a hawk fly into the same spot. I heard Boris' "SQUAWK!" I strained to see the hawk as he flew off. I couldn't be sure if he was empty-clawed. And then … there was nothing but a heavy silence … a horrible end to our day.

Lost, Exotic Bird, Hazel Dell … Reward: We placed an ad in two newspapers; "Lost, exotic bird, Hazel Dell … Reward." I peppered the neighborhood with flyers (except the area southwest of us). We put his cage outside in full view on the deck … just in case he found his way home. Jon, still working on building the barn, called to him by day, we called to him by night, hoping to hear his little whistle … nothing. We missed him immensely!

Sunday came. I thought it might be a good idea to get a paper and check to make sure our ad was in … but I kept forgetting. About 9:30 Sunday evening, a young pregnant woman called and said there was an ad in *The Columbian* right below ours. It read: "Found, exotic bird, Hazel Dell." She gave me the number. I thanked her and got her contact information. My heart was racing and so was I … downstairs to hand the phone to Harry. He called the number. I could hear only one side of the conversation. Harry gave our location. Then, I heard a faint laughing over the phone and watched as Harry's face began to turn red. He was very close to hanging up! Why was this person laughing? A few seconds later, the person identified himself. It was Tom, our next-door neighbor to the southwest! He lives only 800 feet from us. He had found Boris on the roof of his lean-to on Tuesday. He netted him, boarded him at a nearby pet store, and put an ad in the paper. The rest was history. We got our friend back. Boris got his home back. The young pregnant woman and Tom both got rewards. Boris' wings were clipped. Everyone was happy. All was well in our home once again.

Coming Home: As it turned out, we figured Boris could have found his way home eventually because …

When Harry entered the pet store the next day he said, "I'm here for my bird." The lady behind the counter exclaimed, "Oh, you must be HAR-ry!"

Since the pet store wasn't going to sell him, they put his cage in the break room. Every time someone went in to have a bite to eat, Boris would see the food and say, "Harry … HAR-ry!" (I was grateful to have our little bird back again, but also acutely aware of the manner in which I called Harry to dinner.)

Morrie & Jon

1998

(Color the hats lime green)

The Happiest of Holidays to You!

We have a wonderful year of change to report. Only one sad note: Our big old dog, Bo, died of cancer after the New Year. We were devastated. But as so often happens, "Fate" dropped a 7-month, 100-lb loving hairball in our laps within the month. He's a Bouvier des Flandres named Solo. Chatterbox and Boris were the first ones to "make up" to him. Molly, on the other hand, frequently showed up with a mouthful of gray hair! It took her about *six months* to decide he *might* be OK!

In February, I began writing and illustrating little songs and poems for my little niece. I'll be happy to sing one for you ... anytime... *anytime!*

Later, BPA made me an exit-offer that was too good to pass up. Harry and I ran the numbers and figured out how to make ends meet without too many changes. 'Midst the flurry of activity that comes with closing out a major chapter in one's life, I discovered *(a)* Preventive Health Care ... and a whole new group of people who are excited about making a difference in the lives of those they care about... *(b)* weight-training and *(c)* Martha Stewart. Harry's benefiting, too: Besides, having more free time, himself, he actually commented that my cooking has *vastly* improved. (Thank you, thank you, thank you, Martha.) Got to go ... I'm off to bake yet-another apple pie.

Enjoy your holidays!

SUV

In 1998, Marg told me about a new Mercedes ... an SUV. I've never been interested in cars after my first one. But Harry was going gaga over cars all the time. I decided to pull out all the stops and be supportive of my husband. Mercedes gave me a glossy three-foot banner featuring the SUV. I taped it at eye level on the built-in china hutch so I would see it every time I went into the kitchen ... which was a lot. That banner stayed up all summer and fall. I was proud to be so supportive. Harry decided he was going to order one and told me to pick the color. I was very confused: If he was getting a car, I figured he should pick the color. I didn't question him. I picked Forest Green.

Be Happy!

Love,
Kathy & Harry

Solo, Molly, Chatterbox & Boris

There was a five-month wait. We were going to get Harry's new car in the spring of 1998. As we went through the winter, I looked at cars on the road and noticed how dark the blacks, blues, grays, and browns were. The greens were just as dark. At the last moment, I changed from green to white. Harry took it in stride. I was surprised he didn't care about the color of his car. In May, the car came. He took me over to do a test-drive. I thought it strange he didn't just test-drive it himself. When we brought it home, he suggested I drive it to work since it was the ultimate commuting vehicle. Again ... very odd. It took me another five months to realize he had bought the car for me. Sometimes, I'm just clueless!

MUSTARDY CHICKEN SAUCE

Boil for 40 minutes:

      2 Chicken Breasts (4 halves)

Melt in saucepan over low heat:

      6 tablespoons salted Margarine

Blend and add to saucepan:

      3 cups Milk
      6 tbsp Flour
      1½ tbsp Worcestershire Sauce
      1 tbsp Minced Garlic
      1½ tsp Dry Mustard
      1 tsp Salt
      1 tsp Coarse Ground Pepper

Simmer and stir the sauce until it has thickened.

Chop the Chicken Breasts and add to the sauce. Simmer a little more to ensure the flavors permeate the essence of the sauce and then serve over your most special noodles.

This recipe received rave reviews when I made it for a small group of friends last month. It's a basic cream sauce with mustard, garlic & chicken. Hope you like it.

      –K

KATE

'98

WEST HIGHLAND WHITE TERRIER
(360) 573-6909

Poster of SUV

1999

(The card was printed on mottled blue paper.)

THE WATERFALL

We tried to create a creek and waterfall from one pond to the other by ourselves. Do-it-yourself projects make you appreciate the work the professionals do. We had a professional come in and do it right. Can you see three waterfalls? The main Waterfall, which carries the name, is just left of the center of the picture. There is a large 2 x 2-foot steppingstone in the middle of the creek just above the waterfall. The other two waterfalls don't have names, but you can see the ripples in the water below each. The total drop between ponds is about six to eight feet.

It was a good year for landscaping. Our best project was Harry's waterfall and stream. He had it designed and installed this summer. Transplanted grasses, and shrubs give the site a naturalized feel. There's a nice little sitting area near the end of the meandering stream that captures the music of the water.

On a different note, here's something that set me on my ear last year. I was driving to the grocery store with Kyle, our 8-year-old step-great-nephew. I asked, "What's the best thing about Christmas?" He didn't even hesitate: "Getting together with my relatives." (And no one was prodding him!) Sooo ... next time things get a little out of sorts ...

Remember the important things ...

Have a Merry Christmas!

AUNT MIT

I was newly retired and struggling to reinvent myself. I tutored fifth-grade kids in math for a while. Later in the year, I spent some time with dear Aunt Mit who was bordering on kidney failure. She was a woman of strong moral character packed into a tiny and somewhat frail body ... and she was all alone in Lebanon, Oregon, needing some temporary live-in care. I drove down to stay with her during the weekdays. Cousin Diane drove down from Milwaukie, Oregon, to stay with her on the weekends. The doctor told us her condition could be reversed if she drank lots more water. He gave me the amount in liters, I converted it to small glassfuls ... the size available at the retirement facility: She needed fourteen small glasses per day. We made a game of it. After six weeks of good hydration, it was clear she could manage without live-in care. We were all disappointed. We had fun together, but I was glad to return home to my husband.

Aunt Mit's apartment had a huge bathroom just to the right of her front door. When she took a shower, she wanted a little help to keep her steady. I held her arm and stood outside the almost-closed shower curtain. She used the shower wand … not very gracefully. I'd let out a shriek from time to time as the water escaped the confines of the shower stall.

She was in her nineties. It would have been prudent to respect her age, but I'm not entirely prudent. When she was drying off with the bathroom door wide open, I turned toward the front door and, even though there was no one there, I exclaimed excitedly, "Oh … Pastor Dave!" She shrieked. Fortunately, Aunt Mit had a strong heart … and a good sense of humor.

One of her table buddies, Pearl Gilbert, had been an avid gardener all her life and was tee-tering at the brink of a century. Pearl asked me to do a favor for her. She needed help getting her Medicare and immediately got a fast-talking

Pearl's Shovel

When you hurry and worry

through your day,

It's like an unopened gift ...

Thrown away.

--Author Unknown

KATE '99

WEST HIGHLAND WHITE TERRIER
(360) 573-6909

chirper who absolutely could not slow down if her life depended on it. I know how to speak fast-talking-chirpese, so it was easy to get the information, but it sure gave me an appreciation for older people and what it takes for them to process new information.

When Pearl died in 2001, her son Ray came over from the East Coast to settle her affairs. I asked him if I could have her well-used shovel. It is now one of my prized possessions.

2000

(Glue a little white puff ball to the end of Santa's cap.)

Happy Holidays to You!

This little Rat Terrier, Mickey, has stolen our hearts. When we first got him, his legs grew faster than the rest of him so when he leaned over to eat his dinner he nearly toppled into his food dish. Now, he has adjusted and loves to pounce, "box", and race like the wind.

Mickey rose in Boris' esteem when he gently tried to clean some peanut butter off Boris' beak. He rose in Solo's esteem by running circles and cutting corners around him. He's still working on Molly.

We've enjoyed the Southern Oregon Coast a lot this year ... and gardening in Vancouver. Now, a warm December in Southern California and Yuma is looking very inviting.

May your holidays be Safe and Warm too!

kateh@pacifier.com
-- (360) 573-6909 --

RAT TERRIERS

Dorothy (not my neighbor, not my mother-in-law, but one of the people Harry insures) has a home with a barn on 78th Street surrounded by ten acres of hay. It was just down the street from Harry's office. When her husband died, her sons started decorating the sides of the barn with advertising placards. The most spectacular decoration is the huge Kentucky Fried Chicken bucket. It dominates the area next to the barn.

LIVE,

LOVE,

LEARN.

Merry Christmas from

Kathy & Harry

Dorothy's little rat terrier had a litter of puppies. Harry heard about them and suggested I go have a look. I corralled my tea party friend, Carol, and off we went. Dorothy, a practical farmer, took us to one of the outbuildings. The puppies, having been raised on goat's milk, were adorable and fat. Only one of the puppies had a name … Mickey. When he was facing away from us, we could see the three circles on his back. They looked exactly like Mickey Mouse. His face had perfectly symmetrical markings and he was unbelievably cute. There were four other puppies. One had an asymmetrical face.

Spanish Chicken *adapted fr. Betty Crocker*

This recipe was so good it had both
Cathy & Jim Basler raving!

    1 large onion, chopped (1 cup)
    2 cloves garlic, finely chopped
    1 large red bell pepper, chopped (1 1/2 cups)
    1 tsp dried oregano leaves
    1 tsp crushed red pepper
    1 lb. hot Italian sausage
1 3/4 lb. boneless, skinless chicken, 1" pieces
    1 can (28 oz) diced tomatoes, undrained
    1 can (6 oz) tomato paste
    1 can (14 oz) artichoke heart quarters, drained
    1 can (4 oz) sliced ripe olives, drained
    3 cups hot cooked rice

1. Spray inside of 4-quart slow cooker with
cooking spray. Mix all ingredients except
artichoke hearts, olives and rice in slow
cooker.

2. Cover and cook on low heat setting 6 to 8
hours or until sausage and chicken are no
longer pink in center. Stir in artichoke hearts
and olives; heat through. Serve with cooked
rice. *6 servings.*

Christmas 2000

I nicknamed him "The Rabbit." Naturally, I wanted one of the puppies. I went home and talked with Harry about it. I wanted The

Rabbit. He asked why I didn't want Mickey because I kept saying how perfect he was. Well, I assumed since Mickey was named, he was spoken for. Not so!

I was going out of town to a conference for a few days. We decided not to make a move until I returned. I called Harry on the way home from the conference. He said it didn't make sense to get a puppy because we had Molly, the cranky Westie, Solo who was only a year old, and an open-ended visitor

Barn on 78th St

named Bear, a Chow-mix. Bear belonged to Bill's daughter (Bill was our retaining-wall friend). We needed to wait until Bear was gone. Of course, Harry was right, but Bear's departure kept getting delayed. I drove home from the airport and mulled it all over in my head. By the time I hit 78th Street, I had changed our minds. I called Dorothy saying I was two minutes out. I was so excited I drove right past her place. I pulled a U-turn and arrived. Mickey was available. Ten minutes later, Mickey was mine!

MICKEY WRITES HOME TO HIS MAMA

Dear Mom,

Just a little note to tell you I love you and bring you up to date.

My paws are still pretty soft. Every time I get up after a nap, the two people draw straws to see who gets to hold me. Life is good. The one who picked me up a couple of weeks ago keeps saying "Every nap ends with a P!" I don't get it, but I humor her and turn my face up to her and look cute. The next thing you know, off we go outside. Usually I have to poop and pee, so it seems pretty timely. The lady seems to like it when I run off and take care of nature and then run right back to her. She especially liked it the first week when we got to go outside and it was really dark ... I mean really dark! It hasn't been dark for about a week.

You wouldn't believe the other dogs here. There's a cranky one about your size ... I call her Aunt Molly. She had a miserable attitude until I shared my dinner with her. Then there's this HUGE guy they call Solo. He has so much hair ... I could get lost in it. I try to get him to play, but my neck gets sore from looking up all the time ... and besides he says I move too fast and when I do, he steps on me kinda lightly. Finally there's this other dog with a lot of hair and skin. I've adopted him as my official chew toy. He seems to like me, too. We wrestle every night. I usually win. I don't know much people-talk, but I think the people version of winning is "Bear! Be gentle!"

They call me Mickey just like Grams did (by the way, tell her I love her). We played a game the other day. They called it the Come-Game. I won every time. First the man said "Mickey, Come!" I felt a tug on my collar, and when I went to him, I got a treat, and it tasted good 'cause I was hungry. Then the lady did the same thing and I got another treat. I like this place.

We get to go for a walk just about every morning. The first time I went for a walk, I went a mile, then the lady carried me and finally I walked another quarter mile. This is absolutely great. You wouldn't believe how many people I've met. Life is sure super here. The food's pretty good, too. For a few days, they didn't realize I couldn't eat a ton of food at two sittings, but they finally fixed me up with a great big bunch of food and I get to eat ANYTIME I WANT TO EAT! I've hit the mother lode!

Hey, you know the liver Grams gave the lady? Well she cooked it and it came out just like Grams' liver did. It was good. There wasn't very much, though because the lady kept saying "Yum" and putting it in her mouth. She said she was going to tell Grams how great it was.

I know you and Dad will need help mousing during the hay harvest next year, but I don't know if I'll be able to come. You see, every time there's any talk of that, they just smile and say the word "mole." I'm not sure what mole means, but it might mean leaf, 'cause I've been practicing my pouncing on every leaf I can find.

I've got my own crate in the car. It's pretty cool. Well, I've gotta go. I've been at this letter for 45 minutes and my eyelids are getting pretty darned heavy. Is it true that someday, when I grow up, I'll be able to stay awake more than 45 minutes? I have a feeling there's a lot I'm missing!

Love to you, Dad, and Grams,

Mickey

CALVARY CHAPEL

On the last Sunday of the century, Harry's mom asked if I wanted to read the Bible from cover to cover. I said I did and she gave me a syllabus for daily readings. It took me two months to get started, and fifteen months to finish, but it felt good. When she and Aunt Alma came to visit that summer, we went to a Calvary Chapel church just down the street. I liked it and decided to keep going until I could see through the façade. As it turned out, there was no façade and I got hooked. The symbol was a dove, which I then put on the back of every Christmas card.

2001

Nestled ...
all snug in their bed!

Hello Dear Friends,

Three really nice events punctuated our year for which Harry and I are very grateful.

First: Harry's Great Aunt Mit (92) recovered from pneumonia and a stay in a nursing home. She's getting better and looks great.

Second: I got to visit my Brother and his family in England. (Harry opted to stay home.) One day the four of us were driving to the grocery store. My niece (5) and I were in the back seat having an adult conversation about fashion (she was doing most of the talking).   She ended by saying "It takes a shahp eye to put an outfit togetheh."

Third: Harry asked me the pivotal marriage question: *Do you Like to Cook?"* I gave him an honest answer! But, with his encouragement, I've tried harder. My biggest problem seemed to be substituting color for color: no more substituting cayenne for paprika, nor sour cream for whipped cream and certainly no more substituting soda for cornstarch (fortunately I had caught that in time). Gone are the good ol' days!

Have a Very Happy
Christmas!

Harry & Kathy Hoffman

(also shown: Mickey, Boris & Solo)

Woof-Molly

adapted from Readers' Digest Secrets of Better Cooking

A classic French method of preparing eggs, called oeufs mollets yields a lovely little soft-cooked egg, similar to a poached egg, but left whole.

1. Bring eggs to room temperature. Put enough water in a small pan to cover the eggs completely. Bring the water to a full rolling boil.

2. Place each egg on a spoon and gently slip it into the water. Lower the heat and cook for *exactly 6 minutes.*

3. Remove the egg and place it in a bowl of ice-cold water. Gently crack the shell with the back of a spoon, then put the egg back in the hot water for a few seconds. Remove from the water. Gently peel the egg.

A perfect oeuf mollet consists of a cooked wall of egg white with a semi-runny yolk inside. Keep the shelled egg in tepid water until ready to use.

360-573-6909
kateh@pacifier.com

POST-WTC FLYING

The World Trade Center buildings came down in September. I already had my ticket to England. It was a weird time, but planes were finally allowed to resume limited schedules. I was glad to be able to go visit my England family … and equally glad to return home safe and sound.

CRANKY MOLLY – *RIP*

My friends laugh and tell me not to get sick or Harry will run me in to the doctor's office for a final visit. But the reality is, neither of us want our little charges to suffer. Molly had a named disease. I talked with my vet about what to expect and when to take her in for a final visit. I could see the signs coming and made the decision the last weekend of February. Unfortunately, my vet's office was closed, but I didn't want to wait until Monday. I grabbed a handful of kibble ... Molly loved her treats ... and with tears in my eyes, I had her sit and catch treats while I had a discussion with the weekend vet down the street. As soon as he realized it was not a matter of convenience, we got on with it. Molly died happy. Cranky or not, I loved her.

Our friends should probably warn Harry not to get sick!

SOLO AND ELLIE

I joined Harry walking the dogs on the three-mile nature trail down at Klineline Ponds. A young man named Troy would show up most days with his Malemute, Ellie. She and Solo were evenly matched. It was a thing of beauty to see those two behemoths running loose in the field playing "Clash of the Titans" and "Catch Me If You Can." They learned from each other as they went and had some fabulous routines.

2002

While Visions
of Sugarplums

(Color the ribbon on the bone red)

Happy Holidays!

We made some major improvements to our place this year, covering gravel with asphalt, and adding two lean-to's to the big garage. Now I have a potting area and Harry has a covered area for the trailer ... and no dust on the drive!

My brother, Charles, and his family returned from England this Fall season. I've been home-schooling my niece, Ceridwen (1ˢᵗ grade), while Charles and Trish are busy with job and house-hunting. She and I have been having fun reading, and playing with math and vowels. We made a recipe for bread pudding during the lesson on reading, fractions and measurements!

Harry always told me he wanted to play the Base, I gave him a base guitar for his birthday. (Oops, I didn't realize that he meant the stand-up base.) But he kept the base guitar and practices every evening for 30-60 minutes. It has a pleasant, soothing sound. It's fun to hear him getting better all the time.

I got to work on several projects with people at Church this year and loved every minute of it. Vacation Bible School was the high point. It got me back into painting again!

We lost our aunt this year
which makes us even more grateful
for the family and friends around us ...

Have a Blessed Christmas!

Harry & Kathy Hoffman

(also shown: Mickey, Boris & Solo)

Kate's Stuffed Peppers
adapted from Rombauer & Becker's Joy of Cooking

Preheat oven to 350°

Steam for 9 minutes (cut-side down):
    4 large peppers halved & cored

Sauté:
    ½ lb. ground hot Italian Sausage

Add while continuing to sauté:
    1½ cup cooked rice
    ½ large onion, chopped
    1 cup tomatoes
    ½ tsp salt
    ½ tsp. Paprika
    2 tsp Worchestershire Sauce

*Quarter the peppers, place in 13x9x2 dish, dust
with spices* (eg, garlic powder, salt, pepper) *to
your own taste and cover with cooked mixture.*

Top liberally with grated cheddar cheese.

Bake uncovered for 20 minutes.

2002

360-573-6909
kateh@pacifier.com

SWEET TOOTH

Solo was the best-behaved dog we ever had. He was a large dog who could easily see the top of the counter, even though the counters were four inches higher than normal. He was a good dog. He never got into anything on the counter, until ...

One evening, I made cookies, set them out on a paper bag to cool, and went downstairs to watch TV with Harry and the dogs. We heard a funny noise ... an unusual noise. Since all the dogs were with us and we didn't hear the noise again, we continued watching TV. A few minutes later, we heard that unusual noise again. I looked around and saw we were missing one dog ... Solo! I tiptoed upstairs to find that good dog ... who never messed with anything on the counter ... gently taking the edge of the paper bag in his teeth and carefully inching it to the edge of the counter. One, and only one, cookie dropped to the floor. I guess he figured if it's on the floor, it's fair game. I think he managed to get only two or three cookies. He was smiling.

2003

Noel ... Noel

Holly Bear   Harry

Happy Holidays!

Our family nearly doubled in number this year. In June, we adopted a little black Schipperke who knows no fear, has a mind of her own, and had an active mouthful of needle-sharp teeth. Her name is Holly Bear. We now understand the meaning of the adjective "head-strong". We're constantly conditioning her to do the right thing automatically. She's a real pistol!

No sooner did we get Holly than four ducks at school needed a new home. Donald was the only one of the four to survive. He doesn't have a mean bone in his body. Can't fly, but does a good imitation of the Spruce Goose at mealtime (he flaps hard and runs on top of the water). At first, he was half the size of the mallards and they picked on him. By August, he was twice their size and had top billing in the flock: they know with Donald around, they'll get more food!

Our third addition, Toby, is a 3-year-old male Westie with an endearing vocabulary. We've known him all his life. He and Solo are great companions!

Born is the King of Israel!

You are loved by

Harry & Kathy Hoffman

... Solo, Mickey, Holly, Toby, Boris (& Donald)

(Color the halo with blue glitter)

Kate's Spinach Enchiladas   *20 halves*

Preheat oven to 350°.

Have ready:
   1 lb. mozzarella, grated   **10 flour tortillas**
   2 10-oz pkg cooked spinach

For Sauce ... In a heavy saucepan, cook
   1 lb. Italian sausage
Add and sauté:
   2 tbsp olive oil   **¾ cup chopped onion**
   3 cloves minced garlic   **2 tsp chili powder**
Add and simmer for 15 minutes:
   1 qt. tomato puree   **1 tsp salt**
   1 6 oz. can tomato paste   **1 tsp pepper**
                                      1½ tsp cumin

Fill the center of each tortilla with spinach, mozzarella cheese, and 2 tbsp sauce. Roll tortillas and place in an ovenproof dish.   Pour remaining sauce over top and sprinkle with remaining cheese. .
Heat thoroughly in 350° oven .
about 15 minutes. Slice down.
middle of enchiladas. Serve .
with 2 salads and lots of friends.

2003

360-573-6909
kateh@pacifier.com

HARRY GAVE ME A HAMMOCK CHAIR

Harry gave me a hammock chair as a birthday present. He said I had made it easy on him by telling him a month earlier there was only one thing I wanted for my birthday ... a hanging chair. He bought it right away ... the package was sitting in the garage for two weeks, waiting for the big day ... and I didn't notice it.

But wait, there's more ...

When I told him I wanted a hanging chair, I secretly hoped I'd forget it so it would be a surprise ... and I did. A few days before my birthday, my old chair finally ripped in two. I had had it for at least ten years. I went right into the house, got on the computer, did a search and found a place called Hammocks.com. I found the one I wanted and ordered it. I wanted to order a second one for the sunporch but didn't. I had them enclose a mushy gift card from Harry to me and deliver it to the office.

On my birthday, Harry brought home my package, giving me a questioning look. I had to confess all. Every time I look at the one in the sunporch, I think about my screwup and smile.

HOLLY BEAR

We had only two dogs and it was Harry's pick. He looked high and low in the Portland area until he found a litter of Schipperkes. They are compact little black dogs bred as watch dogs for canal boats. We got her in the spring, took her to the pet store, and got a figure-eight cat harness an a new leash. When we put it on and set her down on the green grass, she flopped over and refused to move. Nobody was going to control her ... I should have realized it was a sign!

HOLLY WRITES HOME TO HER MOMMY

Dear Mom,

I just wanted to let you know I miss you, but I'm having a wonderful time in my new home. It was pretty funny the first day because they kept making all sorts of cooing sounds at me. As you can imagine, I thought I'd died and gone to heaven! But the next day, I had to straighten them out. I did my bear cub imitation and they loved it. Then, on a high note, I rolled right into my piranha imitation. That didn't go over too well. I know you warned me, but I thought they could take it. I was wrong!

Too Much!

The Harry is kind of nice. He likes to hold me with one hand for my singing lessons (Christmas card). He says I can go riding in the car with him when I grow up. I forgot to ask you how I'll know when I'm grown up.

The food's not bad here, but they tried to starve me the first two days. They only put a little bit in the bottom of the bowl, but they did soften it in water. Well, my patience won them over. After eating five bowls full of food over one dinner and breakfast period, I finally got them to realize I can really pack it away. Here's a picture of me after dinner. Maybe I had too much to drink!

I've got two other dogs to play with and a bird who isn't nearly as pretty as I am. Looks like this will be a good home.

I had my toenails done last week. It wasn't as bad as you said it might be. In fact, it was kind of nice until the Kathy started in on my back feet. Then I was bored and wiggled like you taught me to do.

Me ... as a Little Kid

This is what I looked like when I was a little kid, just leaving home.

Guess what, Mom. They have water and I already went for a swim! It was terrific!

Say Hi to Grandma and the gang for me.

Your loving Puppy,

Holly Bear

Me and The Harry

P.S. Here's a picture of me and the Harry. He likes me.

2004

The city had no need of the sun or of the moon to shine in it, for the glory of God illuminated it. The Lamb is its light.

Rev 21:23

*W*HAT A YEAR FOR WEATHER! We were happily stranded at the coast by mudslides for a couple days after Christmas. We squeaked home between storms only to lose power for 3 days. It was the worst silver thaw I've seen. 'Glops' of snow and ice as big as grapefruits fell from 120-foot fir trees, ominously hammering the single-pane roof of the sunroom. The house got below 54° (the lowest possible digital readout). Nevertheless, we stayed toasty in the bedroom with the gas fireplace. Three months later, we spent Easter with friends in the sweltering Palm Springs desert heat.

*D*ear Aunt Gerry died this summer. And my Dad died of cancer, suddenly and peacefully, in October. He kept us laughing until the end!

*H*arry has taken up the harmonica. It's soothing and funky, but when he hits some of the high notes it becomes a family affair: the dogs and I join in, howling with gusto! LIFE IS GOOD!

I am the Root and the Offspring of David, the Bright and Morning Star.

Rev 22:16

MERRY CHRISTMAS!
Harry & Kathy
Solo, Mickey, Holly, Boris & Donald

(Color the star gold)

DAD DIED

In October, Dad had a sudden downturn. Colon cancer came back after a five-year reprieve. Because visiting hours were extrem0ely limited in ICU, Dad decided to call friends and family to say goodbye. The nurses were beside themselves knowing he wouldn't be allowed to make long-distance calls from ICU.

*L*EMON *P*OSSET

(Serves 4-6)

Whip: 1   pint of Heavy Cream

Add: 6   tbsp sugar

            3   lemons (juice only)

Whip until thick but not stiff.

Scoop into crystal goblets.   Refrigerate until chilled. Serve immediately.

This is very pretty with a plate of sweet, vivid-red strawberries, in contrast to the surprising tang of the bright-white Posset!

2004

360-573-6909
kateh@pacifier.com

But Dad had a landline and an accountant's memory for numbers. He used his 32-digit long-distance calling card number to call his sister in Texas and some close friends … just to chat. Then, the nurses in ICU needed to know the dosage of the medication he'd been taking for the last few weeks. Not a problem for Dad … He called his doctor's office in Vancouver to inquire!

Storyteller: Dad could spin a story. He was a funny guy. In the early years, his oldest brother, Tom, was a roofing salesman at Sears, in Bellingham. When Dad and the family were in Bellingham visiting

Grandma and Grandpa, Dad called Sears and got Uncle Tom on the line. Using a Swedish accent, Dad was stringing Uncle Tom along saying how he needed a whole new roof for his great big barn out on Van Wyck Road … and his name was "van Berg … Small-v-Capital-B-van-Berg." After a few more rounds punctuated by the name "van Berg … Small-v-Capital-B-van-Berg," arrangements were made for Uncle Tom to come out and give this Swedish fellow an estimate a few days hence. (It would have meant a tidy commission.) Later that night, when Uncle Tom and Aunt Gerry went over to Grandma and Grandpa's for a visit, my older brother Larry (about three years old), having been coached all afternoon, walked up to Uncle Tom and said in his little voice … "Small-v-Capital-B-van-Berg."

I Love You: Dad spent his last few days in a hospital bed in the two-story living room of his home. The windowed wall in front of him was 85% glass. He had a beautiful view of the Lewis River. We each had a chance to say goodbye. One by one, we leaned over Dad, said goodbye, and told Dad how much we loved him. Dad reciprocated. He acknowledged each member of his family. It was a sacred time. Finally, it was just Kevin, Stephen, Mom, and I who hadn't yet had a turn. Kevin stood up, leaned over the bed, and said, "I love you, Dad." We all leaned in closer, hanging on his every word. Dad, weak as he was, lifted his hands to Kevin's face, as he had done with so many others, and said haltingly in a weak voice, "Well … I … sure … don't … love … you!" Everyone burst out laughing, especially Kevin!

Little Comments: As things would come to our minds, we would say them. We never knew what kind of reaction we were going to get. "Dad," I said, "I borrowed your ladder." The accountant in him responded, "Did you sign for it?"

Later, Pat leaned forward over the foot of the bed and said in a loud, steady voice, "Harry fixed the window of your car." Even though he had very little energy, Dad's eyes shot wide open. He listened closely for Pat to repeat what he had just said. "Harry fixed the window of your car." You could just see the relief flood over his face.

Inside, Outside: Kevin had brought a booklet put out by Hospice describing the various phases of the dying process. Everyone had been reading the information, and naturally we were all looking at whatever Dad said or did as a signal he was progressing to another stage of dying. Pat asked Kevin to put a little marker in the booklet corresponding to whatever stage he thought Dad was in. Kevin was the appointed expert. According to one stage, Dad might be expected to look out with a glassy stare beyond the end of the bed and see people who really aren't there ... ones who had preceded him ... ones who were waiting to welcome him to the other side.

While we were all still gathered around the bed, Dad seemed to go into this stage. Of course, we were all proud of ourselves as we recognized the sign. Dad lifted his right hand. It floated in the air, lightly pointing toward the end of the bed ... and the river beyond the windows. He began to speak. We leaned in and listened closely. It was very soft. He said, "Inside ... Outside."

The booklet hadn't said anything about speaking words, but none of us wanted to give up on this theory. Frowning with intensity, we asked him to repeat it.

"Inside ... Outside," he repeated, his hand still hovering. Kevin, taking his job as appointed expert seriously, was the first to recognize Dad was talking about the river and the trees, not about unseen people: "Yes, Dad, that's the river, it's outside ... and the hills and the trees."

"Wait!" I said with disgust, "There's a box elder beetle on the window. Is it on the inside or the outside?"

It was on the inside. We got it with a tissue. Dad was at peace again. He was a practical man who took his jobs seriously.

Enough Said: Dad died peacefully on Monday, October 25, 2004, having had the opportunity to say goodbye to so many of his friends and family. Later, one of the boys said he had heard Dad say: "I never fiddled around with the Commandments."

2005

(Color the halo yellow)

The message included in the Christmas card:

Merry Christmas to all our friends,

This was a wonderful year for doing things together, especially golf and art.

Golfing: Harry has spent a lot of time studying golf videos and practicing on the golf course. He's very serious about improving all aspects of his game. I've finally joined him this year. He's a good teacher.

Mural: We had talked about having me paint a mural on the wall of his office. He wanted a golf scene. After we watched the Masters' Tournament, we decided the subject should be the twelfth hole at Augusta National (Georgia) with the Ben Hogan Bridge in the foreground. Then, he asked me to paint a window frame around the mural. We both loved the effect. The finished piece was about 6' x 8'. His relatives were shopping and found him a coffee mug with the exact scene!

Let the whole earth be filled with His glory.

Ps. 72:19

Harry & Kathy
Solo, Mickey, Holly Bear, Boris & Donald

Stained Glass: About mid-year, Harry decided to renew his stained-glass efforts (after 25 years) by taking a class to get up to speed on current tools. Now, we both collaborate on the design and the quality and color of the glass. Usually, I draw and trace the pattern and Harry runs with it. He's enjoying the challenge and variety; I'm enjoying the energy and dedication he puts into the projects. He's completed a magnificent heron, a clownfish, and some assorted abstract designs, so far.

We're happy, healthy, and grateful. Hope you are, too.

Walnut Truffles
With thanks to Charlotte Morrison for wanting a recipe.

Cream Together:
  3/8 cup **Hershey's Cocoa**
  1/4 cup melted **Butter** (salted)
  1/8 cup **Sour Cream** (or IMO)

Slowly add:
  1 cup **powdered sugar**

Beat until smooth. Roll in waxed paper; refrigerate about 1 hour.

Cut into nice little chunks, roll in **chopped walnuts** (or pecans) and store in refrigerator or freezer.

2005

360-573-6909
kateh@pacifier.com

Sunday School Invitation and Learning My Lesson

Annette, a very congenial lady from my new church, invited me to teach Sunday school. Actually, she encouraged me to pray about it. I did, but I was scared. I wouldn't know what to say to the kids ... and there was no curriculum! Nevertheless, I agreed after she assured me they wouldn't bite. I didn't know the routine, and I surely didn't know the audience. I could give presentations to adults all day long, but it had been a long time since I was connected with more than just a few kids. I dove in and had the time of my life. I would start studying the upcoming lesson on Monday ... day by day, over the course of the week, I'd figure out some fun way to get the point across. Competition was always involved. By the time Sunday came, I was prepared. We had our one-hour class, I'd go home exhausted and take a nap. The next day, I'd start all over again. Sometimes, I'd really stick my foot into it ...

Everybody knows the story of David and Bathsheba. She was on the rooftop taking a bath, he saw her from the castle, he sent for her ... and the rest was history.

We were studying the kings of Israel in the book of 2 Samuel. I felt it was important to lay the groundwork. Solomon's mother was Bathsheba. It made sense to me to start with how David and Bathsheba met. I started telling how David was looking out from the castle to a rooftop below and Bathsheba was ... oh, good grief, I was stuck. I was embarrassed and fumbled with words until I finally got a tiny bit of the idea across ... using words like "friendly." These kids were only 10 and 11 years old ... I didn't know how much they knew about "life." At any rate, I got past the initial meeting. Then, of course, the next thing was David had to repent. And what did he have to repent for ... for sleeping with Uriah's wife, for conspiring to trick Uriah into sleeping with his pregnant wife, and for having Uriah killed on the front lines in battle. I tried hard not to show how uncomfortable I was.

At the end of most classes, I had the kids draw a picture of the lesson to see if they had understood. I was dreading what they might turn in for this lesson. Sweet little Elsa turned in her drawing. With a mixture of relief and horror I saw a rendering of one of David's generals shooting Uriah with a tommy gun. Rather than correct the type of murder weapon used, I decided to count it as a win ... or at least not a loss. I thought there might be a good lesson to learn from this experience but never put it into words.

Later, we were studying the book of Hosea. God set Hosea up to marry a prostitute. I didn't want to use the word prostitute in front of this age group, so I said Hosea married a Strumpet.

Hands went up ... "Mrs. Hoffman, what's a Strumpet?"

Uh-oh ... "Well ... you know ... a Tart."

Hands went up again ... they didn't know. "Mrs. Hoffman, what's a Tart?"

I was breaking out in a cold sweat ... "You know ... a Hotsy-Totsy woman."

No hands, just words: "Mrs. Hoffman, what's a Hotsy-Totsy woman?" They weren't going to quit. I don't remember anything after that, but I vowed to learn my lesson.

2006

You will find Him if you seek Him,
if you seek for Him in earnest.
cf. Jer. 29:13

(Color the infant pale blue)

MERRY CHRISTMAS!

*W*e've been simplifying our lives lately. Harry's stained glass work has been a great hobby; well-suited to his detailed craftsmanship. He likes to select pieces of glass that have personality all their own and I'm cheering him on: First, we collaborate on the design, then I draw it, finally, he builds it.

*H*arry has become almost religious about his golf spending five days each week studying, practicing and/or golfing. We watch the Golf channel regularly. I'll be getting back into the game this spring.

I had an opportunity to put gardening on hold this summer, without getting stressed. It was a good year. In addition, I've always had an inner passion to do some home remodeling (e.g., carpentry) and have finally given in to it. Most of my work has been demolition, but I'm getting my head into design/build mode for 2007. Harry's cheering me on: He claims I can have anything I want, as long as I build it.

Thinking of you with love!

Harry & Kathy

Solo
Mickey
Holly Bear &
Boris the Bird

Try this for a New Year's Resolution:
Pull out a special calendar ... join me
in "decluttering" for 2007!

A Book, a Paper,
A Project or two,
Are sitting there staring
Intently at you.

You won't read or build it ...
You won't even try.
It's time to kiss
That ol' nuisance good bye.

Pull out a calendar
Just meant for you
To write down the "toss-outs"
You'll never get to.

One "toss-out" each day ...
With glee you will shudder:
You're ridding yourself
Of unwanted clutter.

Give some to your friends
Or your family ... or
Donate those things ...
Get 'em out of the door!

One "toss-out" each day
Unless you are tempted:
Your calendar gets filled,
Your closet gets emptied.

At the end of the year,
If faithful you are,
You'll've shed tons of stuff
And you'll be a STAR!

360-573-6909
kateh@pacifier.com

AN OPPORTUNITY? ... REALLY?

Okay, putting my gardening on hold wasn't really an opportunity.

I got up in the middle of the night to do whatever one does in the middle of the night. Our big ol' Sasquatch of a dog was lying at the end of the bed, and I didn't realize it. I tripped over him, stuck out my left arm, fell forward against the wall, and heard a snap. I thought I had broken my arm, but it was just a crack ... just. There was no way I could heft around a Weed Eater, so I gave up and watched my yard explode. Thank good-

ness it happened after the growing season. I was out of commission for three months. When I got the all-clear, I filled up the tank on the Weed Eater and let 'er rip. After filling it two more times, my yard was pristine again. I gained a real appreciation for how easy it can be to get a wayward yard under control ... with manly tools!

And for those who were horrified ... no, the dog was not hurt.

Mickey & Solo Laughing

2007

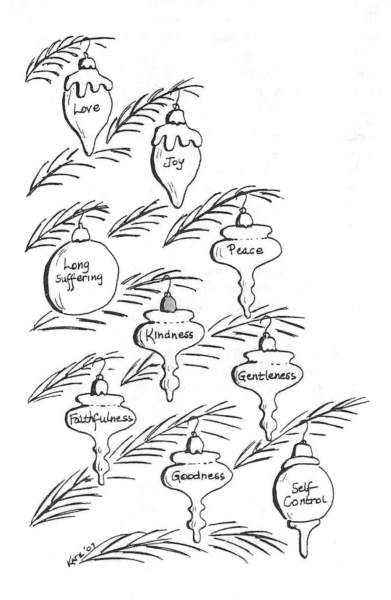

(Color the Kindness-topper gold)

It was a year of change for us. Our big, gentle dog Solo died in February, as did several close friends. Then in September we were stunned when Harry's Mom died of a heart attack. The day before she died, she mentioned that she was "ready to go, but if God let her stay and play with her dahlias for another 5 years, that would be fine, too." We adopted her 14-year old male Schipperke, Toby.

Mickey has learned to roll over and manages to show off whenever we have company ... he's happy to do any trick in his repertoire, even if it's not what we ask for. Holly expends a lot of energy ruling the roost ... even making up rules for the other dogs to follow. She's begun 'attacking' Boris while he's sitting in his cage. Boris just thinks she's comical!

Harry is continuing his passion for stained glass. He's just about finished with a 3'x3' piece in red and white: The State Farm Logo.

I got my State license for insurance this summer and intend to build up my hours to half-time in Harry's office. I enjoyed teaching art classes last spring and I especially enjoyed working with my Sunday School students.

We thank God for good health and good friends.

Thinking
fondly of you
this Christmas
Season!

Harry & Kathy
Hoffman

... Mickey, Holly, Toby, Boris

Doug and Charlotte have been searching for Walnut Creams to no avail. This year, Charlotte and I made "Opera Creams" from the Joy of Cooking, adding walnuts and covering them in semi-sweet chocolate. They were good, but not quite right. Since then, I've adapted the recipe. Both Harry and I like the results.

Kate's Walnut Creams   About 30-40

This recipe is for the Creamy Center. For Nut Creams, add chopped nuts in, on or around the creamy center.

BOIL in a large pan over med. Heat ... **2 C sugar, 1 C whipping cream, ¾ C milk, 2 Tbsp light corn syrup, 1/8 tsp salt** ... STIRRING constantly until mixture reaches 238°, soft-ball stage. (~25 min.)

REMOVE from heat ... let it rest undisturbed until mixture has cooled to at least 160°. (~10-12 min.)

ADD **1 Tbsp butter and 1 tsp. vanilla.**

BEAT constantly until mixture looses its sheen (~5-10 min.)

POUR onto a buttered platter.

COOL first, then CUT into bite-sized portions. *Texture will be sugary.*

REFRIGERATE in a Tupperware container. (~24 hrs.)
This changes the texture from sugary to creamy!

To seal the creamy center:

GRATE **1 lb. of Baker's Semi-Sweet Baking Chocolate.** MELT very slowly in a double boiler over hot water stirring until smooth. DIP to coat each center and set aside for a couple of hours to harden.

2007

360-573-6909
kateh@pacifier.com

Remembering Solo

Brad and Gwen, our next-door neighbors, had a little ten-pound Shih Tzu named Abbie. Our hundred-pound Solo went over every morning. He'd sit there ... a gentle Sasquatch ... outside their sliding glass door, waiting quietly and patiently, until they let Abbie out to play. I had no clue! I thought he was just up in the forest doing his morning business. Brad told me about it after we lost Solo.

Sunday School – Acts of Acts

We were studying Acts of the Apostles. I grabbed all my tablecloths, packed them in a suitcase, and took them to class. Each week, I read a different chapter to the kids. Afterwards, they each grabbed a tablecloth and wore it as a costume. I re-read the chapter as they enacted the action.

My favorite thespian was Elsa in her role as Sapphira. *(Ananias told a lie to the apostles. Peter chastised him. As soon as Ananias heard those words, he fell to the floor and died. Some men took him out and buried him. Three hours later, Sapphira, not knowing Ananias's fate, unwittingly told the same lie. Peter chastised her and instantly, she fell to the floor and died.)* When Sapphira died, Elsa fell in a heap on the floor as if one moment she had a skeleton in her body and the next moment she didn't. We did some of the scenes a second time so the kids could switch roles, but Elsa remained as Sapphira ... instantly dropping like a marionette whose strings had been cut. We did a play for the parents at the end of the first half of Acts. Elsa's timing and execution were perfect. She dropped like a pro.

Geronimo

Harry and I were settling in to watch a movie. It was just about to start, but he put it on pause while he took the dogs out for last call. And there I sat in my recliner, staring at the beautiful face of Wes

Wes Studi as **Geronimo**

Watercolors
Karalee's 4th Grade Class

Students'
Starting Point

Studi as Geronimo. It was the promotional picture for the film. I must have stared for a full three minutes, examining all the details of his facial expression. By the time Harry and the dogs returned, I knew I wanted to paint Geronimo.

At the second opportunity (because I never do things at the first opportunity), I got out some watercolors and got to it. I had seen TV shows about watercolor painting and had a pretty good idea of what to do. I borrowed a page from Harry's playbook and thought: How hard can it be!

I knew nothing about different types of paper. I just jumped in blindly, putting in the shadows and throwing in some browns and reds. Before long, the paper objected by buckling ... a lot. I had no choice but to walk away. I hadn't invested days and weeks like one would with oil paintings. I figured I could just do it over if I didn't like the outcome. It had been fun. But first, I had to let it dry. I came back to it a couple of days later and was stunned. The paper had reverted to its old flat self. I touched up the eyes and called it good!

About a month later, a teacher I knew (Karalie) asked me if I would do a watercolor class with her fourth-grade students. I thought about it and decided it would be fun to do a brightly colored rooster. I got all prepared, but somewhere along the line, I thought it might be fun if we all painted Geronimo. The kids were oblivious to how difficult it might be to paint a portrait ... but they were willing to do it! We broke it into three sessions: Shadows, Sepia, and Final Details. She gave me thirty minutes each day. Each time, the kids got deeply involved in the painting and then totally switched gears after thirty minutes, when it was time for their next lesson. (The promotional picture, my painting, and the kids' paintings are shown in the enclosed collages.)

I'M RICH

Because I was prone to forgetfulness and had left my wallet on the conveyor belt at WinCo, I stopped using a purse. Of course, I'd then leave the house without my wallet. I managed to do that at least once a year. One such time, I really needed a couple of items and I was going right by the store. I grabbed my parking meter bag of change, found it contained a plethora of quarters, and went in to get my necessities, keeping the tally under twenty dollars. I knew it might take a little time, so I started stacking my coins in piles, to make it easier on the checker. The belt started and stopped every time she picked something up. But all my money was ready … stacked in neat little piles suitable for counting … on the belt. I just needed the final tally. When she picked up the second-to-last item, the conveyor belt started moving. I screamed "Aah!" and put the last item against the metal strip. She grabbed the last item and the coins started disappearing through the tiny space between the belt and the counter. I screamed again, "Aah -Aah!" fumbling frantically for the coins, moving them back three inches as the belt moved forward three inches. Finally, the checker saw what was happening and stopped the belt. I was so flustered. I started fumbling in the change purse for more coins to replace the ones swallowed by the belt … I'm good at fumbling, I guess. I must have looked pretty pathetic with my nickels, dimes, and quarters no longer neatly piled up. The man in front of me flipped out a twenty and said he'd pay for my groceries. I assured him I had more quarters in my bag, but he was having none of my protestations. I felt like a waif … a very tall waif. I thanked him again as I was leaving. I went outside, got in my Mercedes, and drove home.

2008

(Color the State Farm logo red)

Merry Christmas!

This year started with a real, albeit small, tornado. Harry had just finished a beautiful 3 x 3 stained glass of the St. Farm logo. He placed it in the window at the office on a Sunday. At lunchtime on Thursday, Vancouver got hit with an unexpected tornado. It went right over our office. For the other ladies and me, it was like having a front row seat in a dinner theater. There was so much debris swirling around we couldn't see the building right next door! The tornado was dipping and striking at random but we were not the random that got stricken … for which we are very thankful. Harry heard all about it when he got back from the golf course.

Our second "tornado" came in April when we adopted a Lab-Doberman mix we call Jud. Jud, as it turns out, is adept at the art of escape. We've seen him *weigh his choices* and take action, whether it's jumping, running or opening lever-handled doors (inward or outward … neither presents a problem for him)! Fortunately, he's getting more controllable every week.

I'm teaching the 2nd-3rd Graders in Sunday School this year. I think the high point of my Christmas season will be Children's presentation of a most unusual and complete sharing of the Good News of Christmas. I hope that you too will discover Jesus in a whole new manner this year.

Look beyond
the hustle and bustle
to find what you're
really looking for
this year!

With Love,

Harry & Kathy

Jud, Mickey,
Holly, Toby, Boris
& Tripod (the 3-legged turtle)

Rediscovering Chicken Broth
Homemade or Store-Bought

Ravioli   We've been enjoying frozen raviolis this year by cooking them like Pot-Stickers. It's easier than the boiling water method and tastier, too.

- Heat a little oil in a non-stick sauce pan.
- Place the raviolis in the pan, turn once.
- Pour in chicken broth to about ½ inch.
- Let simmer for at least 8 minutes (all but about 2-3 Tbsp should have simmered away).
- Sprinkle with your favorite garlic-parmesan mixture, stir and serve at once.

Rice   Substitute Chicken Broth for water in your favorite rice recipe and watch your meals perk up.

Soups   Substitute Chicken Broth for water in your homemade soup recipes to enhance the flavors.

Be sure to let me know if you have a favorite use for Chicken Broth, I'll be looking forward to it.

2008

360-573-6909
kateh@pacifier.com

SUNDAY SCHOOL – THE BIG PARTY

We had a lesson on discipleship. I passed out 2 x 3-inch cards and told the kids to come up with one idea to show they were following Jesus. If you stop and think about it, you might quickly run out of things to write. I started by standing a blank card on the floor. Each student had to come up with one idea and put it to a vote. If the other kids didn't think it was good, the student had to come up with something else. Well, I was just amazed. They did wonderfully. Everyone had five cards. I participated and had to submit my ideas for the vote, too. As each one got voted in, the student would make a half-inch tear in the top and the bottom of their card and we would interlock them, like we were building a tower. I held the penthouse to keep the tower erect and wondered if it would end up higher than I could hold. It was a wavy skyscraper. After four rounds, our time was up even though we were still going strong. Our tower of discipleship ended up being almost four feet high!

The next week was the day of our big Valentine's Day party. I was all prepared with cookies and whipped cream, but I was having doubts … I wasn't sure one small can of whipped cream would be enough. I dashed into WinCo before church, grabbed the nearest can and went to the check stand. I did a double-take because it was about twice the size as the can I already had, but so what, I pondered, I'd just have a little more to take home.

I had taken many of the discipleship ideas from the week before and had made a fill-in puzzle to use for review. I paired the words with the verbs DO and BE so it would be easier to complete. When all the answers were filled in and in the right order, you could read down the middle and see THE GOOD SAMARITAN: our lesson for the week.

We blasted through the lesson. The kids were 100% engaged. It probably had something to do with the thought of cookies and whipped cream.

We spread out a picnic sheet, opened up the big Tupperware cookie container, took out the two cans of whipped cream, passed out napkins and spoons, and we all dug in. Each one in turn put their cookie in the bottom of the Tupperware container, grabbed a can of whipped cream and tried to see who could make the highest pile. Daniel had whipped cream all over his face. Mikaela had whipped cream all over her pants. As she cleaned it up with her napkin, she started snorting and laughing. We all laughed with her and had a great time. Another Daniel, my engineer, managed to hold his second cookie in such a manner his arm and hand looked like a ladle … the whipped cream was supported by his arm. It must have been good for almost two cups!

After the last cookie was slathered with whipped cream, the last can gave out! The can indicated there was enough whipped cream for 120 servings @ 2 tablespoons per serving. In actuality, it was more like 12 servings @ 1.25 cups per serving.

There were six kids (9–11 years old), in addition to Cousin Cathy and me (50-plus years old). We were having a great time, but it looked like we were running late … I told the kids to run out to the restroom, wash their hands, come back for their papers, and they would be dismissed. One minute after they left the room, Cathy and I had the sticky, soggy sheet all balled up and stuffed into the Tupperware container. Quick clean-up!

Cathy and I enjoyed a leisurely walk out to the foyer, talking about how much fun it had been. There we met John, one of the ushers, and discovered the church service had run long. Poor John. Good thing he had raised five kids. He had been standing there innocently when six hyped-up kids had come running out to meet their parents.

*J*UD

Jud was a medium sized muscular Lab-Doberman mix. He must have had a little Vizsla in him as well because he was very clingy. We got him from a client

Jud

who had to drug him to keep him under control. We stopped that practice right away. When the drugs were out of his system ... oh my heavens ... he was a wild dog. We had just finished a long wonderful run with Solo, a gentle well-mannered giant. While we were at work, he would spend his days guarding the patio and the ponds from the chain-link pen on the covered patio. That routine had worked well for Solo, so we put Jud in the pen and went off to work thinking everything was okay.

As I was driving away the first day, I did a quick check to see how Jud was doing, He had hooked his teeth on the chain-link gate and was pulling for all he was worth. He figured he could get the gate open if he could move the hardware just a little. He could ... and he did! Goodness, that dog was clever.

Another time, I was standing on the top terrace watching Jud in the pen. He was facing away from me, sitting a couple of feet from the chain-link fence, looking at the top rail, which was about six feet above the ground. In one fluid motion he sprang from a sitting position, hooked his feet on the top rail and over he went. Well, we didn't want any broken toenails. And we sure didn't want any broken teeth, so we disassembled the pen and moved it up to the barn. At least if he jumped out of the pen, he could still be contained in the barn while we were not home. Every time we came home, he was outside the pen, roaming through the barn. We had to put the water dish half in and half out of the pen because we never knew where he'd be when he needed a drink.

Jud loved to run. I had him on a fifteen-foot expanding leash and he decided he was off to the races. He started running and snapped that leash right out of my hand. He ran up the hill on Tom's property ... brush everywhere. My worst fear was he would get tangled in the brush and I wouldn't be there to help him. (Coyote bait!) But he always returned at night after one of his forays into the wild ... sometimes by two or three in the morning ... but he always returned. And sure enough, several hours later, at dusk, he came sauntering up the road like nothing was wrong ... with only a six-foot line attached to his collar, no handle in sight.

2009

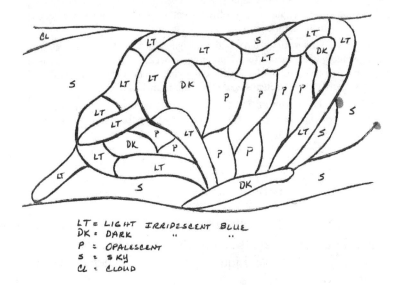

LT = LIGHT IRRIDESCENT BLUE
DK = DARK   "   "
P = OPALESCENT
S = SKY
CL = CLOUD

(Color the knobs on the antennae blue)

THE LUNCH GAME

I had my friend Jennifer and her two children, Elena and Jed (aka My Little Art Students), over for lunch. Both of the kids are very creative and artistic. To tickle their senses, I developed a board game. Once again, imagination failed me and we called it "The Lunch Game."

Before they arrived, tiny bits of a multitude of food items came out of jars, cans, and packages to find their way to cordial glasses, china dishes, and small cut-glass bowls. Tall and medium glass or crystal goblets held other items to give a sense of dimension to the table. Small dinner rolls were cut into about six thin slices to be used as bread for miniature sandwiches.

Merry Christmas Everyone!

We were fortunate to call 2009 a year of peace: our wild dog, Jud, is settling down with exercise, discipline and routine ... and we're healthy and happy. We've been getting a yearning to have another puppy, but our good friends got a Border Terrier so we get a *puppy-fix* from time to time.

In January, Harry and I designed and built a stained glass window of a peacock (close-up of head, neck and feathers). Harry is now working on a window for our living room: Calla Lilies with a butterfly (shown actual size on the front of this card).

Even with all the time he spends on stained glass, Harry finds enough time to go to his Adult Day Care four days each week (aka golf course).

I'm enjoying a variety of things: pruning our ever-maturing estate, working at Harry's State Farm office, participating in small groups at Church, playing with my Art students and teaching Sunday School ... the latter being the most challenging and rewarding.

Small creamers held hot chocolate, apple juice, and lemonade. Just enough for a taste. Teapots and pitchers of replacement fluids were on hand at a nearby table. Liquids were served in demitasse cups and cordial glasses.

Crackers, Cheez-Its, applesauce, black olives, green olives, Greek olives, cucumbers, cheeses, sweet pickles, dill pickles, hot chocolate, apple juice, lemonade, almonds, cashews, Gummy bears, pineapple, banana, maraschino cherry, mini-marshmallows, sourdough bread, carrots, M&Ms, and grapes ... each in its own elegant vessel. We even had teaspoon-sized mixtures of peanut butter and honey served in gold-foil candy cups.

Dessert items were held back: chocolate sauce, ice cream, chocolate pie, whipped cream, and cheesecake.

The playing area of the board game resembled a wagon wheel with two concentric circles and a hub in the center. On the hub was a stack of "Wild Cards." The outer circle had spaces entitling the player to select some luncheon basics: one slice of bread, one olive, one-half glass of lemonade, and so on. The outer circle kept the players hydrated and helped them amass bread for sandwiches as well as little treats.

As we prepare to celebrate
the birth of Jesus,
may you seek and experience
His peace.

With Love,
Harry & Kathy

Jud, Mickey, Holly, Boris the Bird
& Tripod (the reticent turtle)

Each person selected a token. The first person rolled a die to see how far into the outer circle they would travel. We began collecting our lunch, one roll of the die at a time. When we got tired of the outer circle, we voted to go into the inner circle. There were wonderful things in the inner circle. We could get the fillings of a sandwich, combine it with our stored bread, and have a miniature feast. We could also get additional drinks and finger foods.

Along the way, there were squares announcing Wild Cards. Turning over a Wild Card yielded all manner of dessert treasures, including One Scoop of Ice Cream, One Squitch of Turtle Shell, One Sliver of Cheesecake, and One Drizzle of Chocolate. Wild Cards also provided additional lunch items, including One Spear of Fruit, Three Nuts of Your Choice, Three Marshmallows, One Bunch of Grapes, and Select Any Item. But my favorite Wild Card was "YOU WIN! Stop or Continue." No one ever decided to stop.

Cottage Cheese Pie

from Grandma Walsh's Cookbook: A light alternative to cheesecake
by Gertrude Commerford, Puget Sound Power & Light Nutritionist, mid-1960s

2 T lemon juice	1/4 cup hot milk
2 egg yolks	1/3 cup sugar
1 envelope gelatin	2 cups creamed cottage cheese
Graham cracker crumb crust	Strawberry Topping

Put lemon juice, egg yolks and gelatin into blender. Cover and process
at low speed for a few seconds. Remove feeder cap and gradually pour
in hot milk and sugar. Replace feeder cap and continue processing until
gelatin is dissolved (one minute). Turn control to high, remove cover
and gradually add cottage cheese. Process until smooth and clearly
blended. Pour into prepared crust. Chill until set. Top and serve.

If you want to catch up with me, my email
address and phone number are to the
right. You can reach Harry through his
website: www.harryhoffman.net

2009

360-573-6909
kateh@pacifier.com

It took a long time to play the game, but we nibbled along the way.
At the end of the game, to be sure we didn't have any disappoint-
ments, players were allowed to negotiate swaps. Those who had too
much bread were able to swap with those who didn't like cucumbers. It's probably not a very good game for a Covid atmosphere,
but this was ten years before the pandemic hit.

We played, laughed, talked, and ate.
We voted again and went from the inner
circle to the Hub where we collected
our desserts. The size of the slices of
dessert were not predefined; nevertheless, as if by magic, each person got
not only what they earned, but exactly
what they could eat.

It was a labor-intensive game, but it was
fun, and it had a great "WOW factor."

The Lunch Game

LETTER-WRITING SKILLS

In the fall of 2009, after Elena had turned ten, I was talking with Jennifer about home-schooling. She was bemoaning the fact that letter-writing was becoming a lost art. She really wanted Elena to get some practice writing formal letters. It sounded like a fun project. Jennifer's birthday was coming up. Elena and I coordinated the celebration.

From Elena to Kathy (Card Front: An ice cream cone and two lollipops ... "Hi!! YUM!!")

Dear Mrs. Hoffman,

Please tell me when we will go for Ice cream, for my mom's Birthday. My mom's B-day is Oct. 28. Maybe Before my mom's B-day? So Please tell me What time, and what date.

Love, Elena Little

Please WRite Back!

From Kathy to Elena (Card Front: graphic of a 9-scoop cone)

October 16, 2009

Dear Elena,

I'm getting pretty excited about going to Baskin Robbins to celebrate your Mom's Birthday. Here's what I'm thinking about ...

I know your Mom's birthday is on October 28th. I like the idea of doing it before her birthday, but I also know she's trying to meet a school deadline for the month of October. I want us to be able to enjoy ourselves, so I'm thinking it would be good if we plan to go after your October schooling is finished, so that would be in November.

The first time I would be available to go out in November would be Thursday, November 5th. Do you think that would work for you?

I await your reply,
Love,
Mrs. Hoffman

From Elena to Kathy (Card front: purple daisy-on-grass … "Hi!!")

Dear Mrs. Hoffman,

I got the letter from you, and November 5th will work for us. What time shall we meet? Please tell me.

Love, Elena

From Kathy to Elena (Stationery with a stylized beanstalk)

Dear Elena,

I'm glad we've settled on November 5th as the date for our Birthday Party.

Since Ice Cream is a dessert, I think we should have a little lunch first. Would you like to come over here before we go to Baskin Robbins? We could have some of my famous peanut butter and honey sourdough sandwiches.

If that sounds good to you, just let me know. You and your Mom and Jed can come to my house at 11:20. We can have our little lunch and then go for a double scoop or a sundae or whatever we want.

Let me know if that sounds like a good plan.

Love,

Mrs. Hoffman

From Elena to Kathy (Card front: A surprisingly precise drawing of a woman holding a three-scoop ice cream cone and a structurally accurate table with place setting)

Dear Mrs. Hoffman, I got the letter from you. And I also want to say that lunch will work out and the time too! I think everything will work out. I can't wait until we go!

Love,

Elena

("YUM!" ... Drawings of a sandwich and an ice cream cone filled in the rest of the page.)

From Kathy to Elena (Card front: mushroom computer graphic)

October 30, 2009

Dear Elena,

I made a fun game for my Sunday School students. I think you and Jed and your Mom might like to play it. It's called a "Quotefall" ... I will give you the letters and all you have to do is put them in the columns of the Quotefall and then ... PRESTO! ... it forms a quote, or in this case, a Bible Verse. Won't that be fun?

Because of the addition of the Quotefall, I'd like to suggest a slight modification to our plans. Could you and your Mom and Jed come to my house at 11:10? That's 10 minutes earlier than we had originally planned. We can work on our Quotefall (Jed and I can work as a team), then have our little lunch and THEN go for a double scoop or a sundae or whatever we want.

Will this new plan be acceptable?

Love,

Mrs. Hoffman

From Elena to Kathy (Card Front: brown fall leaves ... "Happy Fall Y'all")

Dear Mrs. Hoffman,

I got the letter you gave me. And the timing will work out. When we were trick or treating Jed, Malena, and me were there. I was a tiger, and Jed was a race car driver, and Malena was a butterfly. Malena's dog was a butterfly too. And Tino was a chicken. We got some funny Pictures of Tino and Oscar, They were both chickens. I will see you on Nov. 5th at 11:10.

Love,

Elena

From Elena to Kathy (Card front: preprinted white floral on black)

Dear Mrs. Hoffman,

Thank you for having us over to your house. It was fun eating with you at your house. We loved having Ice cream with you! I will see you in two weeks at our house! Love, Elena

From Kathy to Elena (Card Front: Graphic of bees flying from honey balls.)

Dear Elena,

Thank you for your lovely card! I had a really good time at our little impromptu luncheon, too. Perhaps the best part was rolling peanut butter and honey balls in our hands and eating them. But I really liked laughing so hard when we were eating our ice cream cones, too!

I'm looking forward to coming over to your house in another week, for pumpkin pie. That reminds me of something else related to pie: My brother is coming over for dinner on Sunday. I plan to have an Orange-Pineapple Pie in a Graham Cracker Crust. I've made it once before and it turned out super ... very pretty.

Say hello to everyone for me.

Love,

Mrs. Hoffman

From Kathy to Elena (Card front: Pumpkin image atop a pizza)

YUM-YUM! ...Pumpkin Pie ... I can hardly wait.

Please let me know when I should be over at your house on Thursday, November 19 to play Bingo and eat Pumpkin Pie! Also, let me know if there's something I should bring.

With love,

Mrs. Hoffman

From Elena to Kathy (Hello Kitty stationery)

Dear Mrs. Hoffman,

Thank you for the letter.

Maybe you should come at 11:00. You should bring the cross-stitch stuff and we could talk about it when you come over.

If this sounds good to you please write back, or if it does not sound good, well, just still write back

Love, Elena

XOXOXO

From Kathy to Elena (Plain stationery with a pumpkin graphic)

Dear Elena,

I'm not sure that 11:00 will work for me. Unless it's raining, I'll have to take Jud for a walk Thursday morning. When I get home, I'll have to take a shower. I'm thinking that the earliest I can be there is 11:05.

Please call me if that will be a problem. (Of course, if it's raining none of that will be a problem and I'll be there at 11:00 as expected!)

I'm looking forward to our visit on Thursday, 11/19.

With love,

Mrs. Hoffman

2010

Merry
Christmas

May Your Days be Merry & Bright!

Harry, Kathy, Jud, Mickey, Holly & Boris

Greetings Dear Friends & Family,

Thanks for all the newsy cards and letters you've sent!

We had quite a time with **Stained Glass** again this year. At the beginning of the year, Harry finished the Calla Lily window. Now he's almost through with the last of our 5-window project ... Marsh Iris. I can hardly wait to see the yellow flowers in our south-facing window!

I worked on a **Stained Glass** project with nineteen 9-year-old students at a local Christian school. They designed a 12"x18" scene of the Crucifixion and selected the glass. Harry guided me in building it. Later, it was auctioned for charity. The whole experience was exhilarating: an amazing collaborative effort in teamwork & prayer by the entire class.

Jud, as you know, is an indoor dog, but he loves to run. At the beginning of the year, when he was outside, we cabled him to a wheel from the Airstream. After we sold the Airstream we hooked his cable to a metal protrusion on the patio. The cable held but the connector failed after a month. A second connector failed after another month. Finally, the cable failed. Undaunted, Harry continued to connect Jud to the remaining 6-ft length of cable (hooked to nothing!). Jud was faked out by that ... for about a week. Now, we've run out of cables, connectors, and ideas ... help!

Some other things that made this a year to be thankful for:
- I'm **working** more hours in Harry's State Farm agency.
- Mom turned a healthy, happy **"90"** on 10-10-10.
- Harry had a successful **Lasik** surgery.
- We're having our **retaining walls** rebuilt in concrete,
- Harry is working hard to keep his **handicap** under 20!

My 4th-5th Grade **Sunday School** class finished our Bible Overview – Book by Book. Now we're going through all four Gospels, following Jesus through His 3-year ministry!

May your 2011 be a blessed year!

Hamburger Stew

Anyone who knew my Mother-in-Law knew her Hamburger Stew.
The secret to a great stew every time is ... Stewed Tomatoes!

2 pounds ground beef
2 medium onions, chopped
4 cans (14½ oz each) stewed
   tomatoes
8 medium carrots, thinly sliced
4 celery ribs, thinly sliced

2 medium potatoes, peeled, cubed
2 cups water
½ cup uncooked long grain rice
1 - 2 tablespoons salt
1 - 2 teaspoons pepper

In a Dutch oven, cook beef and onions over medium heat until meat is no
longer pink; drain. Add the tomatoes, carrots, celery, potatoes, water, rice, salt
and pepper; bring to a boil. Reduce heat; cover and simmer for **30 minutes** or
until vegetables and rice are tender.

Uncover; simmer **20-30 minutes** longer or until
thickened. **Yield:** about 15 cups.

cf. Taste of Home's Quick Cooking Magazine
November/December 2003

2010

360-573-6909
kateh@pacifier.com

STAINED-GLASS PROJECT – SCHOOL AUCTION

After Christmas, my friend Peggy asked if Harry and I would
be willing to work on a project with her son Joe's class, perhaps
stained glass, for their Spring auction to be held on April 23rd. We
talked about it for a while, and she suggested a cross.

I thought about it for a week and was starting to buy into the idea
of a cross ... straight lines would lend themselves to a project on
a limited deadline. I contacted Mrs. Morgan, the teacher at Cedar
Tree Classical Christian School, to let her know I was "in." We dis-
cussed timing and expectations. She had nineteen third-grade students. It was the job of those nine-year-olds to decide on a design.

WEEK 1 – MEET STUDENTS, DISCUSS AND DETERMINE THEME

We started with a prayer to make sure the Holy Spirit was guiding our creativity and our teamwork.

I talked about different kinds of stained glass and showed some samples, which got a lot of "oooohs" and "aaaahs" from the students. Some pieces, wrapped on the edges for safety, were passed around.

I told the students the design phase was the most important. One boy jumped up and said, "Let's do a farm." Another wanted to do a pig. Mrs. Morgan and I encouraged them to get out all their ideas. There was a flower, a spider, and another pig (they were studying *Charlotte's Web*). After that, we had a rocket ship and a few other suggestions until one quiet boy suggested a cross. I'd been acknowledging all the ideas, but when he suggested a cross, I paused and said "Oh, that's an *interesting* idea!" We went on with more pigs, birds, and other suggestions and ended with a couple of students saying, "three crosses on a hill."

Mrs. Morgan and I looked at each other. We didn't want to railroad anything. Finally, she asked the class for a show of hands. "How many are in favor of a cross?" she asked. All the hands shot up ... we smiled at each other in relief.

WEEK 2 – 19 INDIVIDUAL DESIGNS; 5 TEAM DESIGNS

We started with a prayer, after which I distributed large pieces of paper for each student. I asked how many knew what a cross looked like. (Everyone did, of course.) Then I had them close their eyes and visualize their cross quietly for one minute. We had one minute of complete silence!

Before we proceeded, we prayed again for guidance and gave thanks for our creativity. I gave them five minutes to sketch a drawing of their cross. All the crosses looked the same, except one. I encouraged them to code their drawings to show the colors of glass they wanted for their pictures. Five minutes later, Mrs.

Morgan went around and held up everyone's work. We had each student describe the facets of his or her drawing.

We had 19 ideas, but we wanted only one. With inspiration that did not come from me, I passed out five pieces of paper and had the students team-up to produce five more drawings. They were given the task of choosing a team captain. It was the team captain's job to make sure each person on the team had an opportunity to contribute to the design. Each team picked the name of an animal as its team name and wrote their own first names on the sheet. They were given five more minutes to design a team cross. They even coded them, finishing at the bell ... all in one hour! I left with five drawings, knowing we still had four too many.

They took their individual drawings home to show their parents (which might inspire a good bid at the auction).

WEEK 3 – DETERMINE FINAL DESIGN AND GLASS SELECTION

I had anticipated they would come up with a design 18 inches high and 12 inches wide ... perhaps a cross with a blue sky, standing on a flat patch of green, with yellow rays coming from the center of the cross. I was so wrong.

Before class started, the school assembled in the courtyard and sang a hymn. The hymn for January was *Be Thou My Vision*. After the hymn, the principal led them in prayer. They pledged their allegiance to the flag and dispersed to their classrooms.

Once in class, I was gathering some papers and said, "Good morning, everyone!" They jumped to their feet, responding in unison: "Good-mor-ning-Miss-uz-Hoff-man." We prayed before we started, asking for God's help with creativity and with a design to please Him and bring Him glory.

We reviewed each of the five team drawings, naming the students on each team. However, since the team names were animals, all further references to the drawings were by team name (e.g., Bengal Tigers). No one had to take any comments personally.

As we looked at each drawing, I asked the class to identify at least three things they liked about the design. Next, we looked at some slides I had brought of other stained-glass projects (from the internet). It was a pleasant break. After that, I had them identify things about which we needed to make a decision in order to determine the design. As they called them out, I listed them on the board. Before we voted, we took another minute to honor God, dedicate the project to Him and ask His guidance. Next, we voted on each of the items listed agreeing on a design: The final piece would be 12 inches high and 18 inches wide with three crosses. The sky would be blue; the crosses would be standing on a green hill with a river cutting through the hill from right to left.

There would be rays, but not coming from the crosses. Amber rays would come from the sun in the upper left corner; the moon would be in the upper right corner; a stylized Cedar Tree emblem would be in the lower right corner. There would be a border.

On the drive home, Be Thou My Vision *kept running through my head. I thought it would be cool to hide the title in coded blocks at the bottom of the design. I suggested it the following week.*

WEEK 4 – FINAL DECISIONS

Surprisingly, the final decisions about our project took a whole class period. But the students stuck with it. Mrs. Morgan and I could tell the whole class was firmly behind the project.

With the design phase finished, I began drawing and color-coding a pattern, labelling the glass associated with each color. Since I had never actually done a stained-glass project, Harry gave me a head start by cutting a lot of the pieces. I had to grind the razor-sharp edges making any adjustments as needed, affix a strip of copper foil around each piece, number the pieces, and number the pattern.

WEEK 5 – BURNISH GLASS AND ASSEMBLE PROJECT

When I arrived, I put down my bags and made a big deal of passing out crumpled squares of tin foil. If I could get them to smooth out the tin foil, they'd understand how to burnish the copper foil around the edges of the stained glass. But really, I was just trying to divert their attention to see if anyone would remember to pray first. They were on the ball! Two girls raised their hands and said, "But Mrs. Hoffman, we haven't prayed yet!" Savvy kids!

With all the pieces pre-numbered and separated by color, things should have run smoothly. The pattern was on the front desk. Each student had to burnish the foil around eight pieces of glass. They were told to come to the front of the room and let me examine their first efforts. If they did a perfect job, they got to put their piece of glass where it belonged on the pattern and burnish the rest of their pieces on their own.

Almost immediately, they started coming to the front of the room. I made a detailed examination of each piece, top, sides, and bottom. The students were very patient, accepted instruction well, and made corrections as needed. When they got my approval, they put their piece of glass on the pattern ... a jigsaw puzzle with numbers. There were about 140–150 pieces. Only two unburnished pieces slipped by me. A couple of sky pieces were put in the wrong place, making it look lopsided. The numbers on many pieces of glass were worn away by enthusiastic fingers. I was getting nervous until Mrs. Morgan repositioned them where they really belonged. After it was finished, the students gave an approving "Wooooo!" I was drained but pleased. When I got home, Harry wanted to show me how to solder the pieces together ... but I needed a rest!

3-WEEK INTERLUDE – STEPS TO COMPLETION

To get from burnished glass pieces to the completed project required three major steps on the front side of the project (and three steps on the back side of the project):

Solder: Solder the pieces together, wait at least four hours, re-solder as necessary (about two or three times) to build up a nice ridgeline and make sure there were no sharp points; clean with glass cleaner, twice.

Copper Patina: Rub all solder lines and the frame with steel wool; vacuum; clean with glass cleaner, twice; apply copper patina with small artist's brush. Let dry overnight.

Wax: Buff all solder lines and frame; apply liquid wax and massage in with hands. Dab off excess and let dry overnight. Buff with rag; detail each piece of glass by removing wax next to the solder line using the burnishing tool wrapped in a soft towel; use toothbrush to complete wax removal from solder lines.

FINAL WEEK – DISCUSS STEPS TO COMPLETION AND SIGN THE PROJECT

When I brought the finished project to the classroom, the students were extremely excited, but they remembered to pray first! After unveiling it in the window, they all started chanting: "Hoot, Hoot, Hoot, Hoot, Hoot, Hoot, Hoot!" Mrs. Morgan had to put a gentle stop to it.

I asked them to tell me the things they liked best about the completed project. Each one spoke up. Every facet of the project was addressed: the coded border, green hillside, accent pieces in the hillside, blue sky, sun and sunset, moon and night sky, size of the three crosses, red center on the main cross, solder lines fanning out from the crosses, Cedar Tree logo. It was very encouraging!

One little guy said he liked the stream. The stream was made of water glass: clear glass with a little ripple in it. I exclaimed I liked it too, especially how the water seemed to move. They didn't understand what I meant, so I told them to move their heads up and down and they'd be able to see it move. I was paying attention to the glass, but when I looked back at the class, their heads were all bobbing up and down. They were getting all excited because they could see the water moving. Pretty funny!

I explained the process of building the project (everything I did during the three-week interlude) and had them scratch their names on the back of the metal frame. Mrs. Morgan and I also signed it. I gave souvenir pieces of stained glass the size of a half-dollar coin to Mrs. Morgan who made them available to the students. (I had ground off the sharp edges and points, because of course, it's still glass!) She cautioned them to be very careful and avoid dropping the glass pieces.

The "stream" fellow came up and asked if I'd write my phone number on his piece of glass. "Well … sure." Then he asked if I'd put my name on it. "… Okay." (He said he was going to copy it onto a piece of paper, take it home, and have his mother write it down on their phone list.) About ten more students lined up to have me sign their pieces of glass. Pretty cute.

Hooting, bobbing, encouraging words, and "getting hit on by a nine-year-old." It was a great ending to the Stained-Glass Project!

EPILOGUE

Cedar Tree Classical Christian School – Vancouver Hilton

2nd Annual Dessert Auction – $35 per person

I was looking forward to seeing the Stained-Glass Project get auctioned off. Friends and family had guessed the final price would be $200 or lower, although one friend guessed between $400 and $550.

Susan Morgan introduced me to her husband, David. He mentioned he'd bought a necklace (a locket on a cord) from one of the students for her. Susan seemed a little surprised. I didn't think much more about it because it looked like he might have paid $2 for it (or maybe $5, because it was for charity). He said his parents were there somewhere ... Susan and David's daughter, Claire, had gotten them interested in buying the Stained-Glass Project. I thought that seemed pretty good ... if they got it, at least it would be in the family.

I went inside where round tables were set up for the live auction. It looked like they expected 200 people. They were all adults. None of the younger children were at the auction. Some older students were there, but only in a service capacity. Before I went back into the silent auction area, I looked around for the Stained-Glass Project. There it was hanging in a hand-crafted, free-standing upright oak frame, with a light behind it for visual accent. In front of the Stained-Glass Project was a picture of the class, Susan, and me. It was an elegant presentation.

I went back to the next room where there were so many things going on: There were eight long tables with silent auction items on both sides. Nice things; bundles of nice things. Lots of walking ... so many worthwhile things being offered.

Older students were walking around selling helium balloons on ten-foot streamers. *Would you like to buy one? ... How much? ... $20.* Yikes! ... I had never been to a charity auction like this one! It turned out there was a certificate in each balloon, good for a gift from $5 to $100. All the balloons would be popped at the same time during the live auction. Fun.

Another student approached me to buy a necklace: a numbered locket on a cord. *Would you like to buy one? ... How much? ... $100.* Yikes, again! No wonder couples were trying to get their acts together before the auction. *But there will be a drawing, and if you win the drawing, you can have your choice of any piece in the live auction.* For just $100 you could have your choice of anything in the live auction. I was crushed: The Stained-Glass Project could go for only $100. Initial reactions aren't always correct. I hadn't done the math. *How many have you sold? ... Oh, we're not the only ones selling, but we've sold 14 so far.* I was elated: The Stained-Glass Project could go for more than $1,400!

Soon it was announced the silent auction would be closing. A little scurrying and then "Pens Down!" Several efficient women swooped in separating the three-part bid sheets, taping the pink copy to the item, circling the winning bid on the white copy, collecting, sorting, and gathering pens. The people swarmed into the next room, the Hilton personnel closed off the rooms and the live auction began!

The first order of business was to find the winner of the necklace drawing. A woman named Tara won. She chose the "Family Weekend on Puget Sound" donated by David and Susan Morgan and Janet and Harley Morgan (David's parents). Tara knew she'd enjoy the weekend for six because she got it last year. Fun to know.

The Kindergarten students had painted tiles, which were then incorporated into a table by the same parent who made the stained-glass frame.

The first-grade class created a colorful framed floral collage. Each student had painted, drawn, and cut out a flower to assemble into a group bouquet.

The second-grade class had painted oil and pastel paintings of birds. They were incorporated into a bookshelf.

The Balloon Pop was fun. Everyone popped their balloons at once.

The older kids gathered together and sold their time: ten students for six hours each. Yard work, housework … whatever one needed. I figured the worst thing about winning this would be planning enough work to keep the kids busy. I wondered how much I would be willing to pay … if I could get it for $360, it would be a steal. When the Student Work Team bidding started, I was right in there. The auctioneer brought up a tall lanky Norman-Rockwell student and had him strike his best strong-man pose. Five auction paddles went up and so did the bids. Another student got down and did push-ups. Three more paddles were raised. I made three bids, but $360 came and went. I wasn't surprised, but I was happy I had a chance to bid. Their former principal (ex-military) won the bid at $540 … still a good deal at $9 per hour if he can keep them moving!

The next piece was a spectacular tile mosaic of Aslan, the lion from the Narnia series by C.S. Lewis. The bidding went right up to about $450. Finally, the auctioneer had the two bidders stand up. One was David Morgan (Susan had helped the students create the mosaic), the other was Tara. They battled for another couple of rounds. The audience started encouraging each of them. They both wanted it, but when the bidding hit $550, Tara got cold feet and let it go. It was very entertaining.

A few more items were auctioned, and it was finally time for the Stained-Glass Project. A minimum bid of $150 was announced. A bid of $200 left it in the dust. $350 came and went. I was beginning to think it might actually bring $400 to $550. How exciting. $400, $450, $500. The bid passed $550. I was stunned. I knew Tara was bidding on it, but I didn't know who the other party was. David and Susan Morgan had stopped bidding much earlier. Back and forth, back and forth ... the bidding passed $650 and was just barely showing signs of slowing. Once or twice, it threatened to stop, but each time at the last minute one of the two would raise a paddle. In the $700s, the bids came at a snail's pace until finally, at $750, the hard-fought battle had been conceded by Tara. Wow! Entertainment! I couldn't tell who had won the bid, but I was sure everyone else in the room would know the person.

The next thing up really interested me. It was called the Paddle Raise ... raise your Paddle and count it as a donation. They started at $2,000 ... no takers. One bid at $1,000, a couple at $500 and more at $100. When the auctioneer asked for a count of the $100 donations, there were seven. He announced there was a $2,000 matching donation, if they could get twenty $100 donations. Up went the paddles. The next count was 18. Only two more were needed. He put out the feelers. Slowly, but not too slowly, one more paddle went up and then another. It was a great moment!

Mrs. Leidy, a grandmother, came up to the microphone to talk about the school. I wasn't paying too much attention until she said something about her grandson, Brennen. I knew him! He was the little guy who had asked for my phone number. After she sat down,

I couldn't resist a quick visit with her, to let her know how much I had enjoyed interacting with Brennen.

They were still going strong, but I needed to get home. On the way out, I asked who had won the Stained-Glass Project. No one knew. I was perplexed. In a last-ditch effort, I asked the woman in charge if she knew who had bought it. She looked it up and said it was the Morgans ... David's folks! I was delighted! What a perfect ending to an exciting evening!

(Pictures of the finished project are on the back cover.)

LASIK

Harry is far-sighted. His glasses were fine for distance, but for close-up viewing he had to tilt his head back a little. This became a real problem when he took up golf. Something had to be done. Laser surgery was the preferred fix.

Dr. Will, the surgeon, asked if he could pray with Harry before starting the surgery.

"Of course!" Harry said, very pleased. A short petition ensued.

Dr. Will had an assistant who talked to Harry non-stop about what was going on ... how many more seconds it would take ... what it would feel like. What a calming effect she had ... mostly on me because they had given Harry a Valium.

Nine minutes after he went in for his Lasik surgery appointment, he was finished. He used eye drops like they were going out of style and continued to do so for two months. He could see without glasses, but still needed magnifying glasses to read at night. He was surprised to see how many wrinkles he had around his eyes. On the brighter side, I was in his blurry vision and looked ten years younger to him.

I was surprised it all went so fast. I got to watch the monitor from an adjoining room with a glass wall separating us. Right in the middle of the surgery, the lights went off and some shiny blue dots started dancing all over the monitor ... not unlike a laser light show. I wondered what was up with that. It was LASER surgery ... DUH!

SUNDAY SCHOOL – AN INCIDENT

I was teaching my students about the book of Job. Cousin Cathy had been sitting in on the classes: "A Bible Overview – Book by Book." There were seven students, and two Junior High helpers. We were having a great time playing a game with three teams.

In the back of the room, Ona (10-year-old girl) was pulling at the drawstring of her tunic. Meanwhile, Peggy's son Joe (wiggly 9-year-old boy) was sitting there minding his own business (uncharacteristically). She winged him with the drawstring. I noticed it, but there's no way it would have hurt him. Next, she pulled it out farther and really whacked him over the head (but it was still only a drawstring). He lost his cool, put his head down between his knees for at least a minute, then came up fuming. His face was beet red. I walked back there to see what was up. Then he took his pencil and flung it at her. He missed her by about two feet, and I was grateful. I asked what was going on. He sputtered something. I told him to go pick up his pencil, letting him know we don't throw pointed objects at people.

We had a meeting of the minds (keeping my voice level and calm throughout):

"Ona, apologize to Joe."

"Sr-y," she slurred.

"Joe, did that sound like it came from the heart?"

"No."

"Ona, apologize to Joe from the heart."

"*Sor*-ry," she said, emphasizing the first syllable and rolling her eyes.

"Joe, did that sound like it came from the heart?"

"No."

"Ona, apologize to Joe from the heart."

"Sorry I hit you."

"Joe, did that sound like it came from the heart?"

"Yes."

"Joe, apologize to Ona ... from the heart."

He began sputtering self-righteously! "What? Why? I didn't do anything!"

"Joe, we don't throw pencils at people. Apologize to Ona from the heart."

"I'm sorry," he said meekly.

"Ona, did that sound like it came from the heart?"

"Yes."

The rest of the class was so interested, you could have heard a pin drop. I followed it up with, "It's a good thing I didn't hit you ... like this" ... (BOP ... Joe got it on the shoulder) ... "or like this" ... (SHOVE ... David, an innocent bystander, was smiling at me bright-eyed ... before and after the shove).

As I was returning to the front of the room with my back to the class, I remarked loudly, "You're lucky I didn't make you kiss and make up!" The whole class exploded with "Ick" and "Yuck." Joe blurted out, "I'd rather eat crushed glass and slam my head in a car door!" I didn't hear it all, so I asked him to repeat it, which he gladly did for everyone to hear.

Cathy and I laughed about it after class. As she pointed out, Ona was probably trying to show off to get the attention of a Junior High boy. I'm so clueless! Poor thing, she must have been completely embarrassed to have to go through the apology routine in front of the older boy.

HONESTY

My sister-in-law, Ann, was dating a handsome Englishman from London. He came "across the pond" regularly. The Big Pond!

Harry and I had Kevin and John, Mom, David, and Ann and Nigel over for dinner. I was at a loss about what to serve for dessert. I always like to mix it up a little. Finally, I decided on tapioca pudding. We hardly ever have it, and it sounded good to me.

When everyone was finished with dinner, I served the tapioca in pretty little crystal champagne glasses. Before I could sit down, Harry said, "What *IS* this?" in an odd voice. When I got to the table, John said in a voice dripping with sincerity, "You know where this would be good, Kathleen? In a re*TIRE*ment home." We all started laughing.

Later in the evening, Nigel asked, "Can I be honest?"

"I'm married to Harry ... I can handle brutal honesty."

He said, "I don't like tapioca pudding."

Well, it was honest. I'm glad I can laugh!

2011

Reach for the Stars

The message included in the Christmas card:

We're very happy and peaceful and we appreciate it! Harry continues to aggressively pursue par. This fall, he broke 90 playing at least three times each week. He read the book Younger Next Year *and passionately believes exercising daily keeps everything on an even keel. He had me read* Younger Next Year for Women. *With the book, my husband's urging, and the need to keep Jud worn out, Jud and I walk together on the treadmill every morning. (If he starts to crowd me, I vary the incline. It keeps his head in the game.)*

Harry's State Farm agency is doing well. We're looking forward to having an extra person in the office after the first of the year. When that happens, it will free me up to start golfing with Harry at least once a week. (Brrrr, why couldn't she start after the weather warms up!)

Life has taken a creative bend this year. I've branched out to constructing 3D stained-glass projects. Now I understand why Harry likes to build model cars and boats. As fun as it is to create a pattern and build it, my passion continues to be Sunday school with the 10-year-olds.

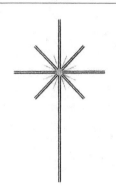

May Your Days be Merry & Bright!

pictured: Mickey, Kate, Holly Bear, Harry, Jud, & Boris the Bird
not shown: "Tripod" the Three-Legged Turtle and "Auto - Get it?" the Otter

I enjoy the challenge of corralling minds and pounding a lesson in via games, puzzles, or plays. I love how they respond to the games, working together in teams, totally focused on accomplishing the task. It's the perfect age for Sunday school! And it continues to be very humbling for me!

We enjoy hearing from you. Merry Christmas!

SUNDAY SCHOOL – THREE'S A CHARM

I had looked at chapter three of every book of the Bible to find a verse I was pretty sure the kids would "get." I was also pretty sure if they didn't get it right, at least they'd be able to get close enough by process of elimination. Mr. Moeller, the head of children's ministry, likes games and was more than happy to join us. For several weeks, I had been getting the kids pumped up about "beating Mr. Moeller." They were all ready for the class!

Pad Thai with Shrimp   Kate & Cathy
                                          Serves 4

Cousin Cathy and I experimented four times last Spring with a Pad Thai recipe until we got it just the way we all liked it. Here's what we found:

- On the first try, we doubled the shrimp and substituted chopped cashews for chopped peanuts (for lack of peanuts). Result: Not enough sauce, rice noodles were rubbery, cashews got lost.

- Second, we tried a powdered mix (doubled it) and skipped the bean sprouts. We put the cashews on top just before serving. Result: The taste was OK but bland compared to the first time.

- Third, we bought Pad Thai from a local restaurant specializing in Thai Cuisine. Result: Big mistake ... our least favorite.

- Finally, we used angel hair pasta, pea pods, doubled the sauce, cooked the cashews (whole) and hoped for the best: GREAT!

½ lb	Angel Hair Pasta
4 T	vegetable oil, divided
1	egg, beaten
1 lb	raw shrimp, peeled and de-veined
2 cups	pea pods, rinsed and tipped
4	scallions, chopped
½ cup	whole cashews
2 pkgs	(3.25 oz ea) *A Taste of Thai* Pad Thai Sauce

Cook Angel Hair pasta according to directions. Heat 2T oil in wok over medium-high heat. Add egg: scramble lightly 20 seconds. Add shrimp: stir-fry until cooked through. Add remaining vegetable oil, pasta noodles and pea pods: stir-fry 4-7 minutes. Add scallions, cashews, and Pad Thai Sauce: stir-fry 1 minute. Complement with a colorful side dish.

2011
360-573-6909
kateh@pacifier.com   www.harryhoffman.net

After we prayed, I told the kids it was supposed to be a Bible review for them, but since they'd been doing so well all year long, it was really a test for Mr. Moeller. I explained there were individual 3 x 5 cards ... one for each book of the Bible. The ones in black were books for which I had a verse. The ones in gray did not have a verse. Three or four kids helped Mr. Moeller put the book cards in order.

The verses were also on 3 x 5 cards. All were set out on the table. Then the kids were each to pick a verse card and figure out which book of the Bible the verse came from. They had to verify it with me before they presented it to Mr. Moeller.

Immediately, someone selected the most familiar card ... "16: For God so loved the world that He gave His only-begotten Son, that whoever believes in Him should not perish but have everlasting life." Everyone recognized John 3:16 ... it was paired with the book card labelled "John." As all the kids started to understand the game, several of them brought verse cards to me, told me where they came from, and went off to see if they could stump Mr. Moeller.

I knew a few of the kids would struggle with the game so some of the verses were downright easy. I told one girl to look for a "1" because sometimes the name of the book was in the first verse. She was immediately engaged. Another little guy needed some major one-on-one. He had picked a verse card with the name of the book used twice but not as a proper noun. I told him to look for repeated words. His eyes lit up … he guessed which book it was. I had him check it in his Bible to make sure he got it right and then he was off to see if Mr. Moeller could get it.

One little guy who is extremely competitive was jumping up and down yelling "Mrs. Hoffman … I stumped Mr. Moeller, I stumped Mr. Moeller!" Twenty minutes later, I made an ill-educated guess with him. He was jumping and yelling "I stumped the Teacher! I stumped the Teacher!" It just kept getting better and better! In the end, Mr. Moeller got all the cards paired correctly and everyone left on a high note!

FAMILY CHRISTMAS – WHITE ELEPHANT GIFT EXCHANGE

The whole family gathered at our house for Christmas dinner and a white elephant gift exchange. I had wrapped a couple extra gifts just in case. We needed them both.

We passed out numbers. Kevin chose first: free-standing, curved glass picture frame. Kevin liked it. So did Mom.

Mom chose next … she stole the picture frame from Kevin. She kept saying how much she liked it until we finally got her to understand it could be stolen by someone else. All of a sudden, she didn't like it anymore!

Kevin chose another gift and got two classic CDs and a juice jug with a cork stopper on a string. Kevin made the most of that. His husband, John, was sitting right next to him and got clobbered by the cork, multiple times.

John chose third: a big jar of Costco mixed nuts. Mom said it was pretty nice. I gave her the eye and the nod until she realized she was the one who brought the nuts!

Auntie Helen chose fourth: an eight-inch-tall clay pitcher, which was good only for placing on a shelf. Nobody knew where it came from. Harry said he'd never seen it. (I had plucked it from our bathroom shelf earlier in the week ... the master bathroom ... the one Harry uses every day! It had been in the same spot for 25 years!)

Trish selected a small box containing a mirrored butterfly. (I made quite a few stained-glass butterflies that year, three had mirrored wings.) She liked it.

My turn: I got an amazing washcloth made by Kevin. He knitted checks on one side and stripes on another by cabling the backside. I'm glad Harry taught me how to cable ... it increased my appreciation for the work Kevin did.

Harry's turn: He picked one of my emergency packages. (I forgot to communicate with him before the game started.) He got a can opener ... Black & Decker ... used ... Oh boy.

Ceridwen's turn (Trish's daughter). She stole the butterfly. Trish didn't want to let it go, but we all convinced her it was the rule!!!!!!

Trish stole the nuts from John.

John stole the washcloth and soap from me.

I stole the can opener from Harry.

Harry opened the final gift: a CD, some floral coasters and a nice little bud vase. I liked the vase, but the floral coasters ... ick.

Kevin had been the first to choose, so he got to have his pick of anything. He had his eye on Ceridwen's butterfly, but (perhaps because he likes his niece) he decided he wanted to keep the vicious juice jug ... and we were finished. Everyone was happy.

Dinner was fabulous: Morton's tri-tip roast from Costco. I had cooked it in advance, made gravy, cut it into bite-sized pieces, and reheated it in the gravy ... it was beyond belief! Kevin brought spicy mac & cheese (heavy on the cream); Trish brought a green salad. It couldn't have been simpler or tastier.

Larry, Leslie, and their son Jonathan stopped by for a visit. They had called earlier to say "no food, no gift exchange." Her sister almost died the week before Christmas. They had to put their holiday on hold, thinking a trip to Seattle might be required at any minute. Nevertheless, they were able to come for a while.

After the party, I decided to put the icky coasters in a white elephant gift exchange next year. The next day, Harry and I both went our separate ways at noon, but he came home first. When I walked in, I noticed the coasters had been opened. He had found a good use for them on the table between our chairs in the TV room. Go figure.

2012

(Color the belt buckle red)

The message included in the Christmas card:

A Very Merry Christmas to Everyone!

Harry completed two specialized stained-glass windows this year. Each is more intricate than the one before. I enjoy designing them with the lucky recipient. Harry enjoys building them little by little each day.

Harry is passionate about exercise. He dedicates three mornings per week to cardio and weights. On alternate days, he plays 18 holes of golf with a men's group. At the first of the year, he brought me into the picture. He and I play nine holes once a week as long as the weather is above freezing. We like playing together.

I've been working at the church. We've been "churching" out of a trailer in the local middle-school for ten years. Now, we have the old JC Penney building downtown. It's been remodeled ... spectacular! They asked for help during the remodel, so I volunteered to do something new to me ... I vacuumed!

Good Health   Good Friends   Good Wishes

Have a Holy, Happy Christmas!

With love,
Harry, Kate, Jud, Holly, Mickey & Boris

My Sunday school class is made up of ten boys and one girl. I've arrived! All those years growing up with six brothers are now paying off. The kids love puzzles, and I try to stay a step ahead of them. Not an easy task!

I exercise on the treadmill in the morning, walking with Jud (9). If I step off, he gets confused, stops, and gets thrown off the back end of the treadmill. There's a small void between the garbage can and the car where he slouches, sheepishly, until I get back on. A 45-minute walk takes the edge off his roaming nature. We both agree Jud is mellowing nicely …finally!

Mickey (12) is the old man now. He's almost completely blind, but trots around our place like he can see perfectly (except for a wall or two). He still has a little peripheral vision … he cocks his head slightly left when he walks. At night, if he jumps into his chair successfully, he sits proudly waiting for a treat.

Boris (18) is a pleasant little bird. I love to hear him cackling like a witch in the evening.

Three-Cheese Cracked Rice
A Thanksgiving Tradition for one year

1. Turn burner on med with copper pot
2. Add 2 cups uncooked white rice
3. Add 2 T butter and increase heat to HIGH
4. Stir violently
5.   Car arrives
       Open door for 92-year-old Mother & Brother
       Dogs escape; hope no one topples
       Get Mother, brother, dogs in house
       Kiss Mother
       Lead Mother to comfortable chair
       Remember rice – grateful that cooking-cousin
          beat you to the scene by 2 minutes
       Smell rice – think of microwaved popcorn
       Dump in 2 cups of water and stir
       Pluck out some "blackened" grains and toss
6. Simmer covered for 20 minutes
7. Add 1/4 cup Cheddar Cheese

8. Add 1/4 cup Feta Cheese
9. Add 1/8 cup Parmesan Cheese
10. Add salt and 'black' pepper to taste and hide
11. Fluff and put in serving dish
12. Announce the name of the dish before passing it
    around.

Three-Cheese Rice

To make **Three-Cheese Rice**, use recipe above, but
replace step 5 with:
5. Add 2½ cups of water and stir

2012
360-573-6909
kateh@pacifier.com   www.harryhoffman.net

Holly (9) sleeps under the bed at night ... on Harry's side. If I approach him while he's reading in bed, startling her, she comes alive like a vicious badger, snarling, snapping at my toes, and protecting Harry ... twelve pounds of attitude.

SUNDAY SCHOOL – THE BIG TEST

It was January 1, 2012, and the kids, who had enjoyed their Christmas break, were back for another week of Sunday school, starting off the new year. They were primed, but so was I ...

I walked into class. The kids were busy getting their pencils and papers. I announced we were going to have a huge test. I had their attention, but they didn't groan. I had to tighten the screws.

"We're going to have a test on Kings ... and Chronicles ..."

Still no reaction, although the little Korean girl, who doesn't know English as well as the other kids, was very silent. Her buddy Dolly asked, "Mrs. Hoffman, can I work with DaeYeon?"

"No. You all have to work separately." I continued, "And Joshua and Genesis and Exodus, and all of Deuteronomy ... and Judges ... and Ruth and Job."

"Mrs. Hoffman, can I read the questions to DaeYeon?" Dolly was really starting to worry.

"No, everyone has to do their own work."

DaeYeon was melting into the table, Aishlyn was shrinking, James and Eli were getting excited, Theresa was still listening.

"But first, let's say a prayer."

We prayed ... it was not part of the ruse. After praying, I passed out the tests ... to James ... to Eli ... to DaeYeon.

"Oh!" I exclaimed feigning surprise, "It looks like it's not a test after all ... it's a game!"

We had 24 pictures and had to figure out which Christmas carol each picture represented. I asked how we should do it ... teams or individuals. Eli, James, and Theresa wanted to work on their own. DaeYeon, Dolly, and Aishlyn wanted to work in a team. We did a practice run at one of the carols. They got it, understood the instructions, and off they went!

I asked the team if I could join them and was welcomed. It turned out the only Christmas carol DaeYeon knew by name was "Jingle Bells." We looked at the page and she pointed to the one she thought was "Jingle Bells." She got lots of praise as we all wrote Jingle Bells above the jingling bells.

We deciphered several more of them. After each answer, the conversation went like this:

"DaeYeon, have you ever heard of (insert name of carol here)?"

"No."

Dolly would retort, "Yes you have, we sang it at the beach."

One picture had "Ag" on each of three bells. Assuming they wouldn't be hearing about the Periodic Table of the Elements for another six years, I told them elements, including precious metals, have symbols.

"Name a precious metal." ... No response.

"What are some rings made of?"

"Gold!"

"Right! The symbol for Gold is Au ... but this says Ag ... It must not be Gold. Name another metal." ... No response.

"Shiny!"

"Silver! ... Silver Bells!"

"Good! Write it down!"

After everyone did about half of them, the independent workers joined our group, and we finished the rest of them.

Sunday School – Understanding Christmas Carols

I handed out a sheet of paper with the lyrics of "Angels We Have Heard on High," "Silent Night," and "We Three Kings." All the girls broke out singing "Gloooooooria, in excelsis Deo."

Silent Night

I got them back on track and we sang "Silent Night" all the way through ... three verses. I told them I was going to sing it to them again and ask them questions ... starting with verse one

> *Silent night, holy night*
> *All is calm, all is bright*
> *Round yon virgin, mother and child*
> *Holy infant, so tender and mild*
> *Sleep in heavenly peace*

"What was 'round yon virgin'?"

"Mother and child!"

"No," I chuckled. "The virgin WAS the mother. What was 'round yon virgin, mother and child'?"

"Jesus!"

"No!" I tittered. "Jesus was the Child. What was 'round yon virgin'?"

"Mother and child!"

"NO!" I laughed. "You already said that. The answer is in the song. Now … what was 'round yon virgin'?"

"Jesus."

"No!" I laughed. "Read the words. What was 'round yon virgin'?"

"Silent Night."

"Yes, you've just about got it. What was 'round yon virgin'? What time of the day was it?"

"Night."

"Yes!"

"Dark."

"What … was … 'round yon virgin'?"

"Bright!!!!!!!!!!!!"

"Right!!!!!!!"

"The star was bright. It was bright all around. Good job!"

"Now let's do the second verse." I sang the second verse reverently as the children listened quietly:

Silent night, holy night!
Shepherds quake at the sight.
Glories streams from heaven afar.
Heavenly hosts sing, alleluia.
Christ the Savior is born.

"How did the shepherds feel?"

"Joyful."

"No," … déjà vu … "… try again. There was a huge angel in front of them. In fact, the whole sky was filled with angels." We took a little break to do the math … because I'm all about math.

"There are six billion people on earth at this time. More people in the past and still more to come in the future. One guardian angel per person." I figured the math was self-explanatory. "Heavenly hosts means a whole lot. The sky was FILLED with lots of angels."

"500 million!"

Oh well, I gave up on the math. When you get that high, a half-billion is about the same as 100 billion. It's a whole lot!!

"How did the shepherds feel?"

"Scared!"

"Right! They quaked. What does 'quake' mean? Think about 'earth quake'."

They got it!

"What did the heavenly hosts sing?"

"Alleluia, Christ the Savior is born!"

"Perfect!"

On to verse three we went:

Silent Night, holy night!
Son of God, Love's pure light.
Radiant beams from Thy holy face,
With the dawn of redeeming grace,
Jesus, Lord, at Thy birth.

They understood "Love's pure light" on the first try. When we came to the "dawn of redeeming grace," they got it. "The beginning of redemption starting with the birth of Jesus and ending with Him dying for our sins and rising on Easter." It was a very successful sojourn.

We Three Kings

"We Three Kings" is a great carol to take apart verse by verse. Everyone knew the three gifts: Gold, Frankincense, and Myrrh. I thought a spelling contest might have been a fun interlude, but let it pass.

I sang the first verse and the chorus:

> *We three kings of Orient are*
> *Bearing gifts we traverse afar.*
> *Field and fountain, moor and mountain,*
> *Following yonder star*

We pulled out a map and found Jerusalem. We talked about the Orient and located Japan, China ... and Korea. We made sure we knew our directions ... north, east, south, and west ... then we imagined the three kings coming to Jerusalem from the Orient.

I sang the second verse:

> *Born a king on Bethlehem's plain,*
> *Gold I bring to crown Him again.*
> *King forever, ceasing never,*
> *Over us all to reign.*

I needed them to discover the nature of Jesus through the gifts of the kings: Gold signifies He is a King; Frankincense signifies He is a Priest/God; Myrrh signifies He is a Sacrifice/Savior. And so we began anew.

"What is Gold a symbol of?"

"Au!"

I couldn't help but laugh!

"Okay, Au is the symbol for Gold, but who wears a gold crown?"

"A King!"

"Right!"

I sang the third verse:

> *Frankincense to offer have I.*
> *Incense owns a Deity nigh.*
> *Prayer and praising all men raising,*
> *Worship Him, God on high.*

We talked about incense and solemn sacred traditions so I could draw a parallel between Frankincense and Jesus as God and Priest.

I sang the fourth verse:

> *Myrrh is mine: Its bitter perfume*
> *Breathes a life of gathering gloom;*
> *Sorrowing, sighing, bleeding, dying,*
> *Sealed in the stone-cold tomb.*

"What does Myrrh represent?"

"Murder!"

We tried a couple of times to understand how important it was to have spices in those days because there wasn't any embalming.

"Mrs. Hoffman, what's embalming?" I let out a faint sigh.

Finally, I was nearing a conclusion, asking again, "What does Myrrh represent?"

"Murder!"

"Well ... I guess it does!" I conceded with another sigh, "Jesus was murdered to save us. Myrrh represents His sacrifice as Savior."

I sang the fifth verse:

> *Glorious now behold Him arise;*
>
> *King and God and Sacrifice;*
>
> *Alleluia, Alleluia,*
>
> *Sounds through the earth and skies.*

We talked about King and God and Sacrifice, but they were already mentally finished ... and so was I.

2013

(Color the baby light-blue)

Sunday School – Another New Year

At the first of the year, I tried to get the kids to realize the true meaning of Christmas. I put "Secular" and "Spiritual" as two column headings.

"Uh, Mrs. Hoffman, what's 'Secular'?" came the first query.

I told them secular was the opposite of spiritual. Then we proceeded to identify things representing the secular side of Christmas (tree, lights, reindeer) and the spiritual side of Christmas (nativity, lambs, manger).

Finally, I asked for the One Person Who represented the spiritual side of Christmas.

Lot's of 'excitement' this year:

- Harry's golf game just got greater ... with two eagles. The first one, on a Par-5, had him stumped ... until he looked in the hole and found his ball. I saw the second last week on a Par-4.

- We collaborated for the first time on a stained glass project for a neighborhood church. I found out I like doing the tedious post-construction detail work.

- I acquired a great little golf cart with a trailer hitch and a small 'bed' on the back. It made yard work so much fun that I finally relandscaped the front yard.

- Jud's still mellowing ... NOT! He loves exploring the gully 3 hours at a time.

- Mickey walks around like there's nothing wrong with his sight, as long as I keep the doors open and the cupboards closed.

- Holly makes me laugh: she hides in the shadows when I call until I get totally frustrated, then she materializes!

- Boris continues to bite the hand that feeds him whenever he gets the notion. In my defense, I thought we were 'dancing', not sparring.

- Tripod has staked out a sunny location on a floating log at the end of the pond. He comes out on warm days, but not long enough for me to count legs.

"JESUS!" they all shouted at once.

And, with pen poised, I asked, "Who's the one person who represents the secular side of Christmas?"

"SATAN!" shouted James.

Aack! They pay attention to EVERY word I say. It took two more false starts before I could get them to give me Saint Nicholas and then Santa Claus.

Sunday school kids ... gotta love 'em!

Let's do it again next year!

Merry Christmas!

Harry & Kate
Jud (10), Mickey (13), Holly Bear (10),
Boris the Bird (17), & Tripod the three-legged turtle (5)

GIRLIE PARTY

After a long hiatus, The Lunch Game was resurrected for another adventure on a Saturday in early December.

There were two eight-year-olds and one eleven-year-old in our Sunday school classes. At 11:00 a.m., James' mom Denise brought her daughter, Erica, and two other girls: Marissa and Peggy's daughter Olivia. While I was finishing preparing the last-minute goodies, I had the girls take six slices of plain white Franz bread and three cookie cutters. They made Jam-Sams: cookie-cutter bread shapes smeared with strawberry jam.

Before we got too excited, we gathered in the front room for a blessing. Then we went to the table to play the homemade board game.

Brown Sugar Candy
This is Mom's favorite!

1 lb brown sugar	1½ tbsp butter
1 cup Carnation Evaporated Milk	1 tsp vanilla.

Stir brown sugar and evaporated milk in pan over medium heat continuously until mixture reaches "soft-ball" stage (when a few drops of the mixture form a soft ball in ice water) ... about 20 minutes.

Rest mixture in pan with bottom submerged in cold water. Gently drop in butter and vanilla. Let mixture cool until butter has melted. Do not stir!

When cooled, beat with long-handled spoon, incorporating air into mixture ... until it barely looses its sheen (about 5-10 minutes). Immediately pour onto buttered platter.
Cool about 5 minutes. Cut into squares.

2013
360-573-6909
kateh@pacifier.com   www.harryhoffman.net

The board game was in the center. It was the third time I had used it, and it was beginning to look a little worse for the wear. Each person had a small area in front of them big enough for a plate and a cup. Every other square inch of the table was filled with fine china, cut glass and stainless steel. There were crystal goblets, cordial glasses, and regular drinking glasses filled with all sorts of wonders!

The object of the game was to land on squares and collect whatever menu item you landed on. But there were still more menu items that didn't show up on the board or in the Wild Cards, so we made a rule: "When you roll the die, you get something for the roll in addition to whatever is printed on the square on which you land." We rolled for the magic numbers and came up with 1=Gummy Butterfly, 2=Cheese cube, 3=Celery, 4=Hershey's Kiss, 5=Potato Salad, 6=Jam-Sam

In the outer circle, the squares leaned heavily to drinks, breads and crackers, and condiments. You could collect a lot of things for your plate, and get a lot to drink, but the good stuff was in the inner circle. Each time you landed on a juice square, you got one-half of a cordial glass of juice. It was mandatory … passing was not an option … if you still had juice in your glass, you had to drink at least half to accept your new portion. (I'm all about hydration, even in a game.)

Neither Erica nor Marissa cared for potato salad and wouldn't you know it, they managed to roll about six 3s each. Even though each serving was about the size of a large grape, each girl had quite a mound of potato salad on her plate. Whenever they rolled a 3, there was a massive groan as all five of us empathized with them. I, on the other hand, had a penchant for landing on sourdough bread … and for rolling 4s (a Hershey's Kiss), producing a massive cheer around the table. By the time the game was over, I had amassed eight of the eighteen bread slices. When the bread and juice portion of the game got a little boring, we all voted to proceed to the inner circle. In we went. Once in the inner circle, there were many, many more Wild Cards for even better things!

Three of the Wild Cards were labelled "You Win! Stop or Continue." This allowed the player complete authority to stop the game completely, but when they realized they'd be stuck with what they had and would miss out on the dessert items, they always voted to continue. We had been at the game for hours when Denise, the other adult, drew the third "You Win! Stop or Continue" card. The girls almost jumped out of their skin pleading with her to continue.

When the game was finally over, we started eating our lunch, but first we had the option to trade with others. Erica and Marissa traded away their potato salad. I knew in advance Marissa didn't eat nuts, so I asked if she'd be willing to trade all my Cheez-Its for all her nuts. She agreed … she put her nuts in the palm of my hand … they were wet! Ick! I traded away some of my bread to Denise for one of her cucumber rounds. Olivia, who had acquired half the Jam-Sams and was trying to mix them with the peanut butter, looked like she needed some bread to get it all under control. She jumped at a trade. We had a blast! We ate most of our lunch, but the wet nuts were carefully sequestered in a far corner of my plate.

When it was time for dessert, everyone cleared the dishes and gathered around the counter while I dished up the pie, depending on how many slivers of frozen pie you had earned or traded. Denise took the mini-scoop and dished up grape-sized scoops to those who had Ice Cream cards. Each person did their own "drizzling" of chocolate sauce and "squitching" of turtle shell. Again, as if by magic, everyone ended up with a normal-sized serving of dessert.

We had a nice visit with Marissa's mom who had come at the appointed end time, but it actually turned out to be an hour before we finished. It was a three-hour luncheon with the last hour dedicated to trading and eating. When we finished as much dessert as we were going to finish, we cleared our dishes, hugged, put on jackets, and out they went! (It only took about half an hour to clean up after they left.)

FAMILY CHRISTMAS – GRAND PRIZE

Harry and I hosted a family Christmas dinner. Three of my brothers and their spouses were able to come. Before we ate, we had a drawing for a Grand Prize. We weren't giving gifts this year … no white elephants gifts either. But … I had a decorative suet feeder I wanted to give my sister-in-law Ann, so I wrapped it up and called it a Grand Prize. I had everyone sign their name on slips of paper and put the slips in a Christmas pot. Ann's was the only one not folded. I had someone hold the pot above my head as I reached in, selected the unfolded slip, and with great drama, announced the winner. Ann was delighted. When she unwrapped it, she was thrilled and exclaimed it was something she could really use.

THE POODLE-OPOLY PARTY

My little friend Elena started coming over to my house for drawing lessons when she was about six years old. She had a ton of talent and no fear. At the time of the Poodle-opoly Party, Elena (14) had become an accomplished artist. Her brother Jed (11) was also quite creative. I've always referred to them as My Little Art Students. When I visited, I was pleased to see a display of stained-glass ornaments I'd made for them over the years. My ultra-competitive nature came out in spades during the Poodle-opoly game (a spin-off of Monopoly). During the game, I made a strategic mistake and out popped a bad word. An apology was in order. Since I was reading a strange book, which used a lot of rapid slang English in long sentences, that style became the basis for my letter of apology. It will make more sense if you take a deep breath and read it out loud as fast as you can.

THE LETTER OF APOLOGY

Kayso, I was like: "Gotta jump in the shower get dressed and get to the Poodle-opoly Party" which I'll call Pooh Party cuz no one can say Poodle-opoly more than once a day and I was in a hurry so I wouldn't be late for work but since I'm the boss's wife it's not that bad so I hurried but not so much that I got all stressed about it because stress isn't all that good for you and I keep trying to melt the stress around me and chill out when things are kinda tough but that doesn't always work but it did this time and I was like: "Hey you dogs you get over to the barn and sit on your mattress while Jud and I go off to the Pooh Party!"

When I got there I was like: "Hi" and "Oh this is gonna be fun and it's a real game and there are snowmen napkins and the pictures look great especially since you can see them from the front door and the hallway and the kitchen from the place where the candy dish is on the counter."

Stained-Glass Ornament

(I had crafted an elaborate stained-glass representation of their old house for Christmas one year: a surprisingly accurate four-inch ornament made with 43 pieces of glass! It was displayed near a dragonfly and a butterfly from previous Christmases. None of their stained-glass ornaments were hanging. We looked all over for paper clips or string so we could get the pieces up in the light.)

And Mom was like: "The stained-glass house is sooo coolz because the light of the candle comes through it and the colors match the picture and whatnot and the dragonfly looks so rad here with those lacy wings even though it belongs to Elena cuz I really like to see it all the time and I'd be so bummed out if I couldn't see it and I'd like to have that little yellow butterfly hanging somewhere so the light will come through it and there must be a hanger somewhere so let's look in all my junk drawers because that's what I like to do when company comes over and maybe we should have something to eat and whatnot."

(Jed and his dad had found an old knife. They removed the cover and Jed was whittling a new cover from scratch. He's a perfectionist. I was sure it was going to turn out great. Once, after a struggle, a little chip sailed through the air and landed near a cup of coffee.)

And Jed was like: "Here's this cool knife my dad found and we took the sides off it and have to smooth it so the new sides I'm whittling will fit" and he was like: "I'm just sitting here whittling and minding my own business and stuff and I'm not really trying to plunk a whit in the candle or in someone's coffee but I've got major skills and can plunk a whit anywhere I want anytime I want without anyone knowing my major skills cuz I rock."

And Elena was like: "This is so much fun we should do everything all at once and you can see all the stuff I'm clearing out of my room because I'm hoping to get my dragonfly back but it's the wrong color because everyone knows orange and pink don't go that great together even though neon is orange and pink and I like neon which is why I'm wearing this cool turq top since turq is my second fave color after hot pink and can't we have a little milk with our cake and ice cream because the scoop of ice cream I got was a ghastly minimal trace and coffee would be great."

(Jennifer landed on my "Marvin Gardens" (aka Cookie) right after my turn. I meant to put a house (aka Dog Toy) on it but I forgot. "DAMN!" just slipped out of my mouth! Elena's eyes popped open as her eyebrows instantly merged with her hairline. I was so embarrassed.)

And I was like: "Oh I'm so polite and cheerful and we're going to play Pooh and I don't really know how to play and I'm probably not very good at it and I want the yellow dog bowl piece because I have a sunny disposition but if you try to win, I'll turn on you" and I did and I was so embarrassed to find that my true colors came out when I missed the opportunity to put a dog bone or at least a few toys on "Cookie" and someone landed on it and I was all "Dee-am" and you can never take that back once it comes out so true colors came out and they weren't yellow and it wasn't a pretty sight.

(Jed got upset when it was clear he was not going to have a ghost of a chance of winning. He and I joined forces and talked a little strategy, but it was too little too late.)

And Jed was like: "I've had enough of this and who needs it" but I needed it and we colluded to get "Naomi" and we got it and we rocked.

(After the game, Elena showed me her drawing portfolio. She had progressed so well! Her work was amazing and detailed. I was stunned. Most of her drawings were pen and ink.)

And Elena was like: "Oh look at my pretty drawings!"

And I was like: "Whoa … Coolz!"

And she was like: "Yep."

And I was like: "Whoa" again.

And she was like: "Yep."

(I was supposed to take their little black poodle home as the Grand Prize ... no way! Also, I got lost going home. With so many turns and curves, my head was 90-degrees off center on the way home ... e.g., when I thought I was going north, I was actually going west. It was pretty awesome to see the sun set in a place where it was not supposed to be.)

Kayso, I was like: "Gotta go."

And they were like: "Kay, see ya" and they totally forgot to give me the grand prize for winning Pooh which was a good thing cuz Harry gets to pick our next dog and said I can't be bringing home another dog. I totally got turned around when I drove away cuz the sun kept shifting in the sky and I was all late for work but got my stuff done by 27 minutes after quitting time which was the exact amount of time I was late for the Pooh party so what goes around comes around.

Kayso, thanks for a great party and whatnot.

2014

A Star ... dancing in the night

A Song ... high above the trees

A Child ... sleeping in the night

Pray for peace, people everywhere!

(Color the ornament gold)

Beginnings and Endings this year:

Harry continues to work on his golf handicap ... calling his time at the club "Adult Day Care". (Hmmm, makes us all wonder.) He finished an extraordinarily detailed window consisting of twelve different kinds of flowers, for our cousin. The number of pieces in the Mum, Aster and Carnation almost ground him to a halt, but "slow and steady" got the job done.

I was proud of my re-landscaping project, thinking all the chips I used would rot right away and turn into compost. Turns out you have to add nitrogen!

As for the dogs, Jud looked like he was slowing down a little, but that never happened. Mickey did slow down, and got very confused; We had to put him down in September ... we said goodbye to the perfect dog. Holly really needs a neon vest: With an independent nature and black coat, she's hard to keep track of during early and late "outings"! Our new dog, Jack, a 2-year-old Border Collie is fast as the wind, but to our great pleasure, he comes when he's called ... Harry's brother & sister-in—law, Jon & Les, trained him well!

Boris decided to be a sweet bird this year. Instead of biting, he nuzzles and trills.

Tripod meandered over to our neighbors' ponds. He may still be there. We'll see.

Merry Christmas!

He will bring us goodness and light.

Harry & Kate

Jud (11), Holly Bear (11), Jack (2)
Boris the Bird (18) & Tripod the three-legged turtle (6)

MICKEY ... 2000–2014

Mickey was one of the best dogs we ever had. He was a little eighteen-pound Rat Terrier and graced us with his love for fourteen years. He had a variety of handles and responded to each of them. We'd call him Little Mickey, Mickers, Mic-Keep, Piggy, Mick, Mickey-the-Mouser, and Mickey Dog. He was "the perfect dog." He was always there ... trusting and loyal.

Acrobatics: Mickey overwhelmed us with his acrobatics when he was a puppy. One time, I saw Carl down at Klineline Park. Carl was a retired veteran who walked the paved trail every morning like clockwork. He always had dog treats in his pocket and Mickey would dance in front of him, with love in his eyes, to get Carl's attention. It didn't take much for either of them. Mickey loved him with or without treats. I let Mickey off his leash and pointed him toward Carl, who was on the far side of the ballpark. Moments later, Mickey recognized him, and it was ON! He took off like a bolt of lightning, running full tilt all the way, leaping into the air when he got close. He had so much momentum he sailed *over* Carl's shoulder landing behind him. He was a tiny bit confused but jumped to his feet, eagerly looking forward to a treat.

Warm Chocolate Melting Cake

6 oz	Dark chocolate
¾ cup	Butter
4	Eggs
3 T	Sugar
½ cup	Flour

This chocolate cake recipe is said to have come from Carnival Cruise. It bakes flat, and can be used as a nice base for pudding.

Melt the chocolate and butter.
Mix the eggs and sugar and whisk for a few minutes. Add flour.
Add the egg mix to the melted chocolate and mix.
Pour the mix in greased mold.
Bake in preheated oven at 390° F for 14 minutes.
*Tip: Make sure the eggs are at room
        temperature and chocolate is warm.*

2014
360-573-6909
kateh@pacifier.com   www.harryhoffman.net

Tricks: Mickey was eager to learn tricks. Harry taught him to jump into his arms from a standstill. He loved his new trick. We had to make sure we were on solid ground … we didn't want to reward his trust with an error!

He loved children: Mickey was a regular at the tea parties. After we had our goodies, the girls always wanted to walk the dogs. There were three choices: Holly, who can't be counted on for being social; Solo, who was exceedingly gentle, but huge; Mickey, who was the perfect gentleman. I'd put a leash on Mickey and tell the little girl to be careful because he was old (regardless of how old he was). Then she would walk down the hill, little Mickey trotting dutifully by her side. It would have been the same outcome without the leash, but at least this way, the girls thought they were getting something. Another time, Mickey was playing Hide-and-Seek with my friend Mary Ellen's grandson. Donny ran around the sofa and waited for Mickey to come out. He didn't come out … he still didn't come out. Donny wondered what happened to him. We were kind of wondering, too. When he turned around, he saw Mickey staring patiently at his back! It happened repeatedly. Mickey was just that quick!

He loved Solo: Solo, the 95-pound Bouvier des Flandres, was three years old when we got Mickey. We didn't know how they'd react to each other because of the tremendous size difference. They seemed to be getting along, so we stopped being overly cautious. One day Harry was horrified to see Solo running around the backyard holding Mickey by the head. AACK! He yelled at Solo to drop him. Then, Harry saw he had been mistaken ... Solo was innocent. Mickey had jumped up, grabbed a mouthful of Solo's neck hair, and was happily hanging on for the ride.

He was CUTE! When I brought him home, he was just too cute. People were consistent about using that adjective. I started timing them ... anyone who met him managed to call him cute within sixty seconds ... usually within thirty seconds! It was that way all his life. Even in his last month when my niece, Ceridwen, went off to college ... her friend Ciera saw him and said he was ... "cute!"

He was endearing: I took him with me to visit Mom each week during his last several years. I would slip her a treat and tell her how to give it to him. He would get his treat from her and spend the rest of the visit on a bed by the back door. (Mom had never allowed pets in the house. It might have been more of a Dad-thing, but Dad had died years earlier, so Mickey and I pushed the envelope and got away with it.) Mickey would get another treat from Mom before we went home. The routine lasted for years. But one day, he was a little lonely. Leaving his post, he walked through the living room to the office to find us! Mom liked it. It was a turning point! From then on, Mickey had towel privileges in various places in the house until finally, the towel stopped coming out and he had a supervised run of the house.

Mom looked forward to his visits. She was thrilled when she'd give him a command and he'd do it. Not wanting to have any contact with dog saliva, she'd concentrate on the treat in her hand and say "Sit ... Sit!"

I'd say, "Mom, he is sitting!"

She would carefully hold out the treat and he would delicately accept it.

He was flexible: Even when he went blind, he was the perfect dog. He knew where things had been so he adjusted himself to living in a world of semi-darkness (he still had some peripheral vision). Once when we were expecting company, I moved the love seat to the right about five feet. The left arm was now where the right arm had been. He walked up to the love seat, thinking it was still in the same spot. Got ready to jump to his special spot and went up in the air and down on the carpet. I felt bad for moving the love seat and not telling him. He NEVER made that mistake again. He used his nose and whiskers to make sure things were as they were supposed to be and found the love seat every time.

Once I told Mickey and Holly to go do their business. They headed off on a trot to the Forest. Up the asphalt driveway, past the barn to the desired location. Holly's legs were shorter than Mickey's, and unbeknownst to him, he was gaining on her. When he bumped her backside with his nose, she turned on him like a cobra … road rage gone bad.

"Oops, sorry," I could almost hear him say.

He was loved: This excerpt is from "A Puppy's Plea" given to us by Bizi Bodi's breeders:

My friend, when I am very old and I no longer enjoy good health, hearing and sight, do not make heroic efforts to keep me going. I am not having any fun. Please see that my trusting life is taken gently. I shall leave this earth knowing with the last breath I draw that my fate was always safest in your hands.

When his blindness took a back seat to poor health, he counted on me to make the right decision. His quality of life had run out. I didn't let him down.

Sunday School – Whipped Cream Everywhere!

During the Sunday school lesson, Denise's son James kept fiddling with the bottom of his shoe. Denise was teaching the class that week. At the end of the lesson, he said, "Mom, my shoes are falling apart."

After the lesson, I told the kids we were going to have a review. We were supposed to use paper plates and shaving cream. They were supposed to write the answers on their plates by putting their fingers in the shaving cream. Well, where's the fun in that? I had gone to Costco to get some really good whipped cream because this was going to be a really good class!

Before we started, I announced, "Anyone who has been touching the bottom of their shoes, go wash your hands!" They all left for the restroom. Then I got smart and told them to bring back a wet paper towel and lay it flat under their dark blue plastic plates. Most of them were ten-year-old boys: I had to show them what I meant by flat because they were all making a mountain of the paper towel and balancing the plastic plate precariously on top. When they were ready, I went around and sprayed a large blop of whipped cream on each plate.

When I filled the plate of the third boy, he imitated a hungry baby bird, so I filled his mouth with whipped cream. All the other boys immediately followed suit. I was the only one talking and it sounded like this: ... Pssst ... "Oops!" ... Pssst ... "Oops!" ... Pssst ... "Oops!" I was laughing; they were swallowing.

Jacob was always incredibly eager and had a tendency to shout out the answers. I knew I had to make sure it didn't happen during our exercise. I told the kids if anyone shouted out the answer, they'd lose a point. If all the kids got the answer right, they'd get a team point. There were nine questions. They'd been storing up points for almost two months and, in another week they would have earned enough for another donut party ... or they could save the points and continue working for something bigger like lasagna, smoothies, or ice cream sundaes. I may not believe in bribing kids with candy, but I do believe in bribes!

We were ready to start. I said we were going to have a practice question first. After a dramatic pause, I rapidly asked, "How-many-prophets-of-Baal-did-Elijah-go-up-against?"

"450!" shouted Jacob. I raised my left eyebrow tilting my head downward. (After years of practice in front of the bathroom mirror,

I had mastered Paulette's eyebrow.) Immediately he realized the error of his exuberant way. With the practice question out of the way, we were cleared for the next nine questions. They went without incident.

Erica was the only student in the third-grade class that week. We merged the classes in time for the whipped cream activity. Erica was not one of the ones to do the baby-bird trick. She was not interested in having any whipped cream in her mouth. I assumed it meant she didn't like the activity. However, after class was over, Denise told me what a great time Erica had in our classroom: She thought writing in the whipped cream was the best thing ever ... she just didn't want to taste it.

After we had written the answers a few times, the whipped cream had un-whipped itself and each plate had a puddle of cream. (I was glad the wet paper towels were flat under the plastic plates!) I can see why the curriculum suggested shaving cream, but I'd use whipped cream again in a heartbeat!

I passed out dry paper towels first and then they used their wet towels to finish wiping their hands, and in some cases, their noses, foreheads, and cheeks! ... and on we went to the next activity.

JACK

We drove down to Scio, Oregon, to see Harry's family. Jon and Les have a sheep ranch where they also raise and train Border Collies. They had a two-year-old lazy Border Collie. When they finally decided he needed a new home they checked with us. We were interested. When we got him, he was an outdoor dog. Everything in our living situation was strange to him. We piled him in a crate in the car and took him home. It took more than an hour to get home. Naturally, with a new dog in new

Jack

229

surroundings, the first thing one thinks of is making sure he has a chance to pee. We helped him out of the car in the garage. He was spooked ... it was big and confining and his buddies weren't anywhere to be seen. We had to get him through the door to the backyard. *Aack ... a door.* He made it out eventually, did what needed to be done, and came when called. We had to leash him up to get him into the house. *Aack ... another door. Aack ... tile floors. Aack ... another door. Aack ... weird-looking dogs.* He was freaked out by everything and everybody until we gave him his box ... a designer crate ... a piece of furniture with metal-fenced sides. Once in the crate with the door shut, he started to feel safe from the rest of his new world. It didn't take long for him to adjust to our quiet life. His first and favorite trick was "Jack-in-the-box!" When we gave the command, he would dart into his crate!

Whenever we took him back to the farm for a visit, Les would round up the other dogs and work some sheep. Jack fell right into step. He had his spot and he liked working with the other dogs. In fact, he liked the farm. When we were ready to go, we looked for him. He was hiding behind the kennel building, peeking around the corner at us, hoping we wouldn't take him away again. Sheesh!

HOLIDAY GREETINGS

Fall of 2014 was filled with exhausting family business. I took a break from tradition and sent this picture of Hungry Man TV dinners to wish family and friends a Happy Thanksgiving:

Yum-Yum ... Almost Done!

2015

(Color the Santa hat red)

In

Everything

Give Thanks!

With love,

Harry & Kate

Jack (3), Cocoa Bean (5), Holly Bear(12)
& Boris(20)

We had a good year. Lots of disruption to "normal".

We started by removing the rotting deck rails and lost Jud in the process. We held out hope for his return. A month later, the deck was re-covered by Pat who then recommended Danny to re-side and re-paint the house. Best people ever! While that was going on, we adopted a Rat Terrier - Chihuahua mix: Cocoa Bean is 5 and was so happy to have a permanent home that he bonded with me instantly. The only time he strayed from my side was when the Danny and his cohorts sat down on the front porch for lunch. Cocoa was always invited! Danny continued his work by remodeling half the kitchen and half the basement. By the time summer came along, he was putting a steel beam in the ceiling and removing all the walls of the back bedrooms. By August the remodeling was finished and I was diagnosed with Lymphoma *(way to bury the leeead, Kate!)* and all I wanted was "normal". It's like we woke up and realized all the wonderful things we have to be thankful for. At the end of the year, our road washed away by the outlet of the Lower Pond. A mammoth road machine got back to "normal".

As for the diagnosis ... Thank you all for your prayers! ... my body has been handling the chemo extremely well and I'm looking forward to a fresh start to life *on April Fool's Day*. I should be able to return to teaching Sunday School at the same time! God is merciful!

Corn & Tomatillo Stew

I don't like to 'lift' a recipe without making changes, but this was amazing ... a flavorful stew recipe which came from my Sister-in-Law, the Vegan. The tang from the tomatillos and jalapeño peppers really makes the Stew.

- 1 large onion, chopped
- 3 cloves garlic, minced
- 4 cups vegetable broth, divided
- 6 ears of corn, shaved (about 6 cups kernels)
- 1 large potato, diced
- 2½ cups tomatillos, husked and chopped
- 1 jalapeño pepper, seeded and coarsely chopped
- ¾ cup chopped cilantro
- ½ teaspoon onion powder
- ½ teaspoon oregano
- 1 teaspoon paprika
   Season with sea salt to taste

1. In a soup pot, sauté onion and garlic in 2 tablespoons vegetable broth over medium heat stirring frequently. Cook for 1-3 minutes, until garlic is fragrant.
2. Add remaining vegetable broth, corn and potato. Bring to a boil then reduce heat and simmer for 10-15 minutes until potato and corn are cooked. Potatoes are done when they are easily pierced with a fork. *[I added frozen corn after step 4 and turned the heat off.]*
3. Add tomatillos and jalapeño pepper. Cook about 5 minutes, until tomatillos are tender.
4. Add cilantro *[I used parsley]*, onion powder, oregano and paprika. Season with salt. Simmer 5 more minutes.

kateh@pacifier.com

2015
360-573-6909
www.harryhoffman.net

WE LOST JUD

Jud went missing on February 21. Just when he was starting to mellow, he ran off and never came back. There are a lot of critters living in and around the gully. We feared the worst. We were on the lookout for him for a month. I was in touch with the Humane Society, online and in person … nothing.

COCOA BEAN (FORMERLY SPOTSO)

Spotso: We were ready to get another dog. The next pick was supposed to be Harry's. After a while, I realized Holly and Jack had really become Harry's dogs. I asked Harry which dog was mine. He thought about it for a minute and then said it probably should be my pick. (It took me more than two years to get a car; I wasn't going to wait another two years for a dog.)

While I was looking for Jud, I came across a little dog who looked a bit like Mickey ... his name was Spotso. I told Harry about him and said I'd had my eye on him for a month. As soon as Harry saw him, he knew I was looking for another Mickey. (Mickey had been gone for six months.) I sent Harry the link to the bio for Spotso. He said I had to have another crate before we got another dog. It seemed to me Harry was sending a clear message!

I called the Humane Society one minute after they opened at noon to see if he was still there. They said he was being shipped to another facility that very day to get "new eyes" on him. Evidently no one had expressed any interest in him since he became available for adoption on February 11. I told them I was serious and ready to come, so they held him for me. It took 45 minutes to get there, but before I met him, I asked to see the "found" dogs, in case Jud was there ... he wasn't. So ...

I went to the socialization room to meet Spotso; a Rat Terrier/ Chihuahua mix; 4.6 years old; pleasant little personality. The Humane Society folks were concerned because they described him as being selective about meeting other dogs. I brought Holly (expecting her to be a bit unpleasant) and Jack (expecting him to be mild-mannered) to do a meet-and-greet. It was a total non-event. They sniffed each other and then went about their own business. (I filled out all the paperwork, bought a crate, forked over some moolah, and took off.)

They also said he was aggressive about his food. Again, it was a total non-event. He didn't seem to care if Holly was sniffing his food, but I kept my eyes and ears open for the next few days to make sure it didn't escalate. He had good manners in the car and responded well to training as though he had had plenty. He stuck with me like glue. Things seemed to be looking up for our relationship.

He was slightly walleyed, with buggy Chihuahua eyes. (Harry tried calling him Wally, but it didn't fit.)

He (the dog) was sitting on my lap in the evening when Harry stood up to leave the room. He (Harry) reached over to pet our new little dog and got a nasty bite. At the same time, I realized he (the dog, not Harry) had peed on my lap. And that's how we realized we had adopted an abused pet. Harry instinctively gave him a pass. It took a full year for the little dog to warm up to Harry.

Cocoa Bean: When I said, "Come!" he'd cower and roll up into a little bean like a potato bug (pill bug, roly-poly). Any time I was serious with him, I got the same behavior. I hoped it would dissipate over time. (It did get a little better after seven years.) With his chocolate brown spots and his pill bug responses, the name Cocoa Bean was a natural.

Cocoa Bean

Cocoa had two inconvenient habits: He would go from zero to one hundred in a high shrill bark when someone drove up … or for no apparent reason. If no one had arrived, I would scold him and tell him to settle down and be quiet. The other inconvenient habit had to do with marking floors. I kept small towels around to clean up puddles. We learned how to live with it. We didn't want to add further abuse to his already damaged upbringing. We were really glad we had installed tile floors everywhere.

Give me a sign: Marg and I had been getting together for years on Saturday mornings to work jigsaw puzzles. Sometimes, we didn't speak a word, other times we'd laugh at the drop of a hat. She and her new husband Keith had two Border Terriers: Bogey and Bacall. If Bacall had to go out, she would get all breathy, then pant and whine until Marg got the hint.

Seven years after I had gotten Cocoa, while Marg and I were deep into working a puzzle, Bacall went through her routine. Marg said what she always said, "What? Do you want to go out? Okay, I'll take you out." And out they went. She came back and we were barely back into our trance when Bacall barked to get in. Marg got up and let her in. We were engrossed in the puzzle … time was flying by. About the fifth time Bacall whined to go out, I lost it. "Boy, she goes out a lot!" I was grateful Cocoa didn't have to go out so often, but at the same time, I realized I had overstepped my bounds. I tried to back-pedal my outburst. When Marg returned, I told her I thought it was very nice Bacall gave her a signal and I wished Cocoa would give me a signal. Within a week, it hit me like a bolt of lightning: Cocoa had been trying for seven years to get it through my thick head he wanted to go out, but all I would do is get up, look out the window, and scold him to settle down and be quiet. Once I was on board with the new signaling system, ninety-nine percent of the "accidents" stopped!

Dogs … gotta love 'em.

SUNDAY SCHOOL – KNOW YOUR AUDIENCE

During Sunday school, we were talking about Jesus healing the leper; then we talked about diabetes and the possibility of losing fingers, toes, or a nose. Loving the age group, I told them it wouldn't be good to pick your nose if afflicted by one of these diseases. They burst out giggling!

SUNDAY SCHOOL – OREOS EVERYWHERE

After summer break, I had a Bible review for the Sunday school kids that entailed looking up the answers. I gave the kids the book and chapter, they did the rest. There were only seven questions. I told them if they answered a question correctly with the right Bible verse, I'd give the class a point. Each point they earned would be worth one second. Then I told them when they were finished with the review, they could use their seconds to stuff their faces with Oreos!

I positioned two kids in Matthew, two in Mark, and two in Luke. If they blurted out the right answer, but it wasn't in their Gospel, they had to forfeit the point. (For example, only Luke contains the reference to there being no room in the inn; therefore, only the kids positioned in Luke could announce that fact.) We went through the questions one by one. They were digging through their Bibles frantically looking for the reference in their assigned books. It was truly an exercise in teamwork and discipline. They all had to work together to earn each point. After every successful answer, I finished with, "Good, you earned another second ... I mean point!" They were really getting revved up.

At the end of class, the parents started rolling into the room. We weren't finished with the review. I asked the kids if they wanted to stop the review or keep going. They all shouted, "Keep going!" The parents were scratching their heads!

When we finished, they had five points out of seven. I told them they could hold their first Oreo in their hand, stuff it in their mouths and grab another, but before they could grab a third, they had to finish their first one. It was very dramatic. Everyone was poised as I gave the countdown: 3 ... 2 ... 1 ... GO! They all stuffed and grabbed another. I counted off five seconds (it went too fast) and looked up to see them chewing for all they were worth. They each got two Oreos in the process.

I told them to clean up the room, and before I knew it, all the chairs, pencils, papers, Bibles, and tables were back where they belonged. It was amazing ... no nagging necessary and everyone left with a smile ... including one lucky dad who got all the leftover Oreos!

PART THREE

Fo-lic-u-lar Lymphoma

They say a good book is one in which the author describes a major challenge or conflict and then details how it was overcome ... maybe this will qualify.

My life came to a screeching pause when I was diagnosed and treated. It's only fitting the Christmas cards and backstories should also come to a screeching pause.

Spoiler alert: I lived to tell about it.

Diagnosis

In the summer of 2015, every time I put my cell phone to my ear, my thumb would rest on a little lump under my jaw. Finally, I realized it might be a good idea to get it checked out. The construction crew was finishing a massive seven-month remodeling job, which started humbly with a simple resurfacing of the deck ... which led to re-siding the house ... which led to tiling the basement floor ... which led to upgrading the kitchen cabinetry and countertops ... which led to remodeling the back bedrooms ... which led to putting a steel beam in the ceiling to support the tile roof. How the inspectors of the 1960s missed the fact the roof support was inadequate is beyond me. I suppose in retrospect, it would have been more appropriate to start with the major structural flaw. But anyway, we had lots of workers keeping us company during spring and summer. Good people. Hard workers.

I had a doctor's appointment but didn't know what to expect, so I asked the contractor to lock up before he left ... it was the last day of our seven-month party. I had already been in for a biopsy and was patiently waiting for the results. It made for some awkward moments: The contractors all knew why I was going to the doctor, but no one was willing to mention the big old elephant in the room!

PREVIOUS BRUSHES WITH MORTALITY

I had had several brushes with mortality ... two of them were surgeries ending with the words "benign" and "not conclusive, so we took it out." Three other brushes had to do with lumps.

First: The first one came when I was in my twenties. I had a lump on the inside of my palm at the base of my middle finger. (My intuition told me if you have a lump anywhere on your body, it means you have the Big C ... and you're gonna die.) I went in to have it looked at, but the advice nurse took one look at it, declared it to be a cyst, and said I didn't need to see the doctor. I'd never had a cyst and didn't know much about them. As I walked dejectedly out of the clinic, I came to the realization I was not okay with her diagnosis. I went back. I broke into tears. It must have scared her a little. She took one look at me and knew I was not okay! About one half hour later, I left the clinic, still shaken, but comforted by the fact the doctor had seen me and had declared it to be a cyst. I still roll my eyes when I think about how fast I lost it.

Second: The second brush with mortality came when I had to have a mammogram re-done. In my limited experience (and with no supporting data), if they tell you to come back for a re-do, it means you have the Big C ... and you're gonna die. I had my original mammogram done in Vancouver. Before I went home, they told me I had to have it re-done the next day at the clinic on the far side of Portland. I went right to the resource center at the clinic and got three books on hormone replacement therapy (HRT). I spent the evening and most of the night preparing myself for the worst. In the wee hours of the morning, I had made a decision ... I was going to have hormone replacement therapy. That decision allowed me to sleep the rest of the night ... all three hours! When I got to my appointment, I was rummy, but prepared. I would need to ask a few questions, but

I was ready to start HRT. I had the second mammogram and was sitting in a small dark office waiting for the doctor. Oops! I didn't have anything to write on. I mentioned it to a nurse. She brought me four sheets of computer paper and a pencil. The doctor came in and found me poised with the pencil at the top of page one.

"Everything's fine," she said.

I was so taken by surprise I asked her to repeat it.

"Everything's fine," she repeated, wondering why I didn't get it.

Evidently, there are a few steps between "a lump or a smear on an x-ray" and "the coffin."

Third: My third brush with mortality was a non-event. I went in for a mammogram a couple of years later … they withheld the results saying I had to have it re-done. After the second one, they were still unsure of what they were reading so I had to have an ultrasound. After that, they said, "Everything's fine." I was an old hand at this. I went home … grateful for having discovered yet another step between diagnosis and death.

THREE LITTLE WORDS

And so, in the summer of 2015, I went in to have a lump in my neck checked out. The doctor felt it and said he'd like to do a needle biopsy. My subconscious said, "Okay … here we go again … there will be several steps to follow before they tell me everything's fine." Since my subconscious was in charge, I followed right along. Besides, I had bedroom furniture and kitchen equipment to put away in my new rooms. There was no sense in wasting time on another big scare that was going to amount to nothing. He did the needle biopsy. No big deal. When those results came back, he said he'd like to schedule me for a surgical biopsy. Okay, fine … I had my surgery.

When I went for the results of the surgery, it was only the third or fourth time I had seen him, but I was ready. He came into the exam room and didn't make eye contact with me. I thought his behavior was strange. Then he "ripped off the bandage" by saying three little words. It wasn't "I love you" ... rather it was "You have lymphoma." He gave me about five seconds to process the words, but my subconscious was flabbergasted. I couldn't think of what to say or what to ask. I was stunned. And then he started talking, telling me what to expect:

... that I'd have to go see an oncologist ... (silently, tears spilled over my bottom eyelids)

... that chemo or radiation might be in my future

... that the oncologist would have to review my file and determine exactly what kind of lymphoma I had (there are at least a couple of dozen kinds) before he could recommend a course of treatment

... that this,

... that that, and finally,

... that it might take about three months.

At last! I'm a mathematician ... I heard a number and jumped on it! Three months ... I could do this ... my life would be back to normal by Christmas. After telling me a nurse would come in soon, he departed, leaving me to compose myself and wash my face. And so I waited ... catching my breath ... in front of the mirror ... staring at my blotchy face.

The nurse did indeed come in soon. I actually felt bad for her having to bat clean-up. I told her there was something good that came out of the visit.

"What do you mean?" she asked.

"I've had my eyeliner tattooed on ... at least my mascara didn't run!"

We had a nice little chuckle as she finished processing my paperwork. Then off I went to start a new life.

CONTROLLING THE DIALOG

I had no control over the events changing my life, but I did have control over how they were conveyed to others. I was determined to keep my attitude positive and hopeful. If I was going to die, I didn't want my last days filled with self-pity, thus, I was determined to find humor in every event. The more I laughed at myself or my situation, the better I felt.

Oddly enough, everything the doctors told me sounded like my condition was a non-event ... until it wasn't.

Re-telling the events seemed to be an exhausting way to go. I found the best way for me to control the dialog was to send out email updates to those who asked. I was oblivious to the seriousness of my condition. These are the steps leading to the eye-opener ... the decision to proceed rapidly with chemo.

May: I found out my friend Megan from BPA had been receiving chemo for Non-Hodgkin's lymphoma. She kept a positive attitude and felt the love from family and friends. I consoled her.

June: I found the lump in my neck and saw a doctor. He took it very seriously and I found myself running in for tests one after another, including an MRI on my neck area. Megan knew it was serious, but I didn't have a clue.

July: *Have you had an MRI ... for me, it was Controlled Terror. Everybody knows what an MRI is ... oh wait, no they don't! All I knew is many people have had MRIs and have lived to tell the story ... and it stands for magnetic resonance imaging ... and you have to lie very still and endure an extremely noisy event in order to have an MRI. That was the extent of my preparation. I didn't know anyone who had had one. I had no frame of reference. It didn't dawn on me to look it up online and see what was supposed to happen. Who knows whether or not it would have made a difference?*

And so I went in on a quiet day ... the technician was the only one there when I arrived. I was asked to lie down on the table, remain very still, and she would slide the table into the machine. Since I was having my lymph nodes examined, my head neck and shoulders had to go into the machine. Before she slid me in, she gave me some earplugs to help with the noise. Here is one of life's basic truths: If you pretend to be confident, you will be. It helped, but I was still bordering on being terrified. The last thing she said to me, and perhaps the most important, was, "Try not to swallow." Who would say that! And there I lay, perfectly still, alone with my thoughts, pretending to be confident, thinking about how badly I wanted to swallow, keeping my eyes closed because I didn't know if I was claustrophobic.

And then it started. The start-up noises were so unusual I wished I had paid more attention to them. After the start-up noises, all I heard was a loud, scary Ha-rang Yang Yang Yang Yang.

The noise continued all through the MRI. After it started, even the earplugs didn't drown it out. It was absolutely terrifying, but I had my job: I was to lie still and try not to swallow. As I lay still, I screamed inside my brain, OH GOD! Unexpectedly, I sensed something familiar was trying to break through. My inner brow furrowed a little as I wondered what ... Ha-rang Yang Yang Yang Yang ... OH GOD! I screamed again, internally ... and once again a familiar something came into my head: ... how great ...? Some words were reaching out to me from my memory. How great is ... Those who love. How great is ... Where were the words coming from? Ha-rang Yang Yang Yang Yang. OH GOD! ... Your goodness. Slowly but surely, the words were coming back to me. One by one they dropped into place. I started to recognize it as a verse from Psalms, one I'd memorized years earlier. (Check out the roof in the 2012 Christmas drawing.) Finally, all the words came together in the right order: "Oh God, how great is Your goodness, which You have stored up for those who fear You, which You bestow in the sight of all mankind on those who take refuge in You." As I lay there absolutely still, I repeated the verse multiple times in my mind ... on those who take refuge in You ... Try not to swallow ... Oh God ... And then, it was too much, I had to swallow. And just as I swallowed, the haranging stopped. Oh no! I'll have to do it all over again. But it turned out to be a rare coincidence. I confessed to the technician. She told me she had enough data for the first pass, but there would be at least one more pass.

When she started the second pass, I was settled enough to focus on how to describe the start-up noises. The first noise was the sound of three deliberate knocks on a medieval castle door, "Knock ... Knock ... Knock." That was followed by a brief pause and the kind of sound you make when you're happily walking down the driveway and a gnat skitters into your mouth. "Pthtt ... Pthtt ... Pthtt." There was another brief pause. And then came the deafening continuous roaring, "Ha-rang Yang Yang Yang Yang."

I conjured up a few more verses from Psalms, but it was still Psalm 31 that brought me the most peace. When the technician started the MRI the third time, I decided this would probably be my last MRI and I wanted the full MRI experience: I decided to open my eyes ... but only for a second. I saw a smudge less than three inches from my forehead. I closed my eyes immediately. As I lay there, enduring the horrendously loud noise, I wondered how the smudge got there. I decided it wasn't a good thing to wonder about.

The rest of the procedure was non-eventful. The haranging stopped. I was pulled from my noisy crypt. I put my earrings back on, and walked out ... but before I did, I told the receptionist the worst part of the MRI was the anticipation.

August: Shortly thereafter, the results of the biopsy came through. I thought they were great ... very passive, but the doctor said he just wanted to "dot the i's and cross the t's." That should have been a signal. At one point, the doctor said I could wait three months, or I could have outpatient surgery and get the tissue in front of a specialist for a closer look. The latter seemed reasonable. He said if I were a member of his family, he'd suggest the latter. We had a plan. At the end of August, I went in for the out-patient surgery.

September: My world came crashing down on me on September 2 when I heard those three little words: "You have lymphoma." Instinctively, I knew what it meant: I had the Big C ... I was gonna die.

Our friend, Doug, sent me a link to a website explaining lymphoma. I don't know what the real words said because the type was small and there were a lot of words, but what I read was: "You have lymphoma ... you're gonna die." I tried to do some web-based research, but the next two articles said the same thing, in the same words: "You have lymphoma ... you're gonna die." I thought it best to knock off the web research for a while.

On the brighter side, Megan sent me a list of things she learned from her recent experience. I could read those words ... they made sense. I had lots to look forward to and Megan's snippets were helpful. The last thing Megan told me in an email was not to worry about the pills. "They have come so far in treatment, especially nausea, you shouldn't worry. Just take the mess." I had a new mantra.

I went to meet with an oncologist six days later. It was scary. While I was in the waiting room with Harry sitting next to me, I was trying very hard to fill in the form they handed me. Gravity was not my friend. I leaned over the form to fill in the first question ... Name, address, phone. I lifted my head and sniffled in strongly. What a time to not have a tissue! I leaned over again, wrote my name, lifted my head, and sniffled in again. There were only six questions, but because of the sniffling it seemed to take forever. The questions were innocuous apparently not designed to convey pertinent information. When I got to question six, still sniffling repeatedly, I read the question. I couldn't believe it. They were asking if I was afraid. I laughed, sniffled, and thought "Well ... duh!" That put me in a much better frame of mind as I went in to meet my oncologist. He said what I had can't be cured, but I might end up being in "Watch and Wait" mode for the rest of my long life. He had a very soothing voice. Everything sounded like it would be years down the road. I was carefree and no longer sniffling.

All the yap-yap-yapping about being in "Watch and Wait" mode came to a halt when my oncologist met with a team of doctors who said I needed chemo ... and I needed it now! My course of treatment was six 28-day cycles with infusions on days 1 and 2 of each cycle. So much for being finished by Christmas. My new target date was April Fool's Day. Marg declared (with one exception) she was going to take me to every infusion appointment ... two days per cycle, four hours per day ... what a friend!

Dr. Chen

Marg is very proactive. She suggested I call Oregon Health Sciences University (OHSU) to get a second opinion. It seemed reasonable. I called and asked if I could have the name of someone who could give me a second opinion. I got five names, within seconds. They were all over the alphabet (C, D, M, S, and Y). I had no idea which one to choose. I asked the young woman on the phone for a little more help. I made it clear I didn't want her to give me a recommendation, but if she were looking for a second opinion, would she choose someone from the beginning, middle, or the end of the alphabet. She said she'd choose someone from the beginning. I had a C or a D to choose from. I asked her if she'd choose someone from the very front or a little bit back in the alphabet. She thought the very front would be good. To let her off the hook, I told her I'd have to think about the names but might be interested in a second opinion from Dr. Chen. If she had been in the restaurant business she might have popped back with: A very good choice.

I sent the request to Kaiser asking for the second opinion. At my next appointment, I told my oncologist I had requested a second opinion from Dr. Chen at OHSU. He told me Dr. Chen was one of the specialists on the team who had reviewed my case.

I started chemo on October 14. My next six months were all planned out!

A month later, I got the results of my second opinion request: *Denied*. I didn't care.

Megan's advice regarding chemo

- This is very personal and everyone wants to be treated differently. Do your best to communicate what works for you.

- This is the time to be a squeaky wheel. Call doctors, radiologists, etc. Don't wait for them to call you. Always follow up.

- Ask about research studies for your targeted specific cancer. Local cancer centers only conduct some of them offered nationwide. You may need to travel.

- Journal – Write down how you feel, what worked or didn't. Document after each treatment because it will likely be the same after each treatment.

- Make sure to have a note taker in each meeting with the doctors. You think you'll remember but YOU DON'T.

- Best advice I got was to shut up and just let people do things because it makes others feel good to be helping. What goes around comes around.

- Chemo brain – it's real ... I had a hard time remembering people's names and what I was doing. The memories do come back but make lists so you don't go crazy.

- Food is important – eat healthy and a variety. Don't eat your favorites right after chemo and limit them.

Megan's advice (continued)

- Best to have someone with you the first chemo session. Go with someone who will just sit there, talk only when you want, will get you water, food and blankets when you need it.

- Distractions help the time and nausea pass – this is a time to read, listen to music, watch movies and do all the things you never had time for.

- Library has online access through Overdrive or Hoopla

- Buy Amazon Prime and/or Netflix and watch TV series.

- Don't waste your precious little energy on cleaning or meals – let others do that for you.

- People understand – don't feel obligated to respond to any voice messages, emails, texts or write Thank You notes. Only do what you can when you have the energy.

- Go bald around those you live with and care for – the faster you get used to it the better for everyone!

- Take nausea meds all the time even before feeling sick.

- Take Prilosec with prednisone and nystein for mouth sores.

- Plan something to look forward to after treatments are over.

PICC Line

I had to have a 51-centimeter PICC line (Peripherally Inserted Central Catheter) put in my arm to keep my veins from getting decimated by the chemo infusions. Our friends, Dick and Carol, the boxer people, drove me to my PICC line appointment. I'd been told it would only take fifteen minutes. Wrong! It took a couple of hours. The first vein fought back and wouldn't let the PICC advance beyond 35 cm. The last thing the nurse said to me was she was glad she didn't have to use my third vein, because "it's a weenie!" A quick chest x-ray showed she knew what she was doing, and we were out of there with instructions: Don't get it wet!

I skipped my shower that night ... denial is my friend ... but I couldn't skip it for six months. The next night, Harry wrapped my upper arm in Saran Wrap with rubber bands at each end. I wasn't going to get it wet! It was a new experience, and I was not coordinated. I showered like a wild woman. Water was going everywhere ... I thought of Aunt Mit. The next night, I wrapped my arm all by myself and found I was way more coordinated after one day of practice. From then on, I put a cotton sleeve over my upper arm and showered calmly. I started laughing at myself and didn't stop for five months.

Symptoms

My brother, Stephen, told me there was a good chance I'd be loose as a goose, too tired to get out of bed, and nauseated by the smell of food. Before I started chemo, I stocked up on Depends, Imodium, and food. I even went to a sports store and bought a swimmer's nose plug. None of those symptoms materialized, but it was nice to have the food pre-made and I was grateful for my brother every time I opened the linen closet (Depends) or the silverware drawer (where I stored my nose plug).

OCTOBER – FIRST CHEMO TREATMENT

During my first chemo treatment, Marg got me settled and then went to a pre-arranged lunch with a friend. I took a little nap. Pretty soon, the monitor started beeping urgently. A nurse came over, shrugged, and said there was just a little air bubble in the line. She flicked it nonchalantly. Noticing my mouth had formed a gaping maw, she thought it might be good to give me a further explanation saying something akin to "if you have an air bubble the size of your thumb, that's bad ... the body can't absorb it ... Hollywood has done us a disservice!" Well, my air bubble was smaller than a split pea, so I closed my mouth. Marg and I skated home quickly in the carpool lane! I was grateful for an easy first day!

This was followed by weekly blood analyses, weekly sessions with a PICC-bandage-changing nurse, monthly pre-chemo visits with the oncologist, and the monthly treatments themselves. I was in the system. I had confidence in my medical team, and I didn't lose my hair. (All my shaving practice in the 1980s was for naught.)

I got used to having hyper leg activity on Fridays after chemo ... It was only one sleepless night per cycle and left me pretty tired on the weekend. Medication kept all the other symptoms at bay. I was a pretty lucky woman!

Stephen was a great fan of Lucille Ball. I had Harry tape four episodes each night. I'd watch them when I was too tired to putz around. After I watched an episode, I'd call Stephen. All I had to do was say the name of the episode and we'd both break into belly laughs.

I had a daily weight chart. It was funny to see a graph of my data. After having steroids on the Wednesday of chemo, my weight would jump about ten pounds and then return to normal by Sunday or Monday. Since I was having weekly bloodwork done, I charted the components of my bloodwork, too. Numbers are fun.

HAPPY THANKSGIVING

I was supposed to limit my exposure to others while on chemo. A quiet Thanksgiving was in order. A week earlier, I asked Harry if he'd go with me to Chuck's Produce and pick up about six dishes. He said he would. We went after dinner on Wednesday night. Our whole family piled into the car (except Boris) and went to Chuck's Produce. Jack, the Border Collie, Holly, the Schipperke, and Cocoa Bean, the Chihuahua-Mix, waited in the car.

Chuck's is only about a mile and a half from home! It was fun. We walked around. First, we came to the soup bar. I had my stomach set on Broccoli-Cheddar soup. I asked Harry if he wanted to get some Broccoli-Cheddar. He said "No!" Holy Smokes! It wasn't going the way I wanted it to. We kept on walking and came to the rolls and desserts. After we got some Cheddar rolls, he asked if any desserts hit my eye. I opted for the Danish Crisps. Boy, they sounded good! Wandering back, we stopped by the deli case and decided to get a little sliced turkey and some green bean salad. Harry walked around the end of the case while I was waiting for the salad. I confided to the young girl I really had my heart set on Broccoli-Cheddar soup, but Harry had vetoed it. When Harry came back, he said "How about some soup?" She piped right in with "The Broccoli-Cheddar soup is very good!" Quickly I responded with, "Okay, we'll take it!" I dished it up before Harry could say a word. I was feeling pretty smug!

We got some cheese-horseradish spread and designer crackers and headed off to the check-out lane where he put his arm around me and gave me an affectionate squeeze. He had never done that before ... but then we'd only been to the store together twice before. Not enough data to judge what was normal, but I knew I had a pretty special guy!

I started Thanksgiving Day by telling Harry how he had been played. It turned out he really wanted the soup but had only said no because he wanted to look around a little first.

We had the cheese-horseradish spread in the afternoon ... when we were together. We had purchased a full pint. Two days later, I looked over as he brought it from the refrigerator and saw there was only about a half inch left! I thought, *Boy, he went right through that cheese spread!* but I didn't say anything. The next day at lunchtime he said, "Boy, you went right through that cheese spread!" Well, the good-natured accusations went flying and neither of us admitted we had anything other than a little bit a couple of times. Then he said he always makes a smooth, level pattern in the cheese, and I said I do the same. "Well, this time it looks like you dug a big hole in it!" he exclaimed, "Did you cook with it?" That's when I had an "ah-ha" moment. I asked if it was a smooth hole, not wanting to hear the answer. AACK! I knew what had happened! We had three dogs who were not shy about exploring whenever we left the room. We were not the culprits. Even though we were both vindicated, our taste for the spicy spread had dwindled to nothing!

December – Third Chemo Treatment

By the time I reached my third chemo treatment, I was looking forward to it. I had been recording a lot of data for two months and was learning how to manage my two biggest problems ... with nausea medication and prunes. I was looking forward to cooking on the weekend. With all the chemo in my system, my body craved hot spicy foods. I had to give Harry a washcloth with his meals ... he's not one for really spicy foods and the perspiration ran off his forehead on those weekends. What a trooper!

January – Fourth Chemo Treatment

Marg had a conflict during my fourth treatment. Jamie from church took me on Wednesday. She had had a heart attack two weeks earlier and recovered so well she had regained driving privileges. She introduced me to chemo brain. It's not so bad ... just a pleasant fog clouding all the salient points you think you're about to make. I think I knew when I was experiencing it. (It's probably a lot like a dog's brain when he's paying attention to his environment and discovers a french fry under the table ... or a puppy who is in the middle of playing, drops to the floor, rolls his head three times, and nods off.)

Carol took me on Thursday. It was interesting to see my chemo site through her eyes. A few years earlier, her chemo treatments were provided in a communal setting ... recliner chairs in a large circle. Mine were in semi-private cubicles.

FEBRUARY – FIFTH CHEMO TREATMENT – "NOT GOOD"

After four cycles, we were pros. Marg was in charge of a money project at church and had been struggling with balancing the numbers. She said it wasn't her forte, but it was definitely mine. We buried our heads deep into the project after I was plugged into my infusion. We were down to the last dozen or so entries. They had to gee-up with the available paperwork ... but it turned out the paperwork wasn't available. We were totally engrossed in our project and getting more frustrated by the minute. When the nurse came by and said, "How's it going?" Marg responded without skipping a beat, "Not good!"

I was mildly aware of the exchange, but only enough to think "Asked-and-Answered." I was trying to regain my focus on the numbers. It took about twenty seconds before I realized the nurse was asking about my infusion. I looked up and saw she had a bit of a frowny face. I responded quickly, "Oh ... me ... just fine!"

Marg and I thought that was the funniest thing ever. The nurse just shook her head and rolled her eyes.

MARCH – SIXTH AND LAST CHEMO TREATMENT

After five months of semi-isolation, I had had my fill of Hallmark movies and had seen every available episode of *I Love Lucy* multiple times. I asked the nurse if a lot of people have an easy time of it, like I had had. She confided most people get pretty sick. Once again, I had so many things to be thankful for ... and I knew it!

Time had been standing still for six months. I was ready to return to the world. In fact, I was looking forward to my sixth and final chemo treatment: the familiar Friday night with restless-leg-syndrome, the weight gain over the weekend, the craving for hot, spicy foods, the sudden weight loss on Monday and most of all ... the promise of returning to normal. Following Megan's and Marg's advice, Harry and I had planned something fun for when I popped out the other side. We're dog people ... we were going to get a Corgi puppy.

PART FOUR

BACK TO NORMAL

2016–2021

2016

(Color the holly berries red)

After I finished chemo in March, we were ready to do something fun. Being dog-people, we decided to get a puppy. It was Harry's pick. He wanted a Corgi. Fate intervened giving us an opportunity to get two puppies rather than just one. Our impulsiveness reared up and we brought home two little 10-week-old Corgi's at the end of June ... Angie and Lucille. They're sisters. They're crazy about each other. Angie has the traditional tri-color look, Lucille has a black face with two brown eyebrows peeking out from the shadows! They have gone through several phases. Usually at least one of them is a good girl, but from week to week that changes. They're favorite trick is to stay 4' from a person with a 3' reach. Sometimes it's just maddening. But Harry takes them out for walk-training faithfully every day. They're getting to the point where I can give a command like down or sit which allows me to traverse that extra foot of territory. Thanks to Harry!

Cocoa was a big dog when we got the Girls. He wrestled with them mercilessly. I warned him they'd be growing fast, but he didn't listen. Now, they're almost as big as Jack (but for the short legs). Cocoa should have listened. Jack hasn't figured out how to play with the Girls yet. When they start tussling, he runs for his bed.

Every morning is a treat. Angie gets out of her pen first and lies in wait for Lucille. Lucy gets out of her bed and cautiously runs to the nightstand. Sometimes she peeks around and gets clobbered by Angie, other times, she peeks around and no one's there. Then she looks up at Harry's chair an instant before Angie pounces on her. One thing's for sure: Every day has a happy start.

Give thanks to the Lord

for He is good,

Give thanks to the God of gods,

Give thanks to the King of kings.

Merry Christmas!

Harry & Kate

Jack (4), Cocoa Bean (6), Angie & Lucille (1) & Boris(21)

Hamburger Beans - A family Tradition

by Dorothy Breeding

The best thing about this recipe (besides the taste) is the warm feeling I have when I make it. Whenever Harry's folks came to visit, his Mom would make this on the first day. Once when we were staying with her at the beach, I heard a rhythmic crackling. I went to investigate. She was measuring and checking the beans. Now every time I check my beans, my heart smiles as I think of her!

1 pound Pinto Beans soaked overnight
1 pound ground beef (not to exceed 20% fat)
1 onion
1 Can Herdez (Mexican Picante)
1 pint tomatoes (Salsa Casera)
Salt to taste

Boil the beans until soft.
Saute the ground beef and onions (drain fat). Add to beans.
Add Salsa and tomatoes and boil on low for about 1½ hours.

2016
360-573-6909
kateh@pacifier.com   www.harryhoffman.net

BIGGER

Shortly after taking my last chemo treatment, I stopped eating any added sugars. No sugar on cereal, no cookies, no cakes … only fruit. Breakfast bars can have a lot of sugar: I started pretending I was diabetic and went for low-to-no-sugar versions (even if they did taste like cardboard). I considered the contents of my sugar bowl to be poison. I was taken aback when I saw the results on the scale each morning. In only two months, I peeled off 25 pounds … and kept it off.

One day, while I was primping in front of the mirror, I threw my shoulders way back and turned from side to side. Foolishly, I asked my Man-of-Few-Words if I was getting bigger, and without pausing to take a breath, he fired back with, "Babe, there are parts of you that are getting bigger that you can't even see."

What a terrible time for him to depart from his Man-of-Few-Words routine!

CORGIS

Harry found a litter of six Corgi puppies in Spokane and started communicating with Doug, the breeder. Doug said we would get last pick so there wasn't any point getting our heart set on any one pup. A few days before the time of the first pick, Doug contacted us and asked if we wanted two puppies …

someone had backed out. It didn't take long at all for us to decide on getting a second pup. We were going in headfirst! Driving to Spokane to pick up a pup seemed a little far, especially since Doug was coming to Longview three weeks later. And so we waited. It was a good thing we waited because I was under the false impression I'd be back to normal when the infusions ended. However, it

Corgi Puppies

was a bad thing we waited because we lost out on three weeks of cuteness … and you really need the cuteness period to tide you through the puppy-teens! It was a hot day in June when we met to take delivery. The pups were adorable. I forgot everything I tried to tell people who bought Westies from me. When you're smitten, you simply can't think straight! Angie was panting. Doug held out a large drinking glass. She drank right from the glass. We thought it was a cute trick. (Later, when we were home, she jumped up on Harry's chair and drank his apple juice. We didn't think it was nearly as cute.)

CORGIS – NOW YOU SEE 'EM ...

When the Girls were five months old ... almost to their teens ... they started expanding their territory. I had a visitor stop by. The Girls were outside with us off-lead, wrestling with each other. We were strolling around on the terraces. All of a sudden it got TOO quiet. The Girls were nowhere to be seen. I shot a glance up to the parking area ... nothing. The next step was to look the other direction to the peninsula ... nothing. I wondered what I would do if they discovered they could jump off the side of the peninsula and have a field day in the wetlands next door. I looked around at the mucky silt in the Lower Pond (drained for maintenance) ... nothing. I was getting

frantic. They were young, quick, and inquisitive. They could have gone anywhere! I started running to the peninsula. As I was running past the bottom terrace, I happened to glance to the left. The sun was sparkling on the Brussels sprouts ... and on the eyes of our two baby Corgis standing still at the base of the plants, watching me race by. Who can help but laugh when that happens!

Runaway Puppies

Several days later, I took them out for a romp. They romped their way to the Lower Pond, which had been drained for maintenance. A rivulet ran through the middle of the area. Then they took to zipping. They zipped to the east toward the peninsula, did a quick cut-and-run, and zipped to the west toward the road and the gully! It was like watching a couple of kids on skateboards: They came up out of the pond bed, did a quick spin, and sailed back down into the muck. They flew over the log at the near end of the pond, did another cut-and-run, and hit the repeat button about a dozen times. (I was sorry the camera was way back at the house!) Each time, they managed to collect a little more muck on their bellies and legs. Even though I was on dry ground well above the pond bed, I felt I still had a semblance of control and started to enjoy their antics.

All of a sudden, Angie decided to expand her pond territory. She padded up the center of the pond bed toward the waterfall at the far end of the pond. That was not a secure area! Fearing she'd climb out of the pond bed and dart up the hill into Rodney's yard and then to parts unknown, my alarm mode kicked into gear. By the time I got up to the waterfall area, they were back down zipping around the log. By the time I came back down to the log, they were up near the waterfall again. And so on, and so on. Finally I decided enough was enough. A few treats and a couple of leashes did the trick. They were back under control.

They made a muck-mess of the patio. I discovered none of our four dogs likes to be hosed off … least of all, Jack. After the hosing and a couple of apple treats the Girls went down for a nap. I got busy on the patio. One hour later, I looked around at a clean patio, with a satisfied smile.

Muddy Puppies

Since hosing the dogs didn't work well, we moved the doggie swimming pool over near the driveway and filled it halfway with water. When they went into the muck a few days later, I plopped them into the pool afterwards. They splashed around and cleaned up nicely. I just had to make sure the water was changed before we started raising mosquitos!

The next time they went into the Lower Pond, it wasn't convenient timing. I grabbed Lucy and carried her up to the house. By the time I returned Angie was nowhere to be found. Experience had shown she would stay in the mucky pond bed and play until I came for her.

She wasn't there. On a hunch, I ran up to the front yard and then to the parking area. She was standing in the forest contemplating the height of the trees. Since I know it's impossible for me to run down a corgi puppy, I sat on the asphalt with a treat in my hand. She trotted right up to me and got leashed up.

We practiced walking the Girls up and down the road on short leads. Each day Harry trained them individually ... Sit, Stay, Heel, Come ... all the basics. I took them out for a nice long walk down the road and back a couple of times. They were more than five months old. It would have been totally ridiculous to assume those walks would tire them out. I let them loose on the terraces, but they decided to explore the other side of the road. They were doing fine until Lucy trotted up to the parking area. Fortunately, I had Angie on a leash. Lucy was going exploring and there was nothing I could say to make a difference. She trotted right through the easement to the neighbor's driveway. I tried to get her back with a treat, but she snagged the treat and jumped back so quickly I couldn't grab her collar fast enough. I parked Angie at the property line (e.g., I hooked her leash to a stake). By the time I raced back to my neighbor's driveway, there was no sign of Lucy. What a sinking feeling! I went to the next house, then came back to the first driveway ... nothing. I turned to go back home, and she appeared out of nowhere. I was down to one-half of a treat ... I made it count. I caught her, picked her up, and didn't put her down until we got home. With Angie, it's all about food, but with Lucy, it's all about freedom!

I was thinking about putting privet hedge and burning bush sticks in the ground in the hopes of having a natural fence around key areas of the property. The only problem was that if they got to the other side ... and you can be sure they would ... I wouldn't be able to get them back!

PUPPIES ... gotta love 'em!

CORGI – ONE LITTLE R

Lucy had been living up to her nickname: Lucy-Fur. She developed a little hop. When we called her, she came to a standstill four feet from us. Our reach was only about three feet. The little vixen left barely enough room to take a little hop back in case we reached for her collar. It was so frustrating ... and so funny at the same time! She'd been perfecting her hop for about a month. Angie took her cue from Lucy-Fur and was working on perfecting her own little hop. But Angie's heart wasn't in it. She didn't seem to mind being on a lead ... she usually came when called.

But that's not the one little R ...

We'd been working hard on the training. Harry took the Girls out every day, individually, to work on obedience. Lucille, who had been hard-headed about doing the down trick, finally decided to come around. When Harry said "Down" she dropped and spread out full-length. Angie, who had been doing perfect downs for the previous couple of weeks, decided to have a brain cramp. We realized one thing by having two puppies at once: They go through phases, and they are never, never, NEVER in sync with each other!

But that's not the one little R ...

After Harry left each morning, I ran the Girls outside to take care of business. When we came back in, the sky was the limit. No boundaries. They had the full run of the house. Cocoa played nursemaid and kept their focus on wrestling rather than exploring the wiring. I practiced patience but kept my eyes on them. I wasn't demanding full compliance with all house rules. Success at this stage meant they would wait for the next trip outdoors to do anything private. We were very successful.

But that's not the one little R ...

These Girls were huge! They were 20 pounds each ... and growing. Since Corgis have pitifully short legs and generously long bodies, they looked lighter than they were. When they came in from outdoors ... wet, dry, muddy, or clean ... they were like little sharks and made a beeline for whoever was sitting in the chair.

But that's not the one little R. Here's the little R ...

Angie and Cocoa Bean were sitting in my lap. Angie had such a pretty little face. She was fussing with Cocoa and vice-versa. All of a sudden, she decided he had overstepped his bounds and our pretty little Angie became a diabolical hellion. Her eyebrows turned down toward her nose, her eyes blazed, she showed her new teeth ferociously (even though they hadn't completely come in yet), and she blasted out a verbal growl earning her one little R in her name ... Angrie.

Corgis! ... They can turn on a dime!

CORGI – FOOTPRINTS

Harry had Nigel over to play pool. I wanted things to be nice for them. I tidied up, moved the birdcage, and cleaned the floor in the pool table room. The next day, I looked at the floors and there were Corgi footprints in the living room ... and around the pool table ... and across the carpet to the sliding glass door. In fact, they were everywhere! I went downstairs to gently confront Harry. He had the nerve to smile.

That irked me a little. Didn't he know how much effort I had expended to make the place look nice for his soiree?

I waited for an explanation, trying not to let my face give away my displeasure. He commented it had been a very hot day and he had opened the doors to let some air move through.

The dogs must have trampled all over the deck and brought in footprints of dew ... but wait, it was late afternoon ... the dew was long gone.

He continued: Angie had discovered the gutters! There was water in the gutters! She liked to play in water. She was splashing away to her heart's content. He had knocked on the window. She stopped what she was doing and came in the house via the sliding glass door in the living room, ran up to see both Harry and Nigel in the pool table room, and wandered back and forth between the rooms.

By this time, I was laughing, too. They had been maturing too fast for me … it was nice to see another sign of puppyhood coming out. It always seemed to be Angie who got into things.

A few days later, we had a downpour. I was heading out to puzzle with Marg but remembered there was water in the gutters … way more than there should have been. Because of the way they were installed, overflowing gutters would mean dry rot and too many problems to enumerate! I went out in the pouring rain and checked the filter. My gutter filter had morphed into a dam due to a buildup of fir needles. A few quick shakes and the debris was gone. The water, which was within one-half inch of the top of the gutter, immediately started flushing with a vengeance. By the time I got into the house it was already down more than one inch. I'm glad Angie pointed out the gutter problem before it became a real nightmare!

2017

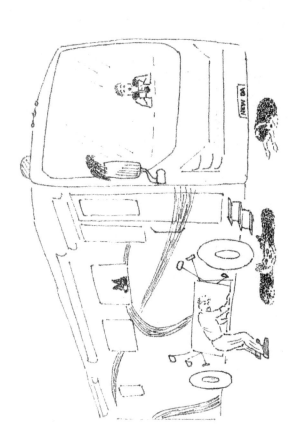

Change is
the only
constant
in life.

Heraclitus
Greek philosopher

Life is taking some major twists and turns.

The timing was right to change churches at the end of 2016. We're now with Messiah Lutheran in Vancouver. It's a very active church in the local community and they make it easy to participate. The first word people use to describe this Church is "Welcoming". Wish you were here!

Harry finally gave notice that he would retire. The big day is December 31. He immediately started looking at motorhomes and the perfect "bus" fell into our laps ... sooner than planned. We picked it up in October and we're getting used to seeing it in our driveway. Soon we'll be seeing it on the road! We're liking the idea of being warm all year round.

Golf is still Harry's passion. He's healthy as a horse. As for me, I joined the Choir at Church and found that singing might be my passion. I'm healthy, too ... just finished my post-chemo maintenance. Things are looking great.

We have some wonderful routines with our pets. For example, every day starts with Boris going out to the Sunporch to enjoy whatever it is that birds enjoy. Then Jack and Cocoa Bean race up and down the long driveway several times. Finally, we take the Girls out to start their day (always on a 25' leash). They start by playing Kissie-Face, then "Clash of the Titans" and end with either biting each other's faces in a full-on jaw-lock or biting each other's butts like the Tai Chi symbol (Yen and Yang). Their games are still evolving. They play "I want what you got" occasionally. Angie has a distinct sneaky side ... she likes taking Harry's Chapstick if she's left alone for more than a minute. Lucy is getting better at coming to us on the first try. Why does dog-training look so easy on TV? Harry's teaching them to sing on command! One thing is certain, they're loveable, always making us laugh.

We'll be embracing change and thanksgiving this year and wish the same for you.

Merry Christmas!

Harry & Kate   Jack (6), Cocoa Bean (7), Angie (2), Lucille (2), & Boris the Bird (22)

Caribbean Oats

Here's what I eat most mornings. It's an anti-inflammatory breakfast that supports my immune system ... and it looks happy! Imagine yourself enjoying a big bowl of Oats under the warm Caribbean Sun.

In a large pot, add:
1 cup Steel Cut Oats (Bob's Red Mill)
4 cups water
½ cup small Pearl Tapioca
1 tsp Turmeric
½ to 1 tsp Cinnamon
1/8 tsp Salt

Simmer 20 minutes covered.

Immediately add and let rest 30 minutes, covered :
¼ cup Goji Berries (festive and nutritious)
½ cup Raisins
¾ cup Shredded Coconut
1 Tbsp Chia Seeds

Serve warm or cold, adding:
1 Tbsp Toasted Diced Almonds
½ cup fruit of choice

Store in Refrigerator.

Serves 6-8

2017
360-573-6909
kateh@pacifier.com

WE LOST ANGIE

It had been a busy day. One activity after another in the morning with a less-than-satisfying round of golf in the afternoon. I was tired and achy and had just finished fixing dinner. I sat down with Harry to eat at about 5:30 p.m.

"How long are you here for?" he asked.

I told him I was in for the night (handbell practice was cancelled for one week). After the third bite, I started to question myself. I struggled to remember which week the practice had been cancelled, finally realizing we had had the previous week off ... I was supposed to be at church at 6:00 p.m. and I was cutting it close! I started eating faster. I knew I could check my email to verify. When I finished my gruel, I lowered my recliner footrest.

(A mental rant: *Stupid electric recliner ... It closed with a couple of unusual clunks and I fussed mentally. I was somewhat disgusted because nothing ever works like you expect it to, even when you pay good money for it. We should have gotten the manual version instead of electric!* Rant completed.)

I jumped up and went upstairs, checked my email and found we were ON for handbells. I went downstairs to change. I could be in the car by 5:45 p.m. and at church with a couple of minutes to spare. With all my movement, I had dogs everywhere: Lucy, Cocoa Bean, Hansel (guest), and Jack. No Angie.

"Do you have Angie?" I asked.

"No, I don't have her," he replied.

"Angie?" I hollered.

"Angie, Come!" he barked.

"Angie!" I bellowed.

I went back upstairs and looked all around, but since there were only three rooms, it was a pretty quick search.

"Angie! Come!" *(I don't know why we continually used the command because she rarely obeyed it. But we always hoped for it to work a first time.)* "Angie! COME!"

Harry checked the downstairs, which was another quick search because all the doors were opened ... nothing. I checked the garage ... nothing. Harry re-checked the upstairs. I re-checked the downstairs. Harry re-checked the garage ... still nothing.

Harry went outside and chanted our mantra: AN-gie ... COME! Still nothing.

Angie had developed explorer tendencies. Only one day earlier, she had toured the neighbor's backyard and front yard, then trotted next door to explore another neighbor's garage. I caught her in the act ... "Angie, Sit!" (That always worked.)

"I'll drive around," I said. "Grab your phone!" It was getting later. I knew I wouldn't make it to practice on time. I started down the hill. We seemed to be continually chasing wayward dogs ... driving in ever-increasing circles from the house until we found them ... sometimes as much as half a mile from home. This day was no different.

Please God, don't let her be a wanderer. Please help me find her.

I drove and drove, passing all the places so familiar to me, remembering each place I had picked up one of our wandering pooches ... it was only too clear why people build fences! I came back home. Harry was there. Angie wasn't.

"Did you check under the bed?" I asked.

"Yes," he replied, curtly. I went back in and, for some reason, checked under the bed ... nothing.

I got the phone number of the director of handbells to text him, saying I was indisposed. Back out on the road I went. Our neighbor Rodney waved to me as I drove by his house. I pulled in to tell him we lost Angie. He said he'd just been talking with Harry and had looked all around in the brush ... nothing.

"Thank you." I was back out on the road, again driving to the school a quarter mile away ... (tick tock ... 6:25).

I met a new neighbor who was watering her lawn outside the cul-de-sac. "Did you advertise on the neighborhood website?" she asked.

"That's next," I replied, forcing cheeriness. I drove on ... checking for traffic ... edging my way along the street looking for movement. I stopped to check with some dog walkers. But no ... no one had seen a Corgi. I tried to take it as good news because each failure closed off one of the many routes away from our house. I drove to another school half a mile away ... still nothing ... (tick tock ... 6:35). Everything pointed to the gully. Had she found a path the coyotes and raccoons used?

Please, God, help me find her!

The path through the gully pops out at a church one mile away. I drove to the church ... (tick tock ... 6:45) ... handbell practice was winding down. As I was driving out of the church parking lot, my phone rang ... it was Harry. "Did you find her?" I asked with anticipation.

There was an unusually long pause. "Yes," he said quietly.

I was relieved and waited for more, but more was not forthcoming. Finally, I asked "Where was she?"

There was another long pause. "Under your recliner."

The Rest of the Story: The recliners were built into each end of a very long, heavy sofa. There was barely enough room under the recliner for a chubby Corgi puppy. Harry said she was wedged in there pretty good. He had to lift the sofa and coax her out from between a couple of rods. He said it wasn't easy, but she was no worse for the wear. It made me wonder if she would ever prefer to lie on the cool tile floor in front of my chair again.

On the brighter side, I had spent a full hour figuring out ways a dog can escape from the house, from the yard, and from the property. Maybe we'll be smarter the next time.

CORGI – CARNIVAL RIDE

One day, I decided to use the treadmill in the garage with Cocoa Bean. But first, I brought the Girls out into the garage, corralled them with a makeshift pen, and threw in some bedding and a couple of toys. Cocoa liked to walk with me ... 3 mph for at least thirty minutes. I watched the Girls for a while, then went back to reading my book while treading.

After eighteen minutes, I was surprised to see Lucy trying to climb on the moving treadmill at a 90-degree angle. It was odd because Angie was usually the escape artist. Both Cocoa and I were stunned because she was trying to get on in a very awkward manner ... and we were full up! Any more bodies on the treadmill and I'd be tripping! We stopped and I leashed up Lucy. I figured if she wanted on so badly, I'd give her a chance. It was her very first time. I punched in 1 mph. She tried to run right off the front. I figured it must have been too slow for her. I got her back on and punched in 2 mph. Again, she tried to run right off the front. Finally, I punched in 3 mph. It must have been too fast because she totally freaked out. She froze with her legs splayed out to all sides. She was not a natural treader.

The next thing I knew, Angie jumped on from the front and rode the treadmill right by Lucy while I tried to assist Lucy. Now, I'm not saying Angie was treading, because she was facing the wrong direction. She jumped on that massive conveyer belt and rode it to the end where she was unceremoniously dumped off into a motley collection of plastic flowerpots. When she hit the floor, she ran around to the front and jumped on again. What a ride!

CORGI – WHO KNEW?

A dog trainer had come to Harry's State Farm Insurance agency to do a little insurance business. As we were chit-chatting, she told me I had to challenge the minds of our little dogs. I asked how. She suggested puzzle toys and games, like fetch. It sounded good to me. Before dinner, I took Angie out on the patio to begin the training. First, I showed her the little squeaky ball, saying, "Ball ... ball." I repeated my efforts a couple more times but couldn't get a good read from her. I moved on to something more challenging. I threw the ball and said, "Get the ball." Angie looked at me like I was a dunce, ran over, snagged the ball, and brought it back to me. I thought maybe it was a fluke. I did it four more times and she brought it right back each time.

Corgis come pre-trained. Who knew?

I told Harry how smart my dog was. He said it was merely a phase. The next night, I sat out with her again and successfully got her to fetch and retrieve five more times in a row. *Pbbth* to Harry's phase idea. However, on the sixth time, she decided five was her limit. I had to get a little more creative. I pulled out a treat and tossed the ball ... "Get the ball!" ... she got it with gusto, brought it back to me and gobbled her little treat. Four more equally energetic fetches later and she was done ... it may be poor grammar, but when they're done, they're DONE!

CORGI – THE GOOD, THE BAD, AND THE PRETTY

The Bad: I let the Girls out in the morning, but I wasn't fast enough. My job was to lead them out of the bedroom into the garage and out to the grass ... all while ensuring there are no noises to wake Harry. They beat me out of the bedroom and took a right turn since I wasn't there to open the door to the garage. Up the stairs they zipped. *OH NO!* There was no way I could run faster than they could. I ran upstairs and started tossing treats as fast and as quietly as I could. They zipped downstairs and followed me out into the garage, but it was too much for Lucy. She didn't make it to the grass. Fortunately, she only had to pee. Angie, on the other hand, made it outside and did what had to be done. I was very proud of my "Angel" but mad at myself for not making it possible for "Lucy-Fur" to get outside in time.

The Good: The next morning I tried something different. I stood an old foam core poster on the bottom step. It wasn't quite as wide as the stairs, but it was imposing. When I let the Girls out, Angie thought a quick zip upstairs would be nice. By the time I caught up with her in the hallway, she was standing there with her face pointed at the foam core barrier as if to say "Huhhh?" We all made it out to the grass with time to spare. Too bad I wasn't keeping score.

The Pretty: In the evening, I let them out while it was still light. Harry asked if I was going to put them on leads.

"Nah," I replied.

While they were doing what had to be done, I changed from my moccasins to my clogs by the patio gate. Things were going well. Lucy came back on her own and got a treat for being so good. When I called her, Angie came back for a treat, too. We all came back to the patio. Lucy and I marched right over to the door. Angie was bringing up the rear. As I let Lucy in, I looked back at Angie who had found a real prize: She snagged one of my moccasins, tilted her head way up, and took off at a dead run. She went to the end of the top terrace and down to the second terrace before I could get Lucy situated indoors. I got out a treat, walked to within ten feet of her, tossed the treat, and said "Drop it." (The book says to do it in a different order, but I did what I had to do at the time.) While she got her treat, I retrieved my moccasin. I waved another treat in front of her and said, "Let's go." I envisioned both of us going to the patio door. But Angie saw the second moccasin, snagged it, tilted her head back and ran to the other end of the pen. I had to laugh at her. Another treat later and peace reigned in our house, once again. (My moccasins dried off after about ten minutes.)

I'm pretty sure I'm trainable, but sometimes I seem to be a little slow on the uptake!

2018

We're Back!

(Color the top of the golf cart red)

Did you miss us at Christmas? We missed you!

We had an exciting time this past winter: we became Snowbirds! On November 1st, we hit the road in the RV (first trip in 10 years) moving monthly around the Southwest. Harry was adventuresome and adaptable. He sought out different golf courses each week. The wind was a big factor all winter … when the golf ball gets up in the air it can change directions radically. Once, Harry whacked it up and watched it turn right, then left, finally landing 4 feet from the hole where he had intended!

I've had two mottos over the last 40 years: "Find Your Place To Be" and "Bloom Where You're Planted". I did my blooming by joining choirs, meeting people, and golfing with Harry. But don't let that fool you, I was homesick for 2.5 months! I'll be better next year and, with pre-planning, you might even get your card before Christmas next year.

Some of the RV parks had a pet limit. The boys stayed home with a friend … we missed them. We took the Corgi Girls. They turned out to be great travelers and learned well … but shed up a storm inside the motorhome! Thank goodness for a Dyson. All long-haired pet owners in RVs understand!

We've already started planning for next winter… another round of monthly moves while staying close to an airport so I can fly home to Vancouver in the first week of December.

Here are some trip highlights:
- Learning how to make the bed in 4 steps
- Visiting a golf buddy in Earp, CA.
- Spotty internet service in a Colorado canyon
- Replacing the floor of the Storage Bay (dry rot) by hand
- Visiting friends/family in Phoenix and Tucson
- Driving 30 and 60 minutes to go *anywhere*!
- Driving through Phoenix with the steps hanging out
- Celebrity Impersonations by *The Edwards Twins*
- Learning how to play Mahjong
- Worst SW winter since 1945 (wind, rain and flooding)
- "Laugh Your Way to a Good Marriage" … YouTube … *Watch it!*
- Navigating the healthcare system in So. California
- Dress shopping in Palm Springs with Vancouver friends

Happy Easter!

Absence made our hearts grow fonder ... of you!

With love,
Harry & Kate
Jack, Cocoa, Angie & Lucy

and Boris (in his new home as of 12/13)

On-The-Road Bean Soup

This bean soup is especially tasty when travelling because it is necessary for living and it uses multiple Costco items, thus creating extra space in a small pantry. The beauty of this recipe is that some ingredients are added after the heat is turned off. They get partially cooked. The result is a crunchy soup!

    2 tbsp Avocado oil
    1 large Costco onion, diced
    1 bulb garlic, diced
    1 quart Organic Chicken Stock
    1 can Costco Organic Black Beans (rinsed & drained)

    2 stalks celery, diced
    1 large pepper, any fun color
    1 can Costco Organic Refried Beans
    1 can Costco Organic Garbanzo Beans (rinsed & drained)
    1 can Costco Organic Tomato Paste
    1 can Costco Organic Sliced Mushrooms
    Salt and pepper to taste

In a stock pot, sauté onion and garlic in oil. Add chicken stock and black beans. Heat to boiling. Remove from heat. Cool slightly. Blend with bullet blender.

Mince celery and pepper finely in food processor. Add to soup. Add remaining ingredients, stirring well to incorporate.

Double the pepper to jazz up the taste!
Whoo-Hoo!

2018
360-573-6909
kateh@pacifier.com

SEXY JACKET

While I was visiting my friend Jordana in Vallejo, she helped me order a sexy brown rabbit jacket on e-Bay. When I got home, I anxiously waited for it to come.

Jordana had already coached me in how to present it to Harry. According to her, I was to ask him to meet me somewhere to have dinner with another couple, but the other couple would mysteriously have a conflict and wouldn't be able to show. Harry and I would stay at the restaurant and have a nice dinner and share a bottle of wine (although we don't drink). Afterwards, I was to take him to a motel where our overnight bags would magically be located. Then the details are a little sketchy, but we would have a wild night, which would serve to spice up our marriage for weeks and months to come.

That's almost exactly what I did ... with a few minor changes.

When I got home, there was a package in the mailbox. I thought it was the slacks I had ordered ... it looked too small to be the jacket. I put it on the counter and went on with my life. The next day, an even smaller package came in the mail. After several texts from Jordana, I worked up the courage to open the bigger package. I was so afraid the sleeves would be too short. It looked as yummy in real life as it did on the website. The sleeves were exactly the right length. I was thrilled. I wanted to run downstairs and show Harry.

Instead, I got my icky somewhat-new blackberry-colored fleece jacket, put it on, and walked into the TV room and stood at Harry's left. "Harry, do you like this jacket?"

Because the light was slightly behind me, it wasn't easy for him to catch the details. He turned his head and said, "Yeh, it looks warm."

"It is."

Then I walked behind his chair and back to the closet to switch jackets. When I returned, I stood in the same spot. The color and size of the jacket seemed about the same in the dimly lit room. I started making conversation about anything except the jacket to keep his eye contact. He glanced furtively at the jacket. We continued to chat, and he glanced at it again. The more we chatted, the more often he averted his eyes to the jacket. Finally, after five times, he said, "Is that a new jacket?"

"Yes, do you like it?" It was probably not the best question because I immediately heard that it looked good on me now that I had lost weight. I became a little flustered.

I went on to tell him the little situation Jordana had tried to orchestrate. And in typical Harry fashion, he said, "For what purpose?" I started laughing. What else could I do?

OVERTHINKING EVERYTHING

I was surprised at how tired I was when we went south in the motorhome. I thought about why I might be tired and realized I was having to put a lot of thought into mundane daily activities. I regained some control by devising a routine to make the bed in four easy steps. I did the same with cooking and tidying up. Putting out a Christmas card was too much for me … I put out an Easter card after we returned home.

2019

We're
Gone!

(Color the Motorhome orange)

I read somewhere that one is supposed to change the location of one's tomato plants from time to time, so I put them by the patio this year, weaving the branches of 18 cherry plants through the pickets in the fencing. I had amazing visions of tomatoes falling all over themselves ... the whole fence turning red and orange through September. But my visions frequently stray from reality. I found out they grow better when they have good soil not just wood chips. (Someone should write a sermon about that.) The poor tomatoes did grow ... slowly but manageably. One day, before taking the dogs for a walk, I discovered my special tomato, *Stupice*, was just about ripe. (I mentally drooled.) Off we went ... down the hill, around the pond, then back up to the house. Lucy, who had been consistently darting out to the cul-de-sac, unexpectedly took a right turn and ran straight to the patio. I had visions of her finally maturing. (Visions again!) By the time I plodded up to the patio, I discovered her munching away on my Stupice! Oh well.

Later that week, as I was sitting on the patio reading, I happened to look up and saw Lucy delicately sticking her snout through the pickets to harvest a little Sweet 100 cherry tomato. There were more tomato stories, but in deference to your sensibilities I'll keep them to myself.

Moving and Shaking: Our family shrunk a bit as Jack went home to the farm in Scio to take on his new role as a cattle dog! This year, we are Snowbirding in CA and AZ (Nov - Mar). I've reconnected with Church people I met last year in Lake Havasu City and Palm Desert. We arrived here just in time! The Hope Lutheran Choir will be singing a Cantata on December 14-15. (I still have choir robe #74!)

If you received the new Snowbird stories of our travels (emailed last week) you will be on the monthly list. But if you did not receive them and would like to be added to the email list please contact me at ***kateh@pacifier.com***. *I'd love to stay connected with you.*

Merry Christmas!

With love,

Harry & Kate

Cocoa, Angie & Lucy

Picadillo-Style Chili

Spiced not spicy, this Spanish-style beef chili is guaranteed to stop the conversation at a dinner party. (With thanks to Martha Stewart.)

30 mins Total Time   30 mins Prep   4 Servings

INGREDIENTS

　　　　2 Tbsp extra-virgin olive oil
　　　　1/2 cup chopped garlic (from 12 cloves)
　　　　1 large onion, chopped (1 1/2 cups)
　　　　2 poblano chiles, chopped, (1½ cups)
　　　　2 teaspoons ground cumin
　　　　1/2 teaspoon ground cinnamon
　　　　2 pounds ground beef (80 percent lean)
　　　　Coarse salt
　　　　3 tablespoons red-wine vinegar
　　　　1 can (28 ounces) whole peeled tomatoes, chopped

　　　　Accompaniments: Green olives, toasted almonds, currants

DIRECTIONS

1. Heat oil in a large pot over medium-high. Add garlic, onion, and chiles; cook, stirring occasionally, until softened, about 5 minutes. Add cumin and cinnamon; cook, stirring constantly, just until fragrant, about 1 minute.

2. Add beef and season with salt. Cook, breaking up meat, until browned, about 5 minutes. Add vinegar and tomatoes with their juices; season with
 salt. Bring to a boil, then reduce heat and simmer, stirring occasionally, until thickened, about 10 minutes.
Serve over rice with chopped accompaniments.

2019
360-573-6909
kateh@pacifier.co

It Was a Day of Running Out Of and Running Into

I took the golf cart up to the end of the Upper Pond with a load of yard debris. It was the very worst spot on the property for the engine to die, but die it did.

I legged it down the hill, past the ponds, up the other hill, past the house, to the barn, grabbed two extension cords and the charger, climbed on the John Deere riding mower, and took off to go charge the golf cart, riding past the house, down the hill, past the ponds, and up the hill. While I was going, I decided to edge the road. Since the John Deere prefers to be warmed up and facing downhill before going into mow-mode, I went all the way up the hill, to the mailbox, and turned around. I had forgotten I still had the bagger connected, but I was being very careful about the blade cover. As I drove down the hill with the mower running, I was looking down to make sure the blade cover didn't bump the opened gate ... but the bagger did! The bagger hit the gate and acted as a fulcrum forcing the mower wheel under the gate. All bets were off. I needed yet another vehicle ... my car.

As I trudged down the hill, I spotted Tom at the top of his hill using some noisy machinery. I tried to get Tom's attention, to no avail. I thought perhaps it would help to go over in person so I turned around and started retracing my steps up the hill. After a few steps, I gave up and turned back around, trudging down the hill, past the ponds, up the hill, to the garage where I got the car.

I drove the car down the hill, past the ponds, up the hill, through the gate, and out to the street where I turned around. Now facing downhill, I edged the car forward slowly, until I could get it close enough to the lawn mower to do something, still not knowing what that something might be.

By this time, Tom had finished his chore. My goal was to get the mower unstuck before Harry came home and discovered my foolish predicament. I asked Tom to come over to see if what I was planning to do was a good plan ... it wasn't. He went into his shop and came along with his come-along. He found a sturdy fir tree, and before long, he used the power of leverage to pull the lawn mower away from the gate. Seconds later, I backed it up and completely freed it. Hearing a noise, I turned around to see Harry arrive. Thankfully, he had missed all the excitement.

I jumped in and hitched a ride with Harry down the hill to Dorothy's carport to show Harry the problem with the cart. He had no solution. He took off driving to the house.

I walked halfway back up the hill to Dorothy's outlet where I had left the extension cords and charger. I hooked up the charger … no power. I walked up the hill to Dorothy's to see if the outlet was on. It was. I got the mower and drove down the hill to go over the dike to the golf cart and thought, maybe I should mow while I was down there. I did, but I quickly ran out of gas. I plodded back up the hill to the Jeep, got in and drove home to get the gas can, hoping I could keep from disturbing Harry with the details of my new predicament.

Eventually, in the comfort of his easy chair, Harry figured out what was wrong with the golf cart. He told me what to do. I went back to remedy the problem. Dorothy's power situation was also rectified. Slowly but surely, all the vehicles made it home to their beds. I slept well all night.

2020

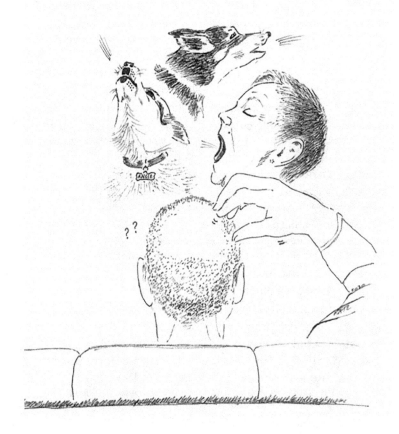

Silent Night

You don't know how prideful you are until you try video yourself. I was invited to be part of a Virtual Congregation singing Silent Night. That means I had to listen to a soundtrack on the computer using headphones, while videotaping myself with a cell phone. How hard could it be. I figured I could do it in one take, maybe two. I waited until Harry was out golfing and this happened:

Take 1:   Oops, my unmentionables were hanging on the chair.

Take 2:   How did I get so many wrinkles?

Take 3:   The camera worked fine but the wrinkles were still there.

Take 4:   Needed to sit on the floor to be positioned correctly in front of the motorhome's fireplace. A video of me getting down to the floor wearing capris ... NOT GOOD!

Take 5:   Oh that Angie! She was not supposed to sing with me!

Take 6:   Still hadn't figured how to sit down gracefully.

Take 9:   Still hadn't figured how to position the camera.

Take 13:   Had a lot of trouble getting the video started, camera positioned and remembering to push the stop button afterwards. (If you don't, the video disappears.)

Take 17:   Started using the headphones

Take 23:   Audio was good but the camera had slipped into Selfie mode. I had a video of the back of the sofa ... Phooey!

My brother sent me an encouraging text , saying "When you record at home you are Singer, Set Designer, Dresser, Make-up Artist, Recording Engineer, Producer, IT, & Lighting Designer!!!"

Take 25:   Camera fell over.

Take 28:   Passable recording but Angie groaned.

Take 29:   Passable recording but Angie groaned ... again!

Take 30:   Oops, a text from my neighbor killed the video.

Take 31:   The Girls really cut loose during the last verse!

Take 34 (final): I put the Girls outside, the camera stayed upright, my face was slathered with Vaseline (to look younger), my lipstick was still good ...but ... because I was sitting on the floor, I ran out of breath. I couldn't get out the last syllable. *"Sleep in heavenly pea ...."* was all I could muster!

Have yourself a

Little Christmas!

With Love,

Harry, Kate, Angie, Lucy & Cocoa Bean

The Versatility of Applesauce

Because of COVID, trips to the grocery store have been minimized. About once a month, I go to Costco or the local grocery store. I stock up on essentials like Harry's apple juice (6 gallons).

Imagine my surprise when Harry said "Why did you buy all that organic applesauce?" Oops! My freezer was already full of applesauce from our Vancouver crop, made hurriedly a month ago before we left for Arizona!

Well, in a COVID era, you don't just turn around willy-nilly and return something to Costco. I started looking for ways to use all that applesauce. Substituting applesauce for oil, one for one, has long been a 'thing' but I had never tried it. When I put it in Harry's brownies, they turned out better than when I used cooking oil! Who knew! Try it, you might like it!

2020
360-573-6909
kateh@pacifier.com

Silent Night will be consolidated into a Virtual Congregation and played at the Christmas Eve Services, 10a, 7p and 9p … PST. To participate in a service, go to *messiahvancouver.org* and follow the link to the service. To watch the taped version of a service, google *"Messiah Vancouver Youtube"* and click on the icon dated Dec. 24th.

EVERYONE HAS A COVID STORY.

Something was happening in China.

In March, we traded up and got a bigger motorhome for our marriage. It came to Tucson to meet us. After a dog show in the RV park, friends and family helped us swap everything from the old motorhome to the new one in two hours, under the blistering noonday sun. We did the paperwork and said goodbye to the old motorhome as it drove away to Vancouver. All our new RV park friends were invited to pop in and see it. Brownies and special napkins were the fare. Together, we discovered the lights and the reclining bed as well as the pop-up TV and the pull-out island. If that wasn't enough to wow the visitors, they got to open a door and see a second bathroom.

People were getting sick and had to go to ICU.

Spanish class was planning a luncheon. I was off to church to practice for the bell choir and the singing choir.

People were dying.

"Nothing is wrong," we were assured. However, within a week, restaurants were closing, church services were being cancelled, all contact with other people was cancelled. YouTube videos showed us how to make masks. Chic mask designs were deemed ineffective by medical personnel. There was even talk about closing state borders. Everything was wrong.

Everyone has a Covid story.

2021

(Color the 150-yard marker pink)

With Covid alive and well in 2021, we continued to hunker down and self-isolate … with the exception of golfing. Harry said he wanted to golf with me at least once-a-week in Tucson so we did. I had a little trouble on a long par 5. I was about 46 yards from the pin. I decided to bash the ball with my putter. As I set up, Harry called out "146". Since I was concentrating on my shot, his comment didn't quite register. As I was addressing the ball, I half-wondered why the green looked so rough. In mid-whack, I realized it wasn't the green, and it certainly wasn't the pin … it was the striped 150-yard marker! That was a stroke I'll never get back! I turned around to see the classic "What Were You THINKING!" look on my hubby's face! Oh well.

Even though golfing is serious business, we still find opportunities to get a little amorous in the golf cart … when wide brims allow (pictured).

It was a real relief to get the vaccination … and the booster. But before that happened, I was scratching my head wondering what to do with my life. I realized it was now or never: I contacted some authors, picked their brains, signed up with a Christian publishing company, and wrote a book. It all started on January 19, 2021. That unleased the creative floodgates and gave me the boost I needed to organize the stories I'd already written. Once the floodgates opened, I got more creative and started painting with acrylics. Between writing and painting, it's been a wonderful year. On July 23, I reached a milestone by submitting my manuscript. And then, it was like the spigot of enthusiasm was turned off and locked! Writing a book is not for sissies … it's all hurry up and wait! To keep my spirits up, I kept thinking "If you build it, they will come". My brother, Kevin, was in the publishing business. He provided lots of insight and encouragement. Finally at the end of October, the day before we took off for Tucson, some books arrived … I was published! I've already started on a second book!

Whack your way

through 2022

and find reasons to laugh!

With love,

Harry & Kate

Angie, Lucy, & Cocoa Bean

Kate's Zingy Fudgsicle

I like to have a little something after dinner, but traditional desserts are out of the question because I am minimizing my 'added sugars'. A while back I read that the Mexican people use hot pepper in their hot chocolate. I find that the cayenne pepper gives my fudgesicle a little lasting zing that finishes my dinner nicely. This fantastic recipe for a protein fudgesicle also gives me a boost of fruit! (I've come a long way since my first smoothie attempt ... using beans ... don't ever do that!)

1 quart Almond Milk
4 Scoops Protein Mix
2 dashes cayenne pepper
2 T Hershey's cocoa
1 T Turmeric powder
2 dashes cinnamon
2 bananas
1 cup unsweetened applesauce
1/3 cup orange juice concentrate (optional)

Blend well. Separate into 8 freezer dishes. Freeze until solid. Eat with a fork.

I use Organic Unsweetened Almond Non-Dairy Beverage Vanilla (Costco; Total Sugars 0g). My Protein Mix is Optimum Nutrition Gold Standard 100% Whey Protein Isolate, Chocolate - gluten-free (Costco 5.64 lb; one scoop equals 2g sugar). The cocoa is 100% Cacao Naturally Unsweetened. I get the Dark Chocolate when I can find it. I don't particularly care for Turmeric, but it's great for keeping my ankles from swelling and has a lot of anti-cancer benefits ... I add cinnamon to temper the taste of turmeric.

2021
360-573-6909
kateh@pacifier.com

CORGI – COME WHEN YOU'RE CALLED!

When we got the Corgis, they were little wild dogs with minds of their own. It was clear we couldn't train them like our other dogs. They needed special handling. We worked for weeks to get them to know their names. Then we started working on the "Come" command. If there wasn't a treat connected with the command, they weren't interested. Life was too short, there were tons of things for them to explore. Eventually, they got better, but they learned to anticipate the reason they were being called. Getting penned up in the barn, being groomed, or getting a bath were not good reasons to obey the command.

Unbeknownst to me, Harry taught them to come to a special signal. Each had her own sound: Lucy's was a kissing sound like smacking your lips; Angie's was shuh. I would call the dogs. "Angie ... Lucy ... Come!" ... nothing. Harry would just sit there in his rocking chair and quietly make his noises "kiss-kiss ... shuh-shuh." The dogs always came on the run, even if they were down at the pond. What's up with that? Harry suggested I try it. Well heck, why not. "Kiss-kiss ... shuh-shuh." They came running to me. I was surprised it worked for me! But it doesn't work as well as it does for Harry ... the dogs are wise to me. No wonder Harry doesn't care to clip toenails. Oh ... that Harry!

2022

Merry Christmas!

Harry turned 75 this year and I'm a year behind him. Our thoughts are dappled with aging.

Trees: Two trees came down this year. After spending a warm winter in Tucson, we came home to a nasty snowstorm followed by two months of rain. The snow was warm and gloppy and weighted down everything. Our iconic leaning cedar took a nosedive into the pond. Branches were poking through the surface everywhere. It was an unsightly mess. Three days later, a dead alder engulfed by ivy came down, totally blocking our driveway. With a little help from machinery and a chainsaw, the tree guy moved the blockage to the side of the road. In keeping with the theme, we discovered our precious dwarf apple trees were well past their prime. Aging … it's not just for humans.

Property: Our home is aging. We've lived here for 36 years. This past summer saw roof replacement on the barn, furnace replacement in the house, and another round of asphalt resealing. I guess you could say our pocketbook is aging.

Choir: Covid protocols knocked out our choir in Vancouver for two years. Every time we take stock of our average age we shudder. Nevertheless, we have a new, energetic choir director fresh out of school. She gently gathered her little charges and assured us our voices would come back with a little practice. Three weeks later, armed with her special tricks, we were older, wiser, and able to hit the highs and lows once again.

Friends: Our pastors aged themselves out of a job. We loved having them shepherd us for 28 years and gave them a massive retirement party to say goodbye.

Weeds: The only good thing about aging in 2022 had to do with weeds. To keep your skin from aging, you need to stay hydrated. To keep weeds at bay during the long, hot, dry summer, I stopped hydrating the front yard. Woo-Hoo! Something finally worked!

Thank goodness for Harry's golfing passion. Golfing is about the only thing that didn't shut down during Covid. Harry golfs with a couple of men's groups three times each week. We golfed together once a week last winter and will start up again after Christmas.

"When we are no longer able to change a situation.
we are challenged to change ourselves."

— Victor Frankl

Have a good year ... and keep reminding yourself:

OLD AGE IS A GIFT!

... With love,

Harry & Kate Angie, Lucy & Cocoa Bean

Cucumber soup

My neighbor Dorothy planted two cucumber plants in the late spring just before the rains diminished. We had a massive run of hot weather, but she had an automatic watering system. Her cucumbers produced like crazy. I was in the right spot at the right time and got to experiment with cucumber soup. Once I added a little chicken stock to it, I knew it was a winner.

2   big fat cucumbers, diced
2/3   cup guacamole
½ – 1   tsp salt
¼   teaspoon garlic powder
½   teaspoon chopped onions
1   tablespoon chicken bouillon
2   cups water

Puree in a Vitamix blender for a frothy soup, or a food processor for a chunkier soup. Served chilled or at room temperature ... Who Cares! ... it's delicious enough either way.

2022
360-573-6909
kateh@pacifier.com

WE LOST ANGIE ... AGAIN

We were having friends over for a pleasant dinner on Sunday afternoon. Preparations were going according to plan until Cathy and Jim came. In a post-Covid world, I enjoy running out to meet people. So do the dogs. I forgot Cathy was not a dog person. We had three dogs jumping everywhere. Harry was fussing with the jacks on the motorhome. He called the dogs ... they came. I led Cathy out onto the deck to enjoy the sunshine and catch up. We were having a pleasant conversation when Harry hollered from the barn, "Do you have Angie?"

"No," I bellowed back, "I only have Cocoa."

And then, the familiar call came from everywhere, "Angie, COME!"

"Did you look in the motorhome and the barn?"

"Yes!"

"Angie, COME ... shuh-shuh!"

Will we ever learn? Moments later Harry was in his car, driving through the easement to the cul-de-sac.

"Where is he going?" Cathy asked.

"We lost Angie," I said, lounging a little too casually on the deck chair, trying to look like a good hostess. It was so unlike Angie to run off when we had company.

Harry came back ... Marg and Keith arrived ... I grabbed the keys to take a turn. Harry stayed behind to entertain. Out to the cul-de-sac I drove. Neighbors two blocks away we're in the garden ... "Have you seen a Corgi?" ... "No, good luck." ... "Thanks." All around I drove in ever-widening circles. I was back to 28th Avenue three blocks from home. I'd met a man named Bob years earlier when looking for Jud. He was blowing off his driveway. I drove up on the wrong side of the street stopping in front of him, "This time I'm looking for a Corgi." People just seem to understand. He hadn't seen her. It was a good sign. I drove home saying the same prayer I had said several years earlier ... *Please God, help me find her.* When I pulled into the garage, Harry came through the door.

"I found her."

"Where was she?"

"In the motorhome." And once again I could feel a mixture of relief and annoyance. I should have checked the barn and the motor-home myself. All I would have had to do is open the door and lean my head in. There are no doors. If she had been in the motorhome, she would have been right there by the front door waiting for me to open it.

He continued, "She was closed in the bathroom." I'd forgotten about the door to the little bathroom! I realized I would have missed her too. My annoyance subsided. We really need to find a command for Angie to cause her to speak. Maybe, "Angie ... SPEAK!"

HAPPY 40TH ANNIVERSARY

The traditional gift for a 40th anniversary is ruby. Our big day came. Harry bought me Ruby-Red Slippers; I bought him dinner. The Ruby-Red Slippers were plastic red-plaid gardening boots. I had to smear a little Vaseline on them to keep them from sticking ... but I didn't do that until two days after our anniversary.

Twigs is a nice little restaurant overlooking the Willamette River. I called to get an early-evening reservation. The earliest dinner reservation was 7:45 p.m. Way too late for us! Instead, I made reservations for 3:00 p.m.

I swear, I thought Harry knew I was planning to wear the boots, with my evening dress. I piled into the car and off we went. When I got out to pay for parking, he noticed the boots, saying with a wee bit of a sneer, "Interesting choice of footwear." My boots rubbed/stuck together as I walked to the pay station, but I didn't quite trip. We walked hand-in-hand toward the restaurant. He said, "If I had known you were going to wear those, I wouldn't have come." As we crossed the street, my boots did the rub/stick thing again, but I stayed upright.

Inside, on the way to the table, I felt like a lumberjack ... walking with my feet apart to avoid tripping myself.

We were seated at a little table for two by a wall with an electric fireplace built into the top of it. If we stood while eating, it would have been so romantic. Harry's back was to the water. Pretty soon, he shifted his chair sideways so he could see the view. It seemed like a good idea ... I shifted my chair, too. We held hands on the table. If we looked to the right, we could see the magnificent iconic Grant Street Pier ... and so we did. Then we looked straight ahead and saw four TV sets in the bar area. We were right at home, holding hands, watching TV, getting ready to have dinner. During dinner, my credit card was in my right boot and his phone was in my left boot. It doesn't get much more romantic than that.

Ruby-Red Slippers

Epilogue

Watch for more stories
as Harry and Kate hit the road in retirement.

Volume Three of the Two Ponds Trilogy:
"Snowbirding from Two Ponds"

CPSIA information can be obtained
at www.ICGtesting.com
Printed in the USA
JSHW050530180523
41875JS00002B/2